THE SIGNS OF OUR TIMES

COLLECTION

THE SIGNS OF OUR TIMES

COLLECTION

MICHAEL SAWDY

**BIBLICAL SIGNS
PUBLISHING**

Published in Plymouth, Michigan, by Biblical Signs Publishing, an imprint of BiblicalSigns.com.

This Book may be purchased in bulk for educational, business, fund-raising, or sales promotional use. For information, please email BiblicalSigns@gmail.com.

Unless otherwise noted, Scripture quotations in this book are taken from the King James Version. Public domain.

All italics in Scripture quotations were added by the author for emphasis.

ISBN: 9781794336575

LCCN: 2018907795 (The Signs of Our Times)
LCCN: 2019901844 (Even More Signs of Our Times)

Cover Design by MichaEL Sawdy.

Printed in the United States of America

FROM THE FOUNDER OF BiblicalSigns.com

MICHAEL SAWDY

THE SIGNS OF OUR TIMES

12 BIBLICAL REASONS WHY THIS COULD BE
THE GENERATION OF THE RAPTURE

THE SIGNS OF OUR TIMES

THE SIGNS OF OUR TIMES

12 BIBLICAL REASONS WHY THIS COULD BE THE GENERATION OF THE RAPTURE

MICHAEL SAWDY

**BIBLICAL SIGNS
PUBLISHING**

TO GOD:

The website and this book would not have been possible without Your unwavering mercy, grace, love, faithfulness, and the guidance of Your Holy Spirit - Who never fails to inspire me. Thank You for everything.

TO MOM:

Thank you for always being there, especially back in the days when I wasn't worth being there for. If not for your prayers and faithfulness, as a Godly mother, I would not be around to write this book today. This book is, no doubt, a testament to your Proverbs 22:6 parenting. I will always love you more than my own life itself.

TO DAD:

Thank you for being there whenever I call on you. You are truly an example of what a Godly father and man should be. Though I was a problem child growing up, you made sure that you coupled love with your discipline. Both have made me the man that I have become today. I am eternally thankful to call you my Dad.

TO BRO:

Though we had fought and argued like cats and dogs growing up, we never let that affect our brotherly love. I'm so happy that you didn't follow in my early footsteps of life, but that you took lessons from the consequences of my many mistakes and charted your own path. I'm so glad that you have drawn closer to the Lord in recent years, and I pray that He will bring you closer to Him each new day - as He has me. Love ya' Bro!

TO FAMILY:

I could not have asked for a better family. I've been blessed by the wisdom of Uncle Jim, Grampa, Uncle Jerry, and Uncle Butch. Aunt Pam, you share my strong faith in God's Word and His Light radiates through you to the entire family. Gramma and Aunt Deb, I'm beyond grateful for your gentle love since the day I was born. Aunt Jude, Tommy, Dawn, Uncle Pat, Uncle Ray, Cindy, Sarah, and Chris S, I'm blessed to have every one of you in my life. Kendall & Kaylee, never forget that God is always there for you when you need Him - as am I. God bless you all. I love you all.

CONTENTS

INTRODUCTION

THE DISCIPLES SAID UNTO JESUS, TELL US... WHAT SHALL BE
THE SIGN OF THY COMING, AND OF THE END OF THE AGE?

- MATTHEW 24:3

THIS WAS THE MILLION-DOLLAR question that was posed to Lord Jesus by His disciples in Matthew 24. I suspect they had no idea that His answer would be referring to events set to take place thousands of years in the future. They had probably assumed that after He died on the Cross, rose from the dead, and ascended into Heaven, that He'd come right back down - so that the Golden Age of their Messianic King could begin. At that time, they were all unaware that He was not only coming to be the Messiah of the Jews - but the Saviour of *all* mankind. They didn't realize that the Father in Heaven had sent Jesus to ultimately reconcile the *entire* sinful human race unto Himself.

While I believe they perceived Jesus' death and Resurrection as the "end of the world" as they knew it, and the dawn of their Messiah's reign on Earth, Jesus was indeed preparing to usher in a new age - just not the one they were expecting. It would become what we now know as the Age of Grace. This is the age in which we currently live. It's the age in which all human beings (Jew and Gentile alike) can repent of their sins, get washed of their sins in Christ's atoning blood, and be reconciled unto our Holy God and Father in Heaven (YHWH).

15

Until our Lord comes again, every man and woman on Planet Earth can begin a relationship with their Creator - through Christ. Though once He returns, the Age of Grace abruptly ends. So, my advice to everyone reading this is to get right with God while the gift of grace is freely given (Ephesians 2:8). Otherwise, if you do not accept Him as the Saviour of your soul in this age, you'll be destined to meet Him as the Just Judge when He returns.

Getting back to the disciples' question... What will the sign of His (second) coming to Earth be, and of the end of the age? Jesus went into great detail to explain what the "Last Days" generation would need to look for. He gave many signs. You will be excited to know that *our generation* is the first in history to ever see *every sign* (pre-Tribulation) that Christ gave being fulfilled. While there have been numerous generations of Christians who believed that they were *the* generation, this book explains why certain essential signs are exclusive only to our day. I'll delve into, what I believe to be, twelve of the biggest signs. Most were given by Lord Jesus in Matthew 24 and Luke 21. I also chose others from elsewhere in the Bible, because they are far too prevalent today to not address.

All of the signs you will read about herald our Lord's Second Coming, so you may be wondering why I subtitled the book: *The Generation of the Rapture* - not The Generation of *His Return*? Because Jesus' return occurs *after* the seven-year Tribulation that is described in the Book of Revelation. The Rapture (described in 1st Thessalonians 4:16-18) is the event that evacuates us believers *out of* this world *before* the Tribulation begins (Revelation 3:10). So, it's definitely something we should be looking forward to! By the time you're done reading this book (believer or not), you'll be looking up to the skies a whole lot more. Like me, you're going to strongly believe that the imminent Rapture of the faithful and return of Christ are so truly "*at the doors*" (Matthew 24:33).

CHAPTER ONE

ANTI-SEMITISM

JESUS SAID, THE TIME COMETH, THAT WHOSOEVER KILLETH
YOU (JEWS) WILL THINK THAT HE DOETH GOD SERVICE. AND
THESE THINGS WILL THEY DO UNTO YOU, BECAUSE THEY
HAVE NOT KNOWN THE FATHER, NOR ME.

- JOHN 16:2-3

GOD LOVES THE JEW. From the beginning, He always has, still does, and always will. You cannot study the entirety of the Bible and come to any other conclusion. Jesus Christ, who was God in the flesh, came down to Earth *as a Jew*.

As believers, we are called to love what God loves and to hate what He hates. On the flipside, Satan has always loved what God hates and has hated - with a passion - that which the LORD loves. Thus it is no wonder that in this world, which is under the control of the devil (John 12:31, 2nd Corinthians 4:4, and 1st John 5:19), the Jews have always been the most hated and persecuted race in the history of mankind. There are countless examples in the Holy Bible, and throughout history, of demonic leaders or even entire nations coming against the Jews to destroy them. We read of the devil's first stance against the Jewish Nation, known as Israel, in 1st Chronicles 21:1 - "Satan stood up *against* Israel."

Since that time, the devil has influenced many wicked men in positions of power, from every generation, to attempt to eradicate Israel and the Jewish people from the Earth. The Book of Esther speaks of the wicked Persian named Haman. He was the Hitler of Biblical times. He sought to destroy all the Jews (Esther 3:6-14). Thankfully, he didn't succeed in his quest. Rather, the LORD had turned his wicked device back upon his own head - *literally*. He and his sons were hung on the very same gallows that Haman had prepared for the Jews (Esther 9:1-5). Whenever Satan thinks that he has the Jewish people right where he wants them, preparing to annihilate them, Almighty God flips the script.

Throughout history, anyone who's ever sought to destroy the Jews has instead been destroyed themself. Every nation that has ever tried to enslave or to kill off their race is no longer a global power. Today, Egypt is just a strip of land among many nations in the Middle East. Babylon is gone. Greece and Rome are shells of their former selves. And when's the last time that any of you have met a real Nazi? I'm not talking about a skinhead teenager who is confused and mad at the world. No... I mean a living breathing member of the Nazi Party? You have not, and you won't, because they're long gone. Hitler's territory has today become 35 separate European countries, and his Nazis are non-existent.

Meanwhile, the Jews have miraculously survived and outlived every powerful empire that has ever sought to exterminate them. While Adolf Hitler and his regime murdered 6-million Jews, they could not put an end to the age-old race of Hebrews. Instead, the Jewish people (well over 6-million of them) are back today where they have always belonged - in their Biblical Promised Land of Israel. Hitler and his Nazis are defunct. Why do you think that is? How is that possible? The answer is simple and short: GOD. He has stated so many times in His Word that He'll curse those who curse the Jews, and that all who attempt to wipe them out will be wiped out themselves. Still, many men have believed Satan's lies.

They believed that God was done with the Jewish people and Israel, as so many ignorant people still believe in our day and age. Satan is the father of lies, and he'll continue to incite hatred and animosity toward the Jews until Christ returns to put an end to him - and his lies - once and for all. One of the most successful lies Satan has ever told is that "the Jews killed Jesus." Hitler used this falsehood to propel himself to power. Sadly, most Christians followed him because of this great deception. The truth is that a tiny group of powerful and corrupt Jews of the Scribes, Pharisees, and Sadducees, were behind the torture and crucifixion of Jesus - not every Jew who has ever lived!

Not even every member of those cliques of "holy" men were against Jesus. Men such as Nicodemus, Joseph of Arimathea, and even Saint Paul had belonged to the Councils of Jewish priests. It was the top brass of those Councils who had really "killed Jesus," along with the turncoat disciple (Judas Iscariot) and the Romans. Yet, Satan has deceived so many to believe that since *some* Jews played a part then *all* Jews must be guilty. The truth is, as I stated earlier, *Jesus Christ was a Jew*. All of His twelve disciples were *Jews*, along with 99% of His earliest followers. Every Book in the Bible was written *by a Jew*, with the exception of only two. There are 66 books in the Word of God we hold today, meaning that 64 of those were penned by *Jews*.

How could all of the wonderful things that you've read about Jesus (which led you to become a Christian in the first place) have been penned by someone who had taken part in murdering Jesus? It doesn't make much sense, does it? None of Satan's lies ever do. Lord Jesus loves His Jewish brethren with the same undying love that His Father in Heaven has for them, as He and Father YHWH are *"One"* (John 10:30). The main reason He comes back down is to save Israel from certain destruction by their many enemies who come against them in the Last Days. So, if He loves the Jews and Israel so much, to make His Second Coming all about defending them, then why are some Christians anti-Semites? Apparently, it's because a lot of believers today just don't know their Holy Bibles.

You can't call yourself a Christian, while holding anti-Semitic views. Christianity and anti-Semitism are completely antithetical. If you harbor hatred toward the Jews, then you are standing with the devil. Like it or not, it is Biblical truth. Genuine Christianity has never taught nor endorsed anti-Semitism of any kind, but that has not stopped wicked men from twisting and perverting God's Word to make it appear so. The Apostle Paul was actually given foreknowledge that some people (even Christians) would attempt to do this. Paul cautioned against believers in Christ becoming too haughty toward the Jews and Israel. He said that there would even be those who would proclaim that God was *done* with the Jewish people, or preach that "the Church" has become the *new* Israel.

In Romans, Chapter 11, he rebuked anyone who'd teach such nonsense. He said, in verses 1 and 2 -

"HATH GOD CAST AWAY HIS PEOPLE? GOD FORBID. I ALSO AM AN ISRAELITE, OF THE SEED OF ABRAHAM, OF THE TRIBE OF BENJAMIN. GOD HATH NOT CAST AWAY HIS PEOPLE WHICH HE FOREKNEW."

Paul went on to explain that we Christians are "grafted into" God's chosen Family Tree after we put our faith in Jesus Christ, but that we by no means *replace* the Jews. He said that if we were to ever "boast" against Israel or the Jewish people, implying that God was "done" with them, then God would be done *with us*. So, if anyone ever tries to feed you the demonic lie that Israel and the Jews mean nothing to God anymore, refer them to that powerful Chapter of Romans. If anti-Semitic Christians continue believing and teaching that false doctrine, then they do so at their own peril.

Sadly, most early Church leaders and Popes were Jew-haters. Many engaged in systematic discrimination against the Jews, and that led to persecution - which led to expulsion and exile - which ultimately led to execution. Prepare to be just as shocked as I was when you read some of these well-known names. First, there was Constantine. Between the years 315 and 337 AD, he had enacted many harsh laws targeting the Jews. John Chrysostom of Antioch, the Archbishop of Constantinople, was not a great "doctor of the Church" like he is revered as today. His views and teachings on the Jews (or "Judaizers," as he had called them) do not reflect the doctrine of the Holy Bible in any way, shape, or form.

Popular saints in Catholicism, such as Origen and Augustine, published what many consider to be anti-Semitic writings. Also, a majority of Popes throughout the centuries of the early Catholic Church were aggressively anti-Semitic. Some of them had called for Jews to be expelled from nations, and to even be put to death. Now, I don't want Catholics reading this to get the idea that this is an attack on the Catholic Church - because it is not. It is simply historical truth that needs to be told.

Martin Luther, the trailblazing reformer who'd broken away from Catholicism to form Protestantism, left the Church of Rome because of disagreements he had with their authority - especially regarding the Vatican's anti-Semitism. Unfortunately, later in life, when he could not convert as many Jews to Christianity as he had hoped, disappointment turned into hatred. His later writings were very hostile toward the Jewish people.

There are many today who do not want to believe this, but his material is available for anyone to examine. Luther published *On the Jews and Their Lies* in 1543. In the pamphlet, he advocates an 8-point plan to "get rid of" the Jews as a distinct group through religious conversion or by expulsion. Some of the worst language reads, "set fire to their synagogues or schools" and "their houses should be razed and destroyed." It is extremely sad that someone like him can be so revered today. Yes, times were different back then; and some say that with Him being raised in an anti-Semitic church, it was inevitable that he would develop such views. Still, for someone with such supposed knowledge of the Word of God, there is no excuse. He should have known better!

Another widely-revered religious figure who taught that God was done with the Jewish people was Muhammad, the author of Islam. A majority of Muslims hold anti-Semitic beliefs, because the unholy Quran teaches them to hate the Jews. Islam's so-called "prophet" once watched as many as 600 Jews being beheaded in Medina in one day. Allah's word instructs Muslims to "*slay the Jew* wherever you find them."

Do not believe the lie that Muslims only burn the Israeli flag because they "don't like Zionists," and not because it is a Jewish symbol. The truth is that whenever they use the words "Death to Israel" or "Kill the Zionists," every Muslim on Earth knows that these phrases are code for "Kill the Jews." They simply substitute "Zionists" for "Jews" so they can openly express their unbridled anti-Semitism publicly, without being condemned. Anti-Zionism *is* anti-Semitism, no matter what they say.

It irritates me when I hear anti-Semitic Muslims crying about prejudice or discrimination against Islam. Many call us Christians "Islamophobic" or "intolerant." Well, they're actually right on one count, because I will *never* "tolerate" a religion whose creed is to "Destroy Israel and the Jews." Muslims won't receive one shred of sympathy from me, as to how they are treated, until they learn to treat the Jewish people and the Jewish State with respect.

They have turned a term that God loves into a dirty word in our generation. I am sure that you have all heard the Muslims and conspiracy theorists call the Jews "Zionists." The term does not mean whatever they want you to think that it means. In reality, a Zionist is someone who believes the Biblical promises of God to return the Jewish people back to their ancient Homeland of Israel. I believe that. So, that makes *me* a Zionist. Many Christians today are Zionists - not just Jews and Israelis. I'd hope everyone reading this book is a Zionist!

Unfortunately, youth today have been programmed to believe that Zionists are "bad people." Does that make me a bad person? Am I part of some global Zionist conspiracy? Nope. I'm simply doing my best to live according to God's Will in this life; and His Will is for everyone to love, support, and defend Israel. Sad to say, many of today's youngsters are doing the complete opposite. Due to enemies of the Jews flooding social media platforms with anti-Israel propaganda, one recent study found that anti-Semitism has skyrocketed about 50% on America's college campuses.

By far, the number one contributor to the rise of Jew-hatred in American universities is the anti-Israel *Boycott, Divestment, and Sanctions* movement. The BDS is an Islamist-inspired campaign against the Jewish State that has led to Nazi swastikas on doors of Jewish students, along with messages such as "Hitler did nothing wrong." Some faculty members make anti-Semitic gestures in the classrooms, and Stars of David with an "X" scratched into them appear on walls, windows, and doors. At rallies, BDS supporters hand out materials that deny the Holocaust, and promote attacks against Jews and "Jew-lovers." BDS'ers protest, harass, or disrupt pro-Israel speakers - sometimes preventing lectures altogether.

While Muslim hatred of Israel dates back about 1,500 years, BDS was started in 2005 by Omar Barghouti. Barghouti has made no bones about the goal of BDS being "the destruction of Israel." Most people today don't realize that Islamic nations were Hitler's greatest allies in his quest to "exterminate" the Jews. The Jewish people were expelled by decree from all Islamic lands and thrown out of many European countries - Spain, France, Italy, England, Russia, Poland, Portugal, and (of course) Germany.

Not long after Adolf Hitler published his grossly anti-Semitic book, *Mein Kampf,* in 1925, he'd become the ruthless dictator of Germany. Between 1939-1945, He devised the "final solution" to eradicate the Jews, culminating in the tragic Holocaust. Between 1933-1941, persecution of the Jews in Germany rose rapidly until they had been stripped of their rights - not only as citizens, but as human beings. Anti-Semitism had reached an all-time high under Adolf Hitler's Nazi Party rule. In 1938, the deportations of Jews to concentration camps (and ultimately the gas chambers) began.

It has been recorded that when trains bound for gas chambers (filled with screaming Jews) would pass by German churches, the congregations would play their music louder so they could drown out the horrific cries for help. This is one of the most disgusting things that I have ever heard in my life. Due to intimidation by the Nazis, most Christians had remained silent during the systematic murder of God's chosen people. With the exception of a handful of courageous believers, like Dietrich Bonhoeffer, the majority of Christendom in Europe stood by and watched as 6-million Jews perished. This, in my opinion, is the greatest stain on Christianity in history. Bonhoeffer was a fearless German pastor who opposed Hitler, and preached the wise words -

"SILENCE IN THE FACE OF EVIL IS ITSELF EVIL. GOD WILL NOT HOLD US GUILTLESS. NOT TO SPEAK IS TO SPEAK. NOT TO ACT IS TO ACT."

Amen. In 1945, he was hung by Hitler for publicly speaking out against the Nazi regime. Bonhoeffer is an inspiration and role model for all believers. As anti-Semitism is again rearing its ugly head in our generation, we must not be afraid to speak out loudly against it. Whether on social media or television, in schools or the public square, the lies and blood libels against the Jewish people and Israel cannot be tolerated! Christians must strongly refute and condemn them. It does not take long in our society for rumours to spread like wildfire, and kids today follow whatever is trending in their world. Germany proved that it takes only one popular voice to gain the ear of an entire nation. Imagine if Hitler had Twitter at his disposal!

If anti-Semitism were to gain a foothold amongst the youth, I shudder to think just how rapidly it would spread. Take a look at Europe today... as more Muslims migrate there, anti-Semitism has shot through the roof. Jews have been fleeing Europe in droves. An eye-opening study by the Anti-Defamation League (ADL) has revealed that 25% of the world - more than *one-billion* people - hold anti-Semitic views. 1/4 of the globe hates the Jew! What can those of us who love God's people ever do about such troubling statistics? We should remember that the Holocaust had happened because virtually all Christians back then did *nothing*. We cannot remain silent like the believers of Hitler's day had done.

If the Jews look to anyone for protection in this evil world, it should be us Christians. We are called by God to be their greatest ally. It is our duty to defend them, because *their* greatest enemy is *our* greatest enemy. That enemy, of course, is Satan. The devil's been targeting God's chosen from the very beginning. When he becomes too frustrated with not being able to destroy the Jewish people, be sure that he will come for us Christians next. And if you haven't been paying attention, he has already begun to.

THE LORD SAID, I WILL BLESS THEM THAT BLESS THEE (JEWS), AND CURSE HIM THAT CURSETH THEE: AND IN THEE SHALL ALL FAMILIES OF THE EARTH BE BLESSED.

- GENESIS 12:3

CHAPTER TWO

CHRISTIAN PERSECUTION

JESUS SAID, THEN SHALL THEY DELIVER YOU UP TO BE
AFFLICTED, AND SHALL KILL YOU: AND YE SHALL BE HATED
OF ALL NATIONS FOR MY NAME'S SAKE.

\- MATTHEW 24:9

2018'S WORLD WATCH LIST, an annual report released by the Christian persecution watchdog group Open Doors USA, revealed that one out of every twelve Christians globally lives in an area where there is high-level persecution. There are over 200-million Christians who live in areas of the world where our Faith is either illegal, forbidden, or punished. Each year, Open Doors tracks and monitors reports of Christian persecution around the world. They will then rank the 50 countries which are the biggest offenders.

Last year, over 3,000 believers had been murdered, more than 1,200 were kidnapped, about 800 churches were vandalized, and over 1,000 Christian women were raped or sexually harassed. In this world, about a half-dozen women are raped, sexually abused, or forced into Islamic marriages under the threat of death for their faith, *every single day*. There were at least 15 Christian teenagers kidnapped and forced into Islamic marriages in 2017 alone. Open Doors' report had revealed that Islamism is still the main driver of

Christian persecution globally. Muslim-majority nations account for 36 of the 50 countries on the list.

While North Korea topped the list, for the 16th year in a row, Afghanistan had given the oppressive atheist country a run for its money. Along with Afghanistan, there were many other countries that had witnessed a dramatic rise in incidents last year. The most notable among them were Egypt, India, Libya, and Turkey. Egypt has been moving up the list rapidly, due to hundreds of heinous attacks on the Christian community in recent years.

Two years ago, in 2016, a Muslim mob in Cairo had stripped down an elderly Christian woman and paraded her naked on the streets. This occurred during an attack in which seven Christian homes had been looted and torched. The attack, in the village of Karma, began after rumors spread that the woman's Christian son had relations with a Muslim girl. Egypt's top Christian cleric said that the 70-year-old woman was dragged out of her home by the mob, who had beaten her and insulted her before stripping off her clothes. As they forced her to walk through the streets nude, they chanted "Allahu Akbar" (which means "Allah is great"). In Islam, Muslim women are forbidden to marry Christian and Jewish men. Yet, Muslim men are permitted to marry Christian women.

In 2011, many churches had been set on fire in Egypt during a national uprising. In another instance of a Muslim woman being romantically involved with a Christian man, an Islamic mob had burned the church of the man. Large groups of Coptic Christians filled the streets to protest the church being burned. The Egyptian army arrived to stop the protests, and killed 25. That tragic event became known as the "Maspero Massacre." The Copts were met with riot police and tanks. As army vehicles charged at protesters, at least six were crushed under the tanks.

There has also been a wave of kidnappings in Egypt, in which young Christian girls are being abducted and forced into Islamic marriages. The girls (as young as 15) are snatched from homes, schools, and sidewalks, by Muslim men who forcibly take them as wives. Families of abducted girls beg the police authorities for help, but to no avail. The crimes have been taking place under the radar in Egypt for about 50 years. In the province of Qena, there were nearly 100 reports of kidnappings and violence against the Copts from 2011-2014. Since authorities investigating the crimes are Muslim, virtually none of the missing girls have been returned to their families.

In 2017, during "Easter" celebrations, Islamists bombed two Egyptian churches - murdering nearly 50 believers. Four months earlier, at Christmastime, about 30 Christians had been murdered when Islamic terrorists bombed the main cathedral in Cairo. The Islamists love to carry out large-scale attacks on major Christian or Jewish Holidays. They also commit scores of attacks against us "infidels" during their "holy" days. On the first day of the Islamic month of Ramadan in 2017, followers of the so-called *religion of peace* murdered over two-dozen churchgoers. 28 Christians lost their lives in that attack, and another 25 were wounded.

A bus was traveling to a church south of Cairo, when three four-wheel drive vehicles pulled up alongside it and opened fire. When the bus came to a stop, ten gunmen wearing fatigues and masks exited their vehicles and then approached passengers that remained alive. Next, came the life or death question...

"Are you Christian?"

When the passengers answered, "Yes," the Islamic terrorists distributed a pamphlet unto them which contained Quranic verses explaining Ramadan. The attackers then ordered the Christians to recite the Shahada from the pamphlet - the Muslim profession of faith. When our brothers and sisters in Christ refused and said, "No. We were born Christian and will die Christian," the terrorists opened fire at close range and murdered those refusing to convert.

Coptic Christians only make up 10% of Egypt's population of 92-million - apparently 10% *too many* for the Islamic nationalists. The Muslims murdering Christians in Islamic nations are not all members of terror groups like ISIS either. Rather, they are regular everyday adherents of Islam. Their "holy" book instructs them to strike terror in the hearts of unbelievers (us Christians and Jews), and to "slay" us wherever they find us. Any Christian who says "we are all children of God," and "Islam is a religion of peace," needs to say those words while looking into the eyes of a Coptic Christian. It is my opinion that the Copts would strongly disagree.

9 out of the Top 10 worst countries for Christians to live are Islamic nations. Those nations are Afghanistan, Somalia, Sudan, Pakistan, Eritrea, Libya, Iraq, Yemen, and Iran. While the African nations of Nigeria, Ethiopia, Kenya, and Central African Republic are not Muslim-majority (like much of the continent), that hasn't stopped Islamist groups from bringing their oppression and terror to Christians in those nations too. Asian nations like Malaysia, the Philippines, Indonesia, and the Maldives show that persecution of believers by Islamists is not exclusive to the Middle East.

Also in Asia, there is another alarming form of persecution - and that is government-led persecution. The number one offender in this category, and the number one most dangerous country in the world for a Christian to live, is North Korea. Public worship is forbidden there. The Christian population, of around 300,000, are forced to hide beliefs and fellowship. Some 50,000 Christians are wasting away in prison or labor camps for their faith.

ODUSA says "it is illegal to be a Christian in North Korea," and believers are often sent to labor camps or are killed if they are discovered. You'd be arrested for carrying a Bible on the streets of North Korea, and for simply saying "God bless you" or "Merry Christmas." Believers who have been fortunate enough to escape the hell of living under Kim Jong Un's atheist regime give horrific accounts of forced starvation or abortions, crucifixion of believers over fires, and Christians being crushed under steamrollers.

There's another government-led persecutor in the Asia region who should be higher on the list, and that is China. The Chinese government regularly orders demolition of churches, because they perceive Christianity to be a threat to the Communist government. Some believers there are ordered to remove images of Lord Jesus, and to replace them with pictures of President Xi Jinping. This year, Xi cemented his position as China's dictator - possibly for life. The Chinese parliament voted to eliminate the term limit for the Presidency, paving the way for Xi to serve indefinitely.

Spokesmen for the President issue statements you'd expect to hear in an End Times film about Antichrist. One of Xi's officials, Qi Yan, has said, "Many rural people are ignorant... thinking God is their Savior. After our cadres' work, they will come to realize their mistakes and will think: we should no longer rely on Jesus, but on the party for help." Another official that's close to Xi made a similar statement, saying, "Christians are ignorant, and need to be taught to worship the State - not God."

Under the leadership of Xi, thousands of Crosses have been forcibly removed from churches, hundreds of churches have been destroyed, pastors and priests have been arrested, and the Bible's even been *banned*. In early 2018, Chinese Christians were unable to find the Bible listed on their country's biggest retail websites. According to *South China Morning Post*, searches for "Bible" on Amazon, Taobao, Jingdong, or Dang Dang, yielded a "no results" response. Search analytics revealed a large spike in the keyword "Bible" on March 30th; but two days later, the analytics showed 0 searches. The data proved that the government began censoring the word on the internet.

Before being banned online, the Holy Bible was prohibited in China's commercial brick-and-mortar stores. It was only available for purchase in church bookstores. Texts of all other major Faiths, such as Buddhism, Islam, Hinduism, and Taoism, are available to purchase in Chinese stores and online. An atheist blogger for the *Patheos* website actually took issue with the Bible ban, writing, "The Chinese policy just adds fuel to the Christians' persecution complex, and no one can say that, in this case, they don't have a valid, even important point."

One of the most surprising countries on the World Watch List would have to be India. I'm sure many think, as I once did, that India is made up primarily of hippie Buddhists and Hindus. That is not the case. In recent years, a very disturbing trend has been forming in the Hindu and Buddhist nations – *radicalism*. Hindu nationalism has rapidly spread across India since the election of Prime Minister Narendra Modi. Under Modi, religious freedom violations against Christians spread unchecked. Last year, Open Doors documented 600+ persecution incidents; but said that most cases remain unreported, so the true number is much higher.

Next door to India, Hindu-majority Nepal has criminalized conversion to Christianity or Judaism. Buddhist nationalism has led to a dramatic and violent rise in hostility toward Christians in the countries of Sri Lanka, Bhutan, and Myanmar.

2018 was the 26th year that Open Doors USA published the World Watch List. Over the past 25 years, just three countries have ever topped the list: North Korea (2002-2017), Saudi Arabia (1993-1995, 1998-2001), and Somalia (1996-1997). The Top Ten nations over the 25-year span were North Korea, Saudi Arabia, Iran, Somalia, Afghanistan, Maldives, Yemen, Sudan, Vietnam, and China. These nations fulfill Philippians 3:18, being "enemies of the Cross of Christ."

A three-year research study, reported in 2016 and conducted by an International Catholic Charity (Aid to the Church in Need), found that Christians comprised 75% of those persecuted for their religion globally. The study revealed that Christians are not only more persecuted than any other Faith group, but that they are also experiencing the very worst forms of persecution. Christians have been martyred for their beliefs more so than any other Faith group over the past two decades. In 2016 alone, a follower of Christ was murdered for their beliefs *every 6 minutes.*

In the Middle East region, the only safe haven for believers is the Holy Land of Israel. While the Western world has not yet seen persecution of Christians reach the violent levels of the Mideast or Asia, I believe we're leaning in that dangerous direction more and more each and every new year. During the administration of Barack Obama, especially following the Supreme Court decision to essentially legalize same-sex marriage nationwide, Americans holding the Biblical worldview were under attack. Believers were taken before courts or fined, fired from jobs, had their businesses shut down, and were even *imprisoned.* What was the crime? Only refusing to violate their deeply held Faith.

In the minds of liberal Americans today, Freedom of Speech and Expression should apply to everyone *except* Christians. When we publicly express our Faith, and take a stand against something which the Bible has deemed immoral, we're told to shut up or are shouted down as hateful bigots. Yet, whenever someone expresses Biblically-hostile, anti-Semitic, anti-Christian, anti-American, or anti-Israel beliefs, they are applauded and celebrated in the media for exercising their controversial Freedom of Speech. This is such gross hypocrisy. One big example of this double standard is the lamestream media's response to NFL player Colin Kaepernick's "take a knee" movement.

When a devout Christian Quarterback, Tim Tebow, had taken a knee in prayer to our Lord during games, the mainstream media would go berserk. Yet, when a "Black Power" Quarterback takes a knee in protest during our country's National Anthem, the same lamestream media cannot praise him enough. MSNBC has said of Kaepernick, "When a NFL player kneels in protest, it's *unifying.*" A few years ago, the same network said (regarding Tim Tebow),

"Kneeling in prayer is *polarizing.*" So, liberals seem to think that bringing God onto a football field is a horrible thing; but they also think that bringing divisive politics into the game is something to be celebrated. Sorry, my liberal friends, I assure you that it's most certainly the other way around.

The folks at MSNBC, and most of the media, are chock-full of double standards. Besides their contradictory opinions on NFL kneeling, another one of their many double standards has to do with us devout Christians refusing to participate in gay marriages. The Bakers, calligraphers, florists, photographers, tailors, or other Faith-based business owners denying services for gay weddings have been demonized as bigots by the media. The PC police are obsessed with forcing believers, like Jack Phillips of Masterpiece Cakeshop in Colorado, to bake a cake for a gay wedding.

Imagine if the Black Lives Matter activists were pressured to make a cake for the Ku Klux Klan. Do you think the media would call them "bigots" or discriminatory for refusing service? I highly doubt it. What if Democrats were forced to make a pro-Trump cake, or to provide services for a Trump Rally? I am sure that the media would be siding with the anti-Trumpers. What if Jews were told they had to bake a cake for Nazis? Obviously, they should *never* be expected to comply. I rest my case. It seems as if only God-fearing Christians are forced to violate their conscience and deeply held beliefs today.

Sadly, even after the landslide Republican Party victory in the 2016 Election, Christians are still under attack across this nation. The messages we are being sent from most liberal Americans are loud and clear: "Christians are NOT welcome" and "Conform OR ELSE." Even powerful corporations use money and influence to force Christians into submission. Apple, AMC, CBS, Coca Cola, Disney, Facebook, Marriott, Marvel, MGM, NBC, NCAA, NFL, Paypal, Sony, Time Warner, Twitter, and Viacom (just to name a few) are all pushing the LGBT agenda. The past few years, these companies all launched boycotts against any States attempting to pass Religious Liberty Bills.

For those not aware, Religious Freedom Laws are passed to protect us Christians and Jews from having to violate our Faith for any reason. All of the Companies that I mentioned above are hypocrites. They say they're fighting the laws in order to prevent discrimination. Meanwhile, they are all guilty of discriminating against those who adhere to Almighty God's Word. They claim to defend freedom, while at the same time, trampling or threatening freedoms of those with whom they disagree. It is nothing short of a war on Christians, plain and simple.

HGTV dropped the Benham Brothers' reality show, before it had even aired, because of their Biblical beliefs. A few years later, their friends, Chip and Joanna Gaines of HGTV's *Fixer Upper*, were demonized in the media for merely *attending* a church that preaches what the Bible says about Gay Marriage. *Duck Dynasty* patriarch, Phil Robertson, whipped up a firestorm in the media for daring to publicly speak what God says about homosexuality. All of these famous believers had come under fire, not for their own cooked up belief system - but for believing what the Word of God says. Sadly, there are many Christians nationally who endure the same kind of pressure from the LGBT Mafia, and who lose their businesses for refusing to violate their Faith.

Christian-owned Timbercreek Bed and Breakfast, of Illinois, was forced to pay a gay couple $80,000 for refusing to host a gay union ceremony. Immediately after Illinois recognized same-sex civil unions in 2011, a gay couple, Todd and Mark Wathen, had inquired as to whether or not Timbercreek would be hosting civil unions. Owner Jim Walder replied, "No. We only do weddings." The men had threatened to sue Walder and he replied, "the Bible trumps Illinois law, United States law, and global law. Please read John 3:16." The couple complained to the Illinois Human Rights Commission and won their case against Timbercreek.

In the Washington Supreme Court, there is a case involving a Christian grandmother. 73-year-old Baronelle Stutzman, owner of Arlene's Flowers, has been accused of "discrimination" against a gay couple. She had come under fire for declining to make flower arrangements for their wedding. Stutzman had served the couple, Robert Ingersoll and Curt Freed, for years; but she declined to do arrangements for their wedding because it violated her beliefs.

The owners of Sweet Cakes By Melissa bakery, in Oregon, were ordered to pay a $135,000 fine after they refused to bake a wedding cake for a Gay Marriage ceremony. The Oregon Bureau of Labor and Industries Commissioner who heard their case, Brad Avakian, said the Christian owners needed to be "rehabilitated." *Rehabilitated*? So believing the Holy Bible is a disease now?!

You should all be familiar with the case of Kentucky County Clerk, Kim Davis, who had actually been thrown into *prison* for refusing to violate her beliefs. Thank God that her story garnered enough media coverage to spark a huge uproar in the Christian community, otherwise she'd most likely still be behind bars today. Simply for adhering to God's Word! The uncomfortable question that believers should be asking today is... how many Kim Davis' are out there as we speak? How many Christians, who've gotten no media attention, are sitting in jail cells right now for refusing to violate their Faith? It is a difficult thought to ponder.

There are so many of our brothers and sisters in the Faith that are being sued and punished by the U.S. judicial system for being *falsely* accused of discrimination. The LGBT community are *not* victims, as they are so often portrayed. Rather, they are the ones who are really discriminating. What if a Christian group tried to hold church services inside of a gay club or resort? Would they be winning a discrimination lawsuit for being denied entry? I'll bet not. How about if a believer walked into an LGBT-themed print shop and asked to have Leviticus 18:22 printed on t-shirts? Would the establishment be forced to make clothing that made them feel uncomfortable? Would they be forced to pay a fine? I think we all know, full well, the answer to these questions is a resounding NO.

If the shoe were on the other foot, Christians would not be winning lawsuits for being discriminated against; and the number one reason for that is because we wouldn't be suing anyone who refuses us service. We just take our business elsewhere. We never set out to intentionally ruin another person's life, or to break them financially, simply because they hold different beliefs than we do. We do our best to influence and inspire others to believe the Word of God, but we don't *force* it on anyone (like we're always falsely accused of doing). Contrarily, as my friends the Benham Brothers point out, LGBT bullies force us to "accept" their lifestyle - then they force us to "celebrate" it - and now they are forcing us to "participate" in it.

If anybody in this country is forcing anything on anyone, it's the LGBT crowd forcing an agenda down everyone else's throat - not the other way around. Every single freedom-loving American, Christian or not, needs to stand united against this evil agenda of bullying others you disagree with into submission. Even Christian children, teens, and college students, aren't safe. School teachers, promoting the LGBT agenda, felt emboldened during the Obama years to discriminate against Christian students who dared object to our society's "new normal."

In 2017, a lesbian teacher in Florida actually forced students in her class to remove their Cross necklaces. One of the students reported that Lora Jane Reidas, her Math teacher, had approached her and said, "I need you to take your necklace off." When the student asked why, Riedas refused to explain and simply said, "It is disrespectful, and you have to take it off." The student says that she did not want to be disrespectful, "so I took it off, but I felt bad because I felt like I was being forced to deny my Faith." Riedas is a Gay-Straight Alliance sponsor, and engages in political activism in her classroom, which is decorated with LGBT propaganda. She has buttons displayed on her desk, facing students, stating "I Love My LGBT Students" and "*Proud* Public Employee."

Think about the left-wing outrage if a Christian teacher ever dared have John 3:16, "Pro-Life," or "I Love My Bible-believing Students" buttons displayed in their classroom. They'd be fired on day one. Yet, Riedas' superiors at the school have seemingly had no problem with her LGBT propaganda on full display. As if all this was not enough to get a God-fearing parent's blood boiling, the teacher also placed LGBT rainbow stickers on her students' folders without their consent. One of the Christian students who removed an LGBT sticker said that "Ms. Riedas' behavior toward me changed for the worse."

When Obama was in power, the Godless teachers across this nation cracked down on students who dared bring Bibles into the classroom. Like Riedas, they'd confiscated Crucifixes and banned God-related clothing. In one instance, a 2nd-grader in Texas had her Bible taken away during "read to myself time." Students were told to bring in personal books from home to read, but apparently the *Good Book* was off-limits. While anything having to do with the Faiths of Christianity and Judaism was being abolished from the schools during Obama's tenure, Islam was being force-fed to your kids. In mandated Common Core textbooks, our Faiths were not taught. When they were mentioned, they were mocked or put down. Yet, an entire chapter (of 30+ pages) was devoted to Islam!

Most major colleges in this country today are infested with far-left atheist professors who don't just question God, but they openly attack Him, mock the Holy Bible, and alienate or publicly disgrace any students who would dare disagree. Go to any secular campus today and tell a professor that you believe in God as our Creator, that Jesus Christ was born of a virgin, that He rose from the dead, and that the Holy Bible is the unerring Word of God. If you are really feeling bold, tell them you believe Jesus is *coming back*. The ignorant Godless "teachers" will shout you down and will laugh you to scorn. If you have never seen the Christian film *God's NOT Dead*, I recommend you do. It's a perfect portrayal of what life is like for believers on college campuses today.

Harvard College, like a majority of this nation's prestigious institutes of learning, had been originally established in 1636 as a Christian University to train clergy. Sadly, they are anything *but* Christian today. In March of 2018, it was reported that Harvard placed the university's largest Christian group on administrative probation for adhering to their Biblical beliefs. Harvard College Faith and Action was disciplined by the Office of Student Life because they "pressured a female member to resign for dating a woman." So, to be clear, a *Christian* group, whose members all believe the *Christian* Bible, asked a member living in unrepentant sin to resign. There is absolutely nothing wrong with this picture. Harvard's powers that be are slapping their God-fearing founders in the face by *punishing* the Faith they used to *preach*.

I like how Andrew T. Walker of *Weekly Standard* described the complete 180 which Harvard has taken from its inception. He wrote, "The shift at the University is so radical that while a few decades ago it took courage to be openly gay at Harvard, these days it takes a great deal of courage to be openly CHRISTIAN." Talk about hitting the nail on the head. Unfortunately, Harvard is not the only college persecuting Christians for their deeply held beliefs. Universities of Vanderbilt, Cal State, Bowdoin, Iowa, and Wayne State have been targeting Christian groups for probation, suspension, and even expulsion.

Vanderbilt's "Tolerance Policy" forced most Christian groups from off of its campus altogether. This is such a disgrace to the fabric of our country, as our very *first* schoolbook was the Bible. How far we have fallen as a Judeo-Christian Nation! Believe it or not, anti-God liberals became so emboldened under eight years of Obama, they are now attempting to *ban the Bible*. No joke. A bill in California, that is expected to pass in the Democrat-controlled

State Senate later this year (2018), aims to ban Faith-based books which "address issues of homosexuality or gender identity."

Assembly Bill 2943 declares Christian books or conferences, dealing with Biblical views on homosexuality or transgenderism, as "fraudulent" under the State's consumer fraud statute. The Bill becoming Law would *criminalize* and penalize all those who dare to share a "Biblical view on marriage." We have been living in an America that's been entrenched in extreme secularism for the past decade. Now, it appears our country has descended into flat out *paganism*. God help us. Even Christians in neighboring Canada are facing extreme pressure from their liberal leadership, led by Prime Minister Justin Trudeau.

In 2017, a Canadian Christian school had been ordered by a Public School Board to "cease reading or studying any Scripture" that was considered as "offensive" to certain individuals. Targeted Biblical verses included all those speaking against homosexuality, fornication, adultery, idolatry, and witchcraft. Battle River School Division, in Alberta, directed Cornerstone Christian Academy to refrain from teaching on Scripture that the board had determined "violates Alberta's human rights legislation." The school's vision statement says, "students will have a good working knowledge of the Bible as a foundation to their education." Unfortunately, their liberal School Board is dead set on changing that.

There have been many more disturbing developments coming out of Canada, and you can read about all of them on my website (*BiblicalSigns.com*). Their Prime Minister, Justin Trudeau, called Evangelical Christians "the *worst* part of Canadian society," and he was one of the very first world leaders to ever take part in a Gay Pride march. America was hell for Christians under Obama, and it's safe to say that our brothers and sisters to the North feel the exact same under Trudeau. We need to pray for Godly leaders to be raised up, not only here in our country - but in Canada, and in every other nation of this world!

While Christians in the West have faced extreme pressure for simply believing what the LORD has to say about things, we have not yet experienced the deadly persecution that our brothers and sisters across the globe have been enduring. Lord willing, we will not anytime soon! Satan has influenced so many around the world to persecute believers, but there is no question that his top recruits have been Islamic terrorists. The next chapter delves deep into the Latter-Day sign of terrorism.

JESUS SAID, BLESSED ARE THEY WHICH ARE PERSECUTED FOR RIGHTEOUSNESS' SAKE: FOR THEIRS IS THE KINGDOM OF HEAVEN. BLESSED ARE YE, WHEN MEN SHALL REVILE YOU, AND PERSECUTE YOU, AND SHALL SAY ALL MANNER OF EVIL AGAINST YOU FALSELY, FOR MY SAKE. REJOICE, AND BE EXCEEDING GLAD: FOR GREAT IS YOUR REWARD IN HEAVEN.

- MATTHEW 5:10-12

CHAPTER THREE

TERRORISM

JESUS SAID, AS THE DAYS OF NOAH WERE, SO SHALL ALSO THE
COMING OF THE SON OF MAN BE.

(IN THE DAYS OF NOAH) THE EARTH WAS FILLED WITH
VIOLENCE (TERRORISM).

- MATTHEW 24:37 & GENESIS 6:11

RECENTLY RELEASED FIGURES FROM the GPI (Global Peace Index) revealed that worldwide terrorism has reached an *all-time high*. According to the Peace Index, the annual number of terror incidents has nearly *tripled* since 2011. That is only seven years from the publication of this book. Also, the breadth of terrorism is spreading; as there are now only 10 countries - out of nearly 250 - that have not been victims of terror in recent years. Deaths from terrorism have risen almost 1000% in the past decade in at least 35 countries. Deaths from terrorism in Europe, and specifically in Belgium, Britain, and France, more than *doubled* since 2012. And according to researchers at the Institute for Economics and Peace, deaths from conflicts in Islamic countries are at a 25-year high.

The majority of the terrorist activity has been concentrated in Mideast Muslim nations, to no surprise. Globally, there have been around 30,000 Islamic terror attacks since the 9/11/2001 tragedy; and well over 10,000 attacks "in the name of Allah," the god of

Islam, in just the past 5 years. That's over 2,000 every year! Since its inception, over 270-million human beings have been murdered by followers of that "peaceful religion" known as Islam. While liberal talking heads love saying, "not all Muslims are terrorists," or "ISIS perverts the religion," facts disagree. Islamic terrorists follow Muhammad's commands in the Quran more faithfully than the majority of Muslims in the world.

The moderate or Westernized Muslims attempt to spiritualize the literal commands of Allah to justify his many calls for "jihad" against infidels. Though, scholars all agree that when Muhammad wrote about jihad, it was never meant to be spiritualized. He had specifically meant to declare physical war on non-Muslims if they refuse to convert to Islam. I'll share some Quranic verses later in this chapter to prove, beyond a shadow of a doubt, that beheading infidels - cutting off their fingers and toes - burning them alive - throwing them off of highrise buildings - burying them up to their heads in sand - and crucifying them - can *never* be "spiritualized." Muhammad meant his words to be taken quite *literally*.

Historically, Muhammad was no "prophet." He was a military leader. He had laid siege to towns, massacring the men, raping the women and enslaving the children. He inspired his followers to battle when they did not feel that it was right to fight, promising them slaves and spoils if they did. He threatened them with hell if they did not. How different from our Holy Lord Jesus Christ and the *real* holy prophets of our true God, YHWH.

Today, most Muslims in America and the Western world are not living like their prophet. That is a good thing! Islamic terror groups, like the Islamic State (ISIS), are Muslims truly modeling their lives after Muhammad. Contrary to the widely held belief, which the lamestream liberal media promotes here in the West, this isn't a small movement of extremists in the religion of Islam. It's a large and growing movement. There are hundreds of Islamic terror groups globally, and it is estimated that 25% of the Muslim population are radicals. This means there are about 300-million Muslims in the world supporting or engaging in terror activities.

There have been more Christians and Jews brutally murdered by Islamists in the 20th century than in all previous 19 centuries *combined*, and roughly 100,000 Christians are murdered for their Faith *every year* by Muslim terrorists.

While prophesying to His disciples the many signs that would precede His return to Earth, Lord Jesus said that the world would be "as it was in the days of Noah." The Book of Genesis, Chapter 6 and verse 5, describes the human condition on Earth in Noah's days. The LORD said that "the wickedness of man was great in the earth, and that every imagination of the thoughts of his heart was only evil continually." He went on to say that all men were corrupt, with the exception of only Noah. In verse 11, we read, "the earth was filled with violence." In the Hebrew translation, the word used for violence can mean "terror."

It is important to note that God's attention is always centered on the Nation of Israel in the Bible. This is what makes Christ's Noah prophecy all the more exclusive to our day and age, because the Hebrew word used for "violence" in Genesis 6 is "HAMAS" - which means "shedding of innocent blood." For over 3-decades, Palestine's leading terror group has been called *Hamas*. It is very interesting that the word used to describe terror, back in the Holy Bible's first Book, is the name of one of Israel's greatest foes!

While Hamas, without a doubt, has committed the most terror attacks against Israelis in modern times, there've been many other groups that have attacked the Jewish State since its 1948 rebirth. Terrorist groups such as Hezbollah, the PLO (Palestine Liberation Organization), Islamic Jihad, Fatah, the Muslim Brotherhood, and ISIS, have all sought the destruction of Israel; but Hamas has, by far, been the most constant threat - hands down.

The Holy Bible interprets the Bible, and God planted a word that would only be truly relevant in this generation back in the very first Book of the Holy Scriptures. Jesus knew that the word "Hamas" was there, as He penned Genesis with YHWH through their Spirit. In Matthew 24, verse 37, He prophesied that the land in and around Israel would be filled with the terror of *Hamas*. For thousands upon thousands of years, there was no group of people called by that name. That is... until *our generation*. Since Israel's rebirth, there've been around 1,400 terror attacks - leaving about 3,500 dead and injuring around 14,000 innocent Israelis. Hamas, Hezbollah, and Islamic Jihad are all the proxies of Israel's biggest enemy on the world stage: *Iran*.

These terror groups all receive their weapon arsenals directly from Iran. The Islamic regime in Tehran is the largest funder and organizer of terrorism globally. If we ever want to truly win the "War on Terror," and destroy the deadly serpent threatening our world, then we must cut off the serpent's head - which is IRAN. The Iranians station the groups that I have mentioned strategically on the borders of Israel. These terrorists receive their marching orders directly from the Ayatollahs, and they serve as hired hands of the anti-Israel regime. The close proximity of these groups to the Jewish State allows Iran to make war on Israel, without ever having the two nations engaged in direct conflict. Iran knows, full well, that they would lose a one-on-one war with Israel.

Sharing a mutual hatred of the Jewish people, the Palestinians - led by Hamas - are more than happy to do Iran's dirty work. They use whatever weapons they can get their hands on to inflict terror upon Israel. In recent years, their weapons of choice have been guns, knives, machetes, molotov cocktails, axes, grenades, flaming kites, vehicles, and rockets. Around 20,000 rockets have been launched into Israel from the Hamas-controlled Gaza Strip since 2001. Over 5,000 of those have been fired upon Israel in the past 4 years alone. Here in America, ignorant liberals scream for "gun control" to prevent mass-casualty terror attacks. What they fail to understand is that mass murderers weaponize anything, as the Palestinians have proven.

Biblically-illiterate politicians do not recognize that we are in a spiritual battle between good and evil, and that guns are simply one of many tools which a terrorist will use to take innocent lives. Banning guns will *never stop* the plague of terrorism. Along with the many weapons that I have already mentioned, which the terror groups threatening Israel use on a daily basis, Islamists have also used planes and pressure cookers. Why aren't Democrats pushing for a "pressure cooker ban" here in America? Such a bomb can leave dozens dead. The truth is that it is not guns, knives, bombs, vehicles, or pressure cookers that have been murdering thousands of innocent people globally. It is the dangerous ideology of Islam. It's the head, heart, and hands behind the weapon that is to blame.

Unfortunately, many cannot comprehend this reality. Liberals will blame anything, and anyone, except the terrorists themselves. When Israelis are murdered by Palestinians, Israel is portrayed as the "bad guy" when they retaliate. When Christians are murdered by Islamists, it is we who are blamed for provoking them with our *Islamophobia*. When Americans are murdered, assault weapons are to blame. When a Muslim couple shoot up an office Christmas Party, "poor vetting" of immigrants is to blame. When an Islamic shooter goes postal at a U.S. Army base, "workplace violence" or mental health are to blame. It seems as if every terrorist attack carried out by a Muslim, especially in the U.S., gets labeled any and every thing other than what it is - *Islamic*.

The civilized world will never defeat the scourge of Islamic terrorism until we can learn to call it what it is. We need to call a spade a spade. I really love how Israeli Prime Minister Benjamin Netanyahu puts it - "If it looks like a duck, walks like a duck, and quacks like a duck, then what is it? That's right, *it's a duck...* It's time the world started calling a duck *a duck*." Can I get an amen?! Politically correct thinking to appease radical Muslims does not work. It never will. So long as the Quran is read by billions across the globe (the book that contains 100+ verses calling for Muslims to "strike terror" in the hearts of unbelievers), they'll always hate us. They'll always want to murder us. You can't get around it. It is just the way it is.

Until the world realizes that Islamic terror is not spawned by radical clerics and mosques, nor by propaganda, or campaigns in the Middle East, but solely by the "holy" book of Islam, terrorism isn't going anywhere. For not one of the most dangerous terror groups in the world today are Christian, Jewish, Buddhist, Hindu, or any other religion for that matter. They are *all* Islamic. Islam is a cancer spreading across the globe. It infects, and systematically destroys, every society it touches. On average, every 12th verse of the Quran speaks of Allah's hatred for the infidels. It calls for our death, forced conversion, or subjugation. Here are examples -

QURAN 2:191-193: "KILL them wherever you find them... Fight them till there is no more disbelief and worship is only for Allah."

QURAN 3:151: "Cast TERROR into the hearts of unbelievers."

QURAN 5:33: "They should be murdered or CRUCIFIED or their hands and their feet should be cut off on opposite sides or they should be imprisoned."

QURAN 8:12: "I will cast TERROR into the hearts of those who disbelieve. Strike off their heads and strike off every fingertip."

QURAN 8:39: "FIGHT with them until there is no more fitna (disbelief in Allah) and religion is all for Allah."

QURAN 9:5: "SLAY idolaters wherever you find them. Take them captive and besiege them. Lie in wait for them in every ambush."

QURAN 9:29: "FIGHT those who believe not in Allah."

QURAN 9:30: "And the JEWS say: Ezra is the son of Allah; and the CHRISTIANS say: The Messiah is the son of Allah; these are the words of their mouths; they imitate the saying of those who disbelieved before; may Allah DESTROY them."

QURAN 47:3-4: "When you meet those who disbelieve smite at their necks till you have KILLED and wounded many of them."

BUKHARI 52:177: "Allah's apostle said, The Hour will not be established until you fight with the JEWS, and the stone behind which a Jew will be hiding will say. 'O Muslim! There is a Jew hiding behind me, so KILL HIM.'"

BUKHARI 52:220: "I have been made victorious with TERROR."

MUSLIM 1:33: "I've been commanded to FIGHT against people till they testify that there is no god but Allah, and that Muhammad is the messenger of Allah."

MUSLIM 19:4294: "Fight in the name of Allah and in his way. Fight against those who disbelieve in Allah. Make a HOLY WAR."

MUSLIM 20:4645: "JIHAD in the way of Allah!"

TABARI 7:97: "The Prophet (Muhammad) declared, 'KILL ANY JEW who falls under your power.'"

TABARI 9:69: "KILLING unbelievers is a small thing to us."

Though politically incorrect when Christians or Jews point it out, the Quran admits that Muslims do not worship the same God as Judaism and Christianity (Quran 109:1-6). Salvation can only be *achieved* in Islam through martyrdom or by murdering infidels (Jews & Christians). The God and Father of Jews and Christians, YHWH, teaches that Salvation is *received* by faith in the sacrifice of His only begotten Son, Jesus Christ - who was crucified on our behalf. Islam's god wants you to die *for him*, while our God died *for us*. What a difference! Our Holy Book's LORD commands us to "do no murder"; while, as I've just proved through the Quran, Allah is *all for* fighting - slaying - murdering - beheading - and committing acts of terror "in his name."

Islam is the polar opposite of Christianity and Judaism; and the main reason Muslims hate us Christians and Jews so much is because their god is *Satan*. Lucifer fell from Heaven because he wanted to BE God (Isaiah 14:13-14); and now, through Islam, he can obtain his age-old desire to be worshipped *as God*. Jesus said that the devil "was a murderer from the beginning" (John 8:44), and there's no other group on Planet Earth with more murderers in its ranks than Islam. Besides Satan, there is another archenemy of YAHWEH mentioned throughout the pages of our Holy Bible - and that is the chief of the false gods, *Baal*.

What didn't surprise me, in my studies, is that the name Allah is derived from the name of Baal. According to the Encyclopedia of Religion, Arabs knew of Baal as Allah long before Muhammad had ever propped him up to be worshipped as the supreme god of Muslims. Before the author of Islam came around, the Arabs had recognized many false gods and goddesses. Each Arab tribe had their own deities. 360 gods were worshipped in their lands. There was a god for every day of their calendar year. Baal/Allah was the name assigned to each tribe's "high god." Baal/Allah was known as the "warrior god" and "moon god." The crescent moon was the symbol for Baal; and today, it's the widely recognized symbol for the religion of Islam and Allah.

Baal was YHWH's chief enemy all throughout the pages of the Old Testament, and Satan is the adversary of God in the New Testament. So, could Lucifer be Baal and vice versa? Biblically, it makes all the sense in the world. It is also important to note that Allah is referred to as "the great *deceiver*" (Quran 3:54 & 8:30). That title should ring a bell in the minds of believers, as someone is referred to as the great deceiver in our Book - and that someone is Satan. So, if Baal is Satan and Allah is Baal, then it is hard for anyone to deny that ALLAH IS SATAN.

The Book of Revelation tells us that the devil will make war on believers, and that we will be slain and *beheaded*. What group of people on Earth do we see beheading Christians today? From medieval times up until a few years ago, the answer was *no one*. Yet, *in our day*, there is a clear cut *someone* - and that would be Islamists. There can be no denying that Islamic terrorism (and the religion of Islam itself) is so truly *of the devil*.

AND I SAW THE SOULS OF THEM THAT WERE BEHEADED FOR THE WITNESS OF JESUS, AND FOR THE WORD OF GOD.

- REVELATION 20:4

CHAPTER FOUR

THE FIG TREE

JESUS SAID, NOW LEARN A PARABLE OF THE FIG TREE; WHEN
HIS BRANCH IS YET TENDER, AND PUTTETH FORTH LEAVES,
YE KNOW THAT SUMMER IS NIGH.

- MATTHEW 24:32

THE GOSPEL OF MATTHEW, Chapter 24, is arguably the Holy Bible's most comprehensive account of the "Last Days" signs that herald Christ's return - that were given to us by Jesus Himself. In verse 34, He told His disciples that "the generation" witnessing fulfillment of His signs would be alive during the season of His Second Coming. In verses 32-34, He mentioned the blossoming of the "*fig tree*" - and that is the most important sign of them all. Without this integral sign being fulfilled, all the rest of His signs could be taking place at once and mean *nothing* prophetically.

The reason being that Jews and Christians have experienced persecution for thousands of years, Earth has experienced a lot of powerful earthquakes, false prophets have been around since the earliest days of Christianity, extreme weather has occurred since the days of Noah, and there've been wars in every generation. But for around 2,000 years, since Christ ascended into Heaven, there was no Nation of Israel on Planet Earth. The "fig tree" that Jesus was referring to was, no doubt, ISRAEL.

Our Lord said that when we witness all of the signs He listed in Matthew 24 taking place, during the generation of the Jewish State's rebirth, we'd *"know"* that His return is *"near."* Throughout history, there have been a lot of Christians who believed that they were *the* generation who'd live to see Him coming in the clouds; but that was impossible with no Israel on the map. I'm glad those generations lived with the hope of seeing Christ come back; but the fact remains that if they lived any time before 1948, there was no way they could be the generation that Jesus had spoken of.

After the Jews had been exiled from their Promised Land by the Assyrians, Babylonians, Romans, Muslims, Turks, and others, they'd been scattered across the globe. Thoughts of their Biblical Homeland ever being resurrected appeared dismal, and virtually impossible. They had one sure and strong hope to cling to though: God's Eternal Word. In the Bible, the LORD had never broken even one promise that He'd ever made to Israel. He had promised in His Word, numerous times, to return the Jewish people to their God-given Land in the Last Days and to reestablish their Nation. The reestablishment of the Jewish State was Jesus' sign of the fig tree blossoming *fulfilled*.

When our Lord eventually makes His imminent return, every believer should know that He comes back down to defend and to save Israel from certain destruction in the Battle of Armageddon. Christ will personally fight and defeat Antichrist, as well as all of the nations who join him in making war on God's chosen Nation. Jesus will then rule and reign from Israel's Capital of Jerusalem, as King of kings and Lord of lords over the entire world. Until there was actually a Nation of Israel on the earth, none of these prophecies could be fulfilled. For over 2,500 years, there was no "Israel." In May of 1948, that changed.

Before I go further, I'm sure many of you may be asking how I can be so sure that the fig tree which Jesus referred to was truly the Nation of Israel? When in doubt, examine the entirety of the

Scriptures to figure it out. When God mentioned the "fig tree" in Jeremiah 24:5, Hosea 9:10, and Joel 1:6-7, He referred to Israel in every instance. There is no one who can argue otherwise. So, that settles that. Now, back to 1948... 70 years ago, on May 14th, the ancient Biblical Nation of Israel was officially reborn. The LORD prophesied, about 3,000 years ago, that the Jews would be exiled from their Holy Land for just over 2,500 Years. After that period of separation, He said He'd return them to their Promised Land. We read in Ezekiel 37:21 -

"THUS SAITH THE LORD GOD; BEHOLD, I WILL TAKE THE CHILDREN OF ISRAEL FROM AMONG THE HEATHEN, WHITHER THEY BE GONE, AND WILL GATHER THEM ON EVERY SIDE, AND BRING THEM INTO THEIR OWN LAND."

In 606 BC, the Jewish exile began. In the exact number of prophesied years later, God would fulfill His age-old promise to the Jewish people. He indeed gathered them from all nations of the world, wherever they'd been scattered, and brought them *back* into their ancient God-given Land. I really love the mathematical prophecy found in the Book of Ezekiel. In Chapter 4, verses 4-6, the LORD said to the prophet -

"LIE THOU UPON THY LEFT SIDE, AND LAY THE INIQUITY OF THE HOUSE OF ISRAEL UPON IT: ACCORDING TO THE NUMBER OF THE DAYS THAT THOU SHALT LIE UPON IT THOU SHALT BEAR THEIR INIQUITY. FOR I HAVE LAID UPON THEE THE YEARS OF THEIR INIQUITY, ACCORDING TO THE NUMBER OF THE DAYS, THREE HUNDRED AND NINETY DAYS: SO SHALT THOU BEAR THE INIQUITY OF THE HOUSE OF ISRAEL. AND WHEN THOU HAST ACCOMPLISHED THEM, LIE AGAIN ON THY RIGHT SIDE, AND THOU SHALT BEAR THE INIQUITY OF THE HOUSE OF JUDAH FORTY DAYS: I HAVE APPOINTED THEE EACH DAY FOR A YEAR (430 YEARS)."

God was speaking of judgment upon Israel, as a whole, but mentioned Judah separately from Israel because (at that time) the Nation was split into two Kingdoms. Judah had represented the Southern Kingdom. There were to be 390 days of judgment upon Israel's ten Northern Tribes, and 40 days upon the two Southern Tribes - which equaled 430 years of judgment against the Jewish State in total. Israel was taken into captivity by the Babylonians for 70 years. So, 430 minus 70 years fulfilled during the captivity = 360 years remaining in the judgment. There are many who have wondered where the remaining 360-year judgment was fulfilled in Israel's history following the Babylonian captivity. We must look to the "7X factor" of God's judgment for the answer.

Biblical scholars cannot find a specific captivity or dispersion to fulfill the 360 years left in the judgment, but a closer look into Leviticus reveals God's seven-times warning (Leviticus 26:18, 21, 27-28 and 33). In the verses, the LORD warned Israel that if they continued in disobedience then He would multiply their judgment by "seven." God always says what He means, and means what He says. So, applying the 7X factor to the 360 years of judgment yet to be carried out against them, 2,520 years of judgment remained.

YHWH gave the Jews the most sophisticated calendar on the earth. It's both a Lunar and Solar calendar. The Hebrew calendar uses a 360-day Lunar (and Prophetic) year, and adds a leap month on specific years to coincide with the Solar cycle. The Bible uses 360-day years for prophecies, and it expects us to add appropriate leap months on schedule. The simplest way we can unravel this prophecy is to first convert it into days - 2,520 years x 360 days = 907,200 days of judgment remaining after Babylonian captivity. We then convert 907,200 days into 365.25-day Solar (Gregorian) years (the .25 adjusts for leap years), and 2,483.78 years remain.

Starting with the 70 years of Babylonian captivity, we arrive at 536 BC. We then add 2,483 years of judgment which are left, plus one year (because there is no 0 BC or AD), and we arrive at

1948 AD! How amazing is that?! The LORD's truly *right on time* all of the time. In the spring of 1948, Israel was officially declared and globally recognized as a nation again for the first time in over 2,500 years. HalleluYah. But wait, there's more! The time period of the Jewish people being exiled from the Holy Land by Babylon to the year the Babylonians destroyed Jerusalem was **19 years**; and the time period of Israel regaining their Homeland in 1948 to reclaiming Jerusalem as their Capital City in 1967 was **19 years**!

God had mirrored the years of exile and return for a sure sign that it was His Divine Hand at work. It was in June of 1967, when Islamic armies surrounding Israel attacked the Jewish State from every border. They were looking to finish what Hitler started by attempting to wipe out the Jewish people and the Nation of Israel from the face of the earth. A small number of Israeli forces were greatly outnumbered by tens of thousands of troops. The Jews not only defended their Nation valiantly, but after only a 6-Day War, they recaptured their ancient Holy Capital of Jerusalem. Islamists controlled the City ever since taking it from Christians centuries earlier. Israel defeated about a half-dozen hostile Muslim nations in less than *one week*.

It is crystal clear to all who study the War that the LORD was with His beloved Nation of Israel. Historians have called Israel's military victory "nothing short of a miracle." The Six-Day War had also mirrored an ancient battle in the Holy Bible to a tee. In Joshua, Chapter 6, verses 3-4, we find that the Israelite Army won the victory at Jericho in only six days -

"COMPASS THE CITY, ALL YE MEN OF WAR, AND GO ROUND ABOUT THE CITY ONCE. THUS SHALT THOU DO SIX DAYS."

By the 7th day, Joshua and his army had obtained the victory - just as the Israeli Army did in 1967. There can be no doubt that the LORD, Himself, fought on behalf of Israel on both occasions. He always has, and He always will.

Now, do you remember when I said Jesus told His disciples that "the generation" to witness the rebirth of Israel would also be the one living during the season of His return? Well, the Word of God tells us that a generation ranges from 70-80 years (Psalms 90:10). In 2018, Israel celebrated the 70th Anniversary of rebirth. 70 years! Biblically, that puts us right at the end of a generation. The number 70 is also very important in Israel's history.

70 Israelites went down into Egypt (Exodus 1:5), Moses had appointed 70 elders of Israel (Numbers 11:16), and Daniel spoke of the prophetical 70 weeks (Daniel 9:24). Lord Jesus sent out 70 disciples to preach the Gospel in Luke 10, the Israelites spent 70 years in Babylonian captivity, it was 70 years from the time that Christ was born to the time of the destruction of Jerusalem's Holy Temple, and on the 70th Anniversary of the Jewish State's rebirth the U.S. Embassy opened in Israel's eternal Capital of Jerusalem.

I truly believe the Lord is at the gates, and ready to make His descent back to Earth. The Rapture could occur any day now, or at any hour, because the "Last Days" prophecies which have yet to be fulfilled are Tribulation prophecies. We believers will not be here for the seven-year period of Hell on Earth. Jesus promised that we would "escape" that hour of judgment which would come upon the whole world (Luke 21:36). He was clear that He would keep us "out of" it (Revelation 3:10).

I can give many reasons why the historic 70th Anniversary of Israel's rebirth could lead to something Biblically monumental on the horizon. For starters, the Hebrew year preceding the 70th year was 5777. The number 777 is attributed to our Father in Heaven, YHWH, for many reasons. It is also attributed to His Father-Son relationship with our Lord Jesus Christ, Israel's Messiah. Written in Hebrew, "YHWH in Yeshua Messiah" gives the number 777. If that, in itself, is not awesome enough, "Yeshua saves" in Hebrew also gives 777. The Holy Name YAHWEH appears as 777 when written in the Hebrew as well. If there were such a thing as the greatest number in the world, 777 would unquestionably be it!

In the Hebrew Year 5777 (which took place on our Western calendar between 2016-17), we celebrated the 50th Anniversary of the reunification of Israel's Holy Capital Jerusalem. Also, 5777 closed out the Biblical "Jubilee Year" (only coming around once every fifty years). It followed the "Shemitah Year" (coming once every seven years), and was the year which an extremely accurate 800-year-old Rabbinical prophecy stated would "begin the season of Messiah's Coming" (in our case - His *return*).

Rabbi Judah Ben Samuel was a respected Talmudic scholar in Germany. Just before he had died, in the year 1217, he prophesied that Ottoman Turks would rule over Jerusalem for eight Jubilees. 8 x 50 = 400 years. Turks had indeed taken control of Jerusalem 300 years after his death, in 1517 - and his prophecy came to pass when they lost the Holy City in 1917 - 400 years later! Amazing. The Rabbi went on to prophesy that, after eight Jubilees, the 9th Jubilee would have Jerusalem being "a no-man's-land." The 9th Jubilee was from 1917 to 1967. He was *right on* again with his prophecy. The City was placed under British Mandate in 1917 by the League of Nations, and it literally belonged to NO nation.

Rabbi Samuel then stated that, in the 10th Jubilee, "Jerusalem would be controlled by Israel" - and the City *has been* ever since the Six-Day War of 1967! His prophecy concluded with "*then* the Messianic End Times would begin." The "then" refers to the end of 10th Jubilee and beginning of the new, which would be 2017! If this Rabbi was 100% accurate about everything else, we should take his Messiah prophecy very seriously.

I expect 2018 to be significant for Israel, prophetically, due to a fascinating 7-8-7 pattern. Biblically-relevant things concerning Israel, over the past century, have occurred in a year ending with a 7 - followed by a year ending with an 8 - and followed by a year ending with a 7. So, a year ending in an 8 would most likely be the year of the next big event concerning Israel.

In **1917**, the 400-year rule of the Ottomans over the Land of Israel ended; and British Prime Minister Balfour penned a historic declaration for a Jewish Homeland in Israel. In **1948**, the Nation was reborn. In **1967**, Israel miraculously won the Six-Day War and had reunified Jerusalem. With 2018 ending in an 8, could the thought-provoking 7-8-7 pattern continue? It already may have. After U.S. Presidents promising to do so for nearly 25 years, but never following through, President Donald Trump finally moved America's Embassy to Israel's eternal Capital in 2018. That was, as he would describe it, HUGE.

There is one last thing that bears mentioning. On November 14th, 2016, just after the kickoff of the year 5777, the Moon made its closest approach to Planet Earth in nearly 70 years. It will not be that close again until the year 2034. The 5777 Supermoon was extremely rare, and was the largest in our century. I mention the celestial event because of the significance of the last time that the Moon and Earth had been in such close proximity. The year just so happened to be 1948, which was the year that the fig tree had re-blossomed! Are you looking up yet?!

The Word of God teaches that "He appointed the Moon for seasons" (Psalms 104:19). A "season" in the Bible doesn't always mean spring, summer, fall, or winter. A season could also be His appointed time for grace, mercy, sowing, reaping, wrath, war, or prophetic fulfillment. Given all of the recent signs in the Moon, including the Blood Moon Tetrad of the recent Shemitah Year, I suspect we are living in a season of something truly historic. Any believer who can ignore the signs occurring all around us must be spiritually blind. God has been trying to alert us to something big coming on the horizon, and I truly believe that the "something" will be a *Someone*.

Will this generation, which is coming to a close, finally be the one that's raptured, endures the Tribulation, and witnesses Jesus' long-awaited return? I believe the answer is YES. Israel is finally back where they've always belonged, and the nations of the world are allying together to make war on the Jewish State - just as they are prophesied to. This means Israel's returning Messiah and their ultimate defender in the Armageddon battle is coming back down *soon*. One of the main reasons the nations come against Israel, in the end, is their obsession with the Jews' Capital of Jerusalem. That is what the coming chapter is about - the past, present, and future of the Holiest City on God's green earth.

FOR THE LORD WILL HAVE MERCY ON JACOB, AND WILL YET CHOOSE ISRAEL, AND SET THEM IN THEIR OWN LAND: AND THE STRANGERS SHALL BE JOINED WITH THEM, AND THEY SHALL CLEAVE TO THE HOUSE OF JACOB.

- ISAIAH 14:1

CHAPTER FIVE

JERUSALEM

THUS SAITH THE LORD OF HOSTS; I WILL BRING THEM, AND
THEY SHALL DWELL IN THE MIDST OF JERUSALEM: AND THEY
SHALL BE MY PEOPLE, AND I WILL BE THEIR GOD, IN TRUTH
AND IN RIGHTEOUSNESS.

- ZECHARIAH 8:8

DECEMBER 6TH, 2017, WAS a historic day for the United States
of America and for God's chosen Nation of Israel. In what I call
the greatest day of Donald Trump's Presidency, the POTUS gave
a live address to the Nation and to the world officially recognizing
Jerusalem as Israel's Capital. He also announced that he'd keep
one of his most important Campaign promises to direct the State
Department to begin preparations for moving our Embassy from
Tel Aviv to Jerusalem. The move was met by rejoicing of Holy
Bible-believers, expressing thanks to the 45th President.

Of course, the anti-Semitic Muslims, liberals, atheists, and all
Biblically-ignorant Americans, harshly criticized and condemned
Trump. At the end of the day, the only opinion that ever matters is
that of Almighty God. His Word makes crystal clear that Trump's
actions, regarding Jerusalem, were undoubtedly pleasing to Him.
I expected to see violent protests in Palestine, and in the Muslim
world at large, following the President's announcement. They are

always looking for an excuse to act like carnal animals. Islamists who hate Jews, Christians, Israel, and America - with a passion - rioted and burned our flags in the streets of Gaza, Turkey, Jordan, and across the Mideast. Hamas terrorists in Palestine threatened to "open the doors of hell" against the Jewish State.

Why the uproar over Trump's Jerusalem proclamation and his announcement to finally move our Embassy to Israel's Capital? Because the Muslims want our God's most Holy City, the most important piece of real estate to the Jews, to be the future Capital of Palestine. They were angry Trump publicly acknowledged the over 4,000-year-old Biblical truth that Jerusalem is the God-given property of Israel *alone*. It has *never* belonged to the Palestinians. It has never belonged to anyone else, in God's eyes, except Israel. Jerusalem may have been occupied by strangers, over the course of thousands of years, but it has *always* belonged to *His* people.

Historically, Jerusalem has always been, currently is, and will forever remain, the Capital of the Jewish Nation. There can be no one who examines the history and facts regarding Jerusalem that could ever say, with a clear conscience, that the Palestinians have a claim to any piece of the Holy Land. There is not one shred of evidence on Planet Earth to support that. So, no matter how many anti-Israel resolutions the Godless United Nations have passed or will pass, the LORD has made it abundantly clear that Jerusalem - and the entire Land of Israel - was gifted to the Jewish people as an "everlasting possession." It does not matter what the Muslims say or what world leaders may think. No one can ever change the facts or unalterable truth about the Holy Land of God.

The UN, Islamic world, and the global media, refer to Israel's most treasured ancient cities as "illegal settlements" or the "West Bank" to deny Israel's claims to the Promised Land - which date back over 4-millennia. They refer to Israel as an "occupier" of land that they think belongs to the Palestinians, on the grounds of Israel reclaiming some of its Holiest Land in 1967's Six-Day War.

Since Jews were not "exterminated" from the Land in that War, as the allied Muslim nations hoped, the Palestinians who left (before the war) chose to remain in nearby Islamic nations. They refused to return to their homes, as long as Jews remained in the Land. Today's Palestinians falsely claim their ancestors were forced out, that Jews occupy their land, and that they have a "right to return."

The truth is that the Palestinians do not want to return to the Land and live alongside the Jews, just as the Muslims of 1948 and 1967 did not. They want what the terror group, Hamas, wants: to drive the Jews out of the Land and into the Mediterranean Sea. That is why every so-called Peace Plan between the Israelis and Palestinians has failed, because Muslims do not want peace with Israel. They want Israel *gone*. The only peaceful future Palestine desires is one where there is *no Israel*. They are going to be very disappointed in the end, because God says that will never happen. He says that "Israel abides forever" (Joel 3:20).

There is not one inch of the Biblical Holy Land that belongs to Palestine. Not even one centimeter. Israelis aren't "occupying" anything, but rather they are exactly where the LORD has always determined them to dwell. The Land which God deeded to them is actually supposed to be 300,000 square miles. That is a far cry from the mere 8,600 square miles that make up the modern-day Nation of Israel. The question we should be asking in the conflict between Israel and Palestine today is: if Israel currently possesses just under 9,000 square miles of land, then who is possessing the other 18.5-million acres of the Jews' Promised Land?

It is only in discovering the answer to that question when we come to the realization that there truly are occupiers in the Middle East today, and Israel is certainly *not* one of them! Yet, the world is always calling for tiny Israel to give up Land-for-peace - *never* their Muslim neighbors. This is primarily due to our generation's Biblical ignorance, lack of historical knowledge, or just unbridled anti-Semitism. As to who is occupying the other 291,000 square miles of Israel's God-given Land, we must examine the original borders of Israel - mapped out by the LORD in the Scripture.

The promise of the Land inheritance had first been made to Abraham in Genesis 15:18-21, renewed to his son Isaac, and then to Isaac's son Jacob (Israel) in Genesis 28:13. The Land had been described, in terms of the territory, in Exodus 23:31. Other verses in our Bible describing the Land allotment are found in Genesis 17:8, Numbers 34:1-15, Deuteronomy 1:7 - 11:24 - 19:8, Ezekiel 47:13-20, Judges 20:1, 1st Samuel 3:20, 2nd Samuel 3:10 - 17:11 - 24:2-15, 1st Kings 4:25, 1st Chronicles 21:2 and 2nd Chronicles 30:5. Some of these verses reveal that the modern-day nations of Palestine, Egypt, Iraq, Jordan, Lebanon, Saudi Arabia, Sudan, and Syria, are all occupying Israel's Land - *not the other way around.* How I wish that this world would get educated in history!

The real conflict in the Middle East today should not be over the lie that Israel has "illegal settlements" on so-called Palestinian land, but should be about how the Palestinians (and *all* of Israel's neighbors) are illegally possessing Holy Land that God has given solely to the Jewish people. As I previously mentioned, the total area of land making up the modern-day State of Israel is less than 9,000 square miles. The size of the country is equivalent to the size of New Jersey. Meanwhile, many of the Islamic nations that I mentioned (who are always shouting at Israel to give up land to Palestinians for "peace") are *much* larger.

Saudi Arabia is nearly one-million square miles, Iran is over 600,000, Egypt is around 400,000, Turkey is over 300,000, Iraq is nearly 200,000, Syria is over 70,000, and Jordan is about 35,000 square miles. How come Palestine's fellow Muslim nations aren't offering up land for their so-called "refugee" brothers and sisters to dwell in for a future Palestinian State? They have far more land to spare than Israel. Think about it, if the Islamic countries loved Palestine (like they claim) as much as they hate Israel, Palestine could be a much bigger piece of real estate than Israel is today.

Egypt, Jordan, and Saudi Arabia all neighbor Palestine. These three nations have 1,440,000 square miles of land combined. You mean to tell me they can't each shave off a sliver of land to create a nation-state for the Palestinians? They can't spare 5,000 square miles between the three of them? It'd solve the Israeli-Palestinian conflict *today*. At the end of the day, they really don't want peace between Jews and Arabs. They want war. They desire Israel to be destroyed. But there is no denying what God wants, and that's for the Jews to remain right where they are.

The LORD promised that once He returned the Jews to their ancient Land, they "would never again be removed" (Amos 9:15). He says Jerusalem and the entire Holy Land is the "property of Israel" about 1,000 times in the Bible. Allah, the god of Islam, on the other hand, mentions Jerusalem 0 times in the Quran. *ZERO*. Jerusalem is known as the "City of David" and "City of the Great King (Jesus)." When Christ returns to Earth, His feet stand upon the Mount of Olives - located on Jerusalem's eastern border. He will then personally do away with the enemies of Israel. In the end, it will be Israel and God versus the entire world - *literally*.

Zechariah the prophet, in Chapter 12 of the book bearing his name, says, "all nations will come against Jerusalem" in the Last Days. That prophecy inches closer to fulfillment, as almost every nation on Earth opposed the President's Jerusalem announcement. In World War 3, which the Bible calls Armageddon, the LORD gathers all nations of the world to battle in the valley of Megiddo. It is in this final battle between the armies of God and armies of Satan that He'll judge the nations, and destroy anyone who came against Israel. In Joel 3:2, God warns the nations to not have a hand in dividing Israel's Land. Yet, in our day and age, that is the number one goal of the United Nations.

They have long been pushing, and now stronger than ever, for the division of Israel - specifically Jerusalem. All nations of this world, who are rebelling against the Word of God, will someday pay the price for their disobedience. God judges the nations of the world according to how they treat His beloved Nation of Israel. If they bless the Jewish State, they'll be blessed. If they curse Israel, they will be cursed (Genesis 12:3 and Numbers 24:9). The reason God gets so angry with nations for attempting to divide His Holy Land is because of just that... it is *His Land* - not United Nations' land, not Palestinian land, not Islamic land, not Christian land, not American land, not European land, and not even Jewish or Israeli land for that matter. It is the LORD's Property.

It is His to give, and His to take. It's the only God-given piece of real estate on the planet, and YHWH has deeded the Land as an "eternal" gift to just one nation: *Israel.* Even the Jewish State cannot place any land on the negotiating table in a future "peace" agreement with the Palestinians, because it is not theirs to deal - only God's. The basis for Palestinians claiming that they have any right to the Land is actions of an anti-Semitic Roman emperor of old, called Hadrian.

In 130 AD, after Jews had been expelled from their Promised Land by the Romans (about a century after Christ's death on the Cross), the Land was renamed "Palestine" by Hadrian. He chose the name because it represented an ancient enemy of the Jews, the Philistines. Hadrian paganized the Holy Land and desecrated the Holy City, Jerusalem. He decreed Roman maps would no longer use Biblical names of "Judea" or "Israel" for the Land. He erased the names in an attempt to scrub from history any Jewish claims to the Holy Land. Hence, due to Hadrian's hatred for the Jews, we have a society today deceived to believe the ancient Land belongs to Israel's enemies (Philistines-Palestinians) instead of its rightful owners - the Hebrews.

Jewish presence in the Holy Land, and specifically Jerusalem, is a presence far surpassing the rule of any other nation, people, race, or religion, since the dawn of time. You'd have to go back to 3500 BC to find the very first Jewish settlement in Jerusalem. If you're not good at math, that is over 5,500 years ago. Around the year 1865 BC, we read of Melchizedek - King of Jerusalem (then known as "Salem" - Genesis 14:18-20). Melchizedek is believed to have been the Lord Jesus Christ, coming down to commune with Abraham (Abram) - the forefather of Israel (Hebrews 7:1-3). In Joshua 18:28, we read that Jerusalem would be the inheritance of the Tribe of Benjamin - one of Israel's twelve sons.

In 1000 BC, King David claimed and declared Jerusalem as the Capital of Israel. In 960 BC, King Solomon (who was David's son) erected the first Jewish Temple in Jerusalem. In 721 BC, the Jews expanded the City. Biblically and Archaeologically, we have every proof that David, Solomon, and virtually all of the Kings of Israel, had ruled and reigned from Jerusalem (2nd Samuel, 1st & 2nd Kings, 1st & 2nd Chronicles). In 586 BC, when Jews were in captivity under the Babylonians, Jerusalem was all but destroyed. Between 539-516 BC, Cyrus the Great conquered the Babylonian Empire and had allowed Jews to live safely in Jerusalem. He also permitted their new Temple to be built.

Between 445-425 BC, Nehemiah the prophet rebuilt the walls of the Holy City. Between 332-141 BC, Alexander the Great had conquered Jerusalem and instituted Greek rule over Jews there. In 141 BC, the Hasmonean Dynasty began and Jews had once again expanded the City. In 63 BC, Roman General Pompey had taken Jerusalem and instituted Roman rule over Jews. In 37 BC, King Herod restructured the Temple and also added retaining walls. In the year 0 AD, our Lord Jesus Christ (Israel's Promised Messiah and King of the Jews) was born. Shortly thereafter, He was taken to Jerusalem to be presented to the LORD (YHWH). In 33 AD, Christ was crucified by the Romans in Jerusalem.

In 70 AD, Roman forces all but destroyed Jerusalem and had demolished the Temple. In 135 AD, the Romans rebuilt Jerusalem as the Jews lived under Roman rule. In 614 AD, the Persians had captured Jerusalem. In 629 AD, the Christians captured Jerusalem from Persians. In 638 AD, Islamic armies took it from Christians. Between 661-974 AD, Jerusalem and the Jews were under harsh Islamic rule. In 691 AD, Muslims had brazenly built their Dome of the Rock directly atop the site of the destroyed Temples. From 1099-1187 AD, Crusaders captured and ruled over the Holy City. From 1187-1259 AD, the Muslims captured Jerusalem back from the Crusaders and ruled over the Jews.

Between 1229-1244 AD, Crusaders had recaptured Jerusalem from Muslims on two separate occasions. In 1250 AD, Muslims captured Jerusalem again, tore down the walls, and persecuted the Jewish people. During the course of the next few centuries, the Muslims nearly wiped out the Jewish population in Jerusalem. In 1516 AD, the Ottomans captured Jerusalem. Between 1538-1541 AD, the walls of Jerusalem had been rebuilt. Between 1517-1917 AD, Jews in the City lived under the rule of the Ottoman Empire. In 1917, the British captured Jerusalem in World War 1 and the Balfour Declaration was signed. The Declaration called for Jews to be able to rule over themselves in their ancient Homeland, and for Jewish people across the world to be able to return to Israel.

In 1948, the Nation of Israel was reestablished. After around 2,500 years under the rule of foreign occupiers, the Jews finally had rule over half of ancient Jerusalem and much of their original Promised Land again. In 1967, Israel recaptured the other half of Jerusalem and reunified their God-given Holy Capital. From 1967 until today, Jerusalem has been the property of Israel - never to be divided again! Hopefully, now that those of you reading know the historic connection between the Jewish State and Jerusalem, you can understand why us believers rejoiced over President Trump's Jerusalem Declaration and Embassy Move. His public recognition of the Eternal City as Israel's Capital didn't just reflect a modern reality, but recognized 5,000+ years of Jewish history.

At the end of the day, Israel needs no peace with Palestinians. The only peace Israel will ever need is that which their returning

Prince of Peace can bring. Until He comes again, may the LORD continue to bless and defend Israel; because their many enemies are rising up against them. In the next chapter, I will explain just who exactly these prophesied enemies are.

THE LORD GOD OF ISRAEL HATH GIVEN REST UNTO HIS PEOPLE, THAT THEY MAY DWELL IN JERUSALEM FOR EVER.

- 1ST CHRONICLES 23:25

CHAPTER SIX

THE ENEMIES OF ISRAEL

THEY HAVE SAID, COME, AND LET US CUT THEM OFF FROM
BEING A NATION; THAT THE NAME OF ISRAEL MAY BE NO
MORE IN REMEMBRANCE.

- PSALMS 83:4

THE BIBLE PROPHESIES THAT many nations will come against
God's chosen Nation of Israel in the season leading up to Christ's
long-awaited return. Since the reestablishment of the Jewish State
in 1948, there've been numerous nations that have hated and even
wanted to destroy Israel. Though, it was not until December 21st,
2017, that we unquestionably witnessed a 2,500-year-old "Latter
Days" prophecy come to pass before our very eyes.

In the previous chapter, I had explained why Jerusalem is the
God-given Capital of Israel. In the Book of Zechariah, Chapter 12
and verse 3, the prophet says, "all the people of the earth will be
gathered together *against Jerusalem*." Last year, on that 21st day
of December, the United Nations had convened to *literally* gather
together against God's Holy City. The Global body represents all
nations of Earth, and they held an emergency session to vote on a
historic anti-Israel resolution. The session had been called for by
the anti-Semitic leader of Turkey, Recep Erdogan, and some other
Islamic world leaders. They put forth a measure condemning the

U.S. recognition of Jerusalem as Israel's Capital, and calling on Trump to rescind his decision to move the Embassy there.

Around 200 nations had voted on the measure, and the vote would have major implications regarding End Times Prophecy. It had publicly determined which nations oppose Israel on the world stage, and which nations support the Jewish State. Over 75% of the world went on record as being for or against God's Nation.

Anyone who carefully studies the Word of God knows that it declares Jerusalem to be the "eternal possession" of Israel nearly 1,000 times. Every nation that had voted against Jerusalem being Israel's God-given property was publicly opposing the LORD and welcoming His judgments. For God has said that all nations who contend with or oppose Israel are, in reality, contending with and opposing *Him* (Isaiah 49:25). Thus, He promised to judge, curse, and even destroy, *all nations* that come against Israel (specifically, the City of Jerusalem). 128 nations of the world set themselves up for coming destruction in the future.

Of the 172 nations that voted, only seven (yes, only 7) voted on the side of Israel and the United States; and thus voted on the side of Almighty God. This very small number, while extremely disappointing, is actually encouraging. I believe that it may fulfill another Biblical prophecy pointing to the Rapture of the Church, and the imminent return of Christ. In the Book of Micah, Chapter 5 and verse 5, we read how the Messiah of Israel (Jesus) will "be our peace" when the enemies of Israel invade the Holy Land. It goes on to say, "We will raise against them (the enemies of Israel) *seven* shepherds, even *eight* commanders." This is an interesting connection to the UN Vote, as seven nations stood with Israel and the United States - amounting to "eight" allies of Israel in total.

The rest of the world stood *against* the LORD's people. The seven righteous nations were Guatemala, Honduras, Micronesia, Marshall Islands, Nauru, Palau, and Togo. I am sure that most of you have probably never even heard of half these nations. Do you know who *has* heard of them, and who knows them *quite well*? Almighty God. Nations that we're familiar with today, the LORD is not too concerned with blessing. I speak of America's so-called allies like Canada, France, Spain, Germany, Italy, and the United Kingdom. Some of you may be shocked by my "God doesn't care to bless them" statement, and so I'll explain.

Just as all human beings have to get right with God on their own, so too, each nation of the world must put themselves on the right or wrong side of the LORD. U.S. allies that I've mentioned sided with the likes of Iran, Russia, North Korea, China, Turkey, and Syria in the UN Jerusalem Vote. That's *not* good company. In God's Sight, that makes some of our nation's allies just as wicked as the world's most evil regimes. America must be very careful to always remain on the side of Almighty God, as a Judeo-Christian nation, and to always support Israel. Our future depends on it.

Besides the 128 nations who'd voted against the Jewish State, and seven that stood with Israel, there were 35 nations who had "abstained." This meant that they did not want to be on record as voting one way or the other. These are *lukewarm* nations, who are just as much of a disgrace to God as the 128 nations who voted against Israel. The LORD says many times, throughout His Word, that you're either "for or against Him." There is no in the middle. There is no on the fence. You're either hot or cold. You're either a sheep or a goat. The UN vote had made clear that 163 nations of this world are oblivious to God's Word, and don't take His threats of judgment for opposing Israel seriously.

They're going to find out very soon just how true the Bible is, and they're going to deeply regret standing on the wrong side of history. They will all have to answer to Lord Jesus someday for their anti-Israel actions. Many people today do not realize that the main reason why He returns to Earth, in the end, is to *personally* do away with the enemies of Israel. The first time, He came to be the Messiah of Israel's eternal souls. Next time around, He will come as the roaring "Lion of the Tribe of Judah" to physically fight against those nations threatening the mortal lives of Israelis. The inhabitants of the earth who do not accept Jesus as the Lamb, who brings us God's peace, will eventually meet Him as the Lion, who executes God's wrath. How do YOU want to meet Him?!

The Book of Revelation is crystal clear that when all nations of the world come against Israel, to destroy the Jewish State, the armies of Heaven descend to Earth with Christ Jesus leading the charge. Before our Lord makes His descent, there are some other things concerning Israel that have to occur according to prophecy. Joel 3:2 says that nations of the world will be judged for dividing God's Holy Land. The number one goal of the UN, for nearly five decades, has been to divide up Israel's Promised Land (namely, *Jerusalem*). The United Nations is now more anti-Israel than ever before in their history, while at the same time...

❖ The Assad regime in Syria murders its own people.

❖ Iran amasses nuclear weapons to target Israel and the US.

❖ Islamic nations are persecuting and murdering Christians, bulldozing churches, throwing gays off buildings, raping children, and sexually abusing or mutilating women.

❖ Russia continues to obtain global power by force.

Yet and still, the number one agenda of the United Nations is to target *Israel*. The UN is, no doubt, under the influence of Satan himself. According to the UNHRC (UN Human Rights Council), Israel is "the worst human rights violator in the world." No joke. I have never read one news report about Christians, homosexuals, women, or the Muslims complaining about mistreatment in Israel. So, why does the UN believe that the Jewish State violates human

76

rights *more than* China, North Korea, Russia, and Syria? Why is Israel *worse* than the Islamic nations that threaten, persecute, and murder anyone who does not live by their Quran? I believe it has got to do with the fact that Muslim-majority nations make up ¼ of the UN's member states.

While 25% of the world may not seem like a big number, it is when they vote together on everything having to do with Israel - or should I say, everything *anti*-Israel. Every time a resolution is brought up against the Jewish State in the UN, the close to sixty Islamic nations are guaranteed to vote against Israel - *guaranteed*. That 25% becomes a one-sided majority in UN councils, panels, and committees. As long as this remains the case, Israel will not get a fair shake in the biased UN. Throughout the past decade, the UNHRC has condemned Israel more so than any of the other 192 UN member states.

There've been about 80 resolutions and decisions demonizing Israel; but only around 30 on Syria, less than 10 on North Korea, just 6 on Iran, and a big fat ZERO on Saudi Arabia, Russia, and China. So, just to recap, the democratic Nation of Israel has been condemned by the UN almost *twice as much* as all of the world's most notorious and murderous regimes *combined*. As of this year, the UN Security Council has passed over 250 resolutions against Israel - more than any other nation of this world. In 2016 alone, the General Assembly adopted 20 resolutions singling out Israel - and only 3 resolutions on the rest of the world *combined*. Those 3 consisted of just one-a-piece against Iran, North Korea, and Syria.

The corrupt United Nations masquerades as an organization that promotes peace and human rights, but is nothing more than a biased body of unGodly nations that are being used by the devil to threaten God's people. In 2016, UNESCO adopted one of their most detestable anti-Israel resolutions to date. The resolution was not just an attempt to delegitimize the Jewish State, but to erase and rewrite history. UNESCO would give Islam precedence over

Judaism and Christianity, even though our Faiths far outdate the "religion" of Muhammad. The resolution denied all Biblical and historical connections of the Jews to Jerusalem. The UN will now only refer to the Temple Mount and the Western Wall by Muslim titles, and no longer by their Hebrew names.

A special section of the resolution states that the sites are now "only sacred to the Islamic faith." What a blatant utter falsehood, and disgraceful denial of world history! The Temple Mount is the holiest site in Judaism, as it is believed to be where the LORD's Divine Presence is manifested more than any other place on this earth. The Bible refers to the holy hill as "Mount Zion," and it is where both Temples of the Jews had stood. The Western Wall is what remains of the second Temple. To say that neither of these sites have connection to the Jews is to not only deny the Word of God, but to also completely ignore over 4,000 years of history.

The Land the UN dubs "Palestinian territory" had been gifted to Israel by the LORD as an everlasting possession. Go and look up *everlasting* in the dictionary. You'll find that it means eternal, endless, never-ending, and abiding forever. Get the picture? Well, the Biblically-illiterate UN sure doesn't! Besides the collection of anti-Israel haters in the UN, there are also specific nations of the world that are prophesied to war against the Jewish State.

One of those countries, Turkey, was the main sponsor of the 2017 Jerusalem Vote (which I opened this chapter addressing). It just so happens that Turkey is identified in the Bible as one of the nations that'll be on the front lines of the Latter-Day war against Israel. Turkey's President is one of the most anti-Semitic leaders in the world. He's publicly criticized, condemned, and threatened Israel. He hosts terror groups who are bent on Israel's destruction, and pushes anti-Israel resolutions at the UN. That explains why President Obama was so anti-Israel. He referred to Erdogan as his "closest friend on the world stage."

Next up is Russia. Believe it or not, it is not a Muslim nation that is prophesied to lead the Islamic confederacy against Israel in the Last Days - it is Russia. The Eurasian nation, throughout the past decade, has threatened the Jewish State many times; and has allied with the exact nations that the Bible prophesied it would in the Latter Days. Earlier this year, there was a summit in Istanbul to discuss cooperation between three specific nations. The three leaders that had met and forged an unholy alliance were Erdogan of Turkey, Hassan Rouhani of Iran, and Vladimir Putin of Russia. Ezekiel 38:5-6 names Iran (Persia) and Turkey (Togarmah) as two of Russia's closest allies in its military campaign against Israel. How accurate is the Holy Bible?!

The prophecy was written over 2,500 years ago, and Russia's President (currently Vladimir Putin) is described as "Gog" in the prophecy. The war on Israel, that Putin (or whomever the leader will be at the time of the battle) leads, is called the "Gog-Magog War." *Magog* refers to ancient Magogites. They are modern-day Russians. Ezekiel also mentions the names "Rosh, Meshech, and Tubal." *Rosh* translates to Russia, *Meshech* translates to Moscow (Russia's Capital), and *Tubal* is modern Tubalsk - also located in Russia. There can be no doubt that Russia is the key player in one of the final wars against Israel.

I say "one of" the final wars, because Gog-Magog is not the same as the Battle of Armageddon. I don't want any of you to get confused when I refer to it as the "Last Days War." I believe this war will be a prelude to the war to end all wars, which is fought in and around the valley of Megiddo (which involves all nations of the world). The Gog-Magog battle is fought on the mountains of Israel, which would most likely be on the border of Syria in the Golan Heights region. I also suspect that the Islamic confederacy mentioned in Psalm 83 could be included in Gog-Magog, or they will attack Israel and fail. The latter scenario would surely lead to Russia entering the battle as the chief military leader.

It is no wonder that Russia is prophesied to be the strongest military power in the Last Days, because Vladimir Putin's regime currently possesses the most nuclear weapons in the world today - even more than the United States of America. As of 2017, Russia had approximately 2,000 nuclear warheads deployed. Thanks be to God that even one-million nuclear bombs are powerless against Israel's ultimate Defense Force: the LORD God Almighty.

One of the closest allies of Russia on the world stage today, and undoubtedly the number one modern enemy of Israel, is Iran. The Ayatollahs of Iran have been itching to go to war with Israel for decades. The Islamic regime's leaders have long threatened to "blow Israel off the map." The supreme leader of Iran, Ayatollah Khameni, had revealed in a televised speech that Iran's reason for participating in the 2015 "Nuclear Deal" with world powers was "*not* for eventual peace." He said that the long drawn out talks were an opportunity to build up his nation's nuclear arsenal to use against Israel "*soon*."

Iran's so-called moderate President, Hassan Rouhani, has also publicly called for the "destruction of Israel." Even after he had signed the horrible Nuclear Deal with Obama and world leaders, both Rouhani and Khameni had chanted "death to America" and "death to Israel" on live TV. The Book of Ezekiel says "Persia" (modern-day Iran) will be one of the most threatening enemies of Israel in the Last Days. Another prophecy about Iran, also found in Ezekiel (32:24), has come to pass in our day. The prophet said that the nation would be an exporter of *terror*. The Islamic regime in Tehran is the biggest funder and organizer of terror worldwide, especially against Israel.

Finally, no document regarding the enemies of Israel could be complete without mention of Palestine. The Jewish State's hostile neighbor has been a constant thorn in Israel's side; and not just through terrorism, but in the United Nations as well - where they dirty Israel's good name in the realm of public opinion. Year after year, Palestinian leadership has tried to influence world leaders to support and aid their cause against the Jewish State. They've long sought, through UN pressure or force, to take Israel's God-given Land as their own. I allude to this subject of "Land-for-Peace" in the previous Israel chapters, and will again in the "Earthquakes & Extreme Weather" chapter.

Gaza in Palestine is the home base of the terror group *Hamas*. They're responsible for murdering thousands of innocent Israelis, many of whom have been women and children. In 2014, they had fired 5,000+ rockets into Israel. Yet, the global mainstream media demonized the Jewish State for retaliating against those so-called "poor Palestinians." How many other nations of the world would just sit on their hands when 5,000 missiles were being fired across their border? The short answer is *none*. Still, the world is always urging Israel to show restraint against terrorists. It's unbelievable.

In early 2018, as Israelis were preparing for celebrations of the 70th Anniversary of their Nation's rebirth, Hamas was staging an attempted invasion of Israel's border with Gaza. While Hamas was telling the global media that the Palestinians were preparing to hold "peaceful protests" along Israel's border fence, they were - at the same time - telling the Palestinian people to prepare for "the beginning of the capturing all of Israel." The Spokesman for Palestinian President Mahmoud Abbas had reiterated Hamas' *real* reason for organizing the protests (which were really riots) - "The message of our people is clear: Israel will be *removed*."

At the same time these threats against the Jewish State were being made by Palestinian leaders, under the guise of "peaceful" protests, the lamestream media was selling the narrative (as they always do) that Israel was the *aggressor* and that the Palestinians were "poor and defenseless protesters" under fire. Nothing, and I mean *absolutely nothing*, could be any further from the truth. For six weeks, tens of thousands of Palestinians had stormed Israel's border - rolling burning tires toward the security fence - throwing grenades, molotov cocktails, pipe bombs, rocks, bricks, and axes. They'd brandished guns, machetes, wire cutters for the fence, and even flew flaming kites over the border to start fires in Israel.

The Palestinians who were killed by Israeli forces for rushing the border fence, in an attempt to breach it, had all been carrying weapons. They were mostly all card-carrying members of Hamas. Of course, the media conveniently left that out - posting headlines that read: "Israel kills dozens of Palestinians." Not one word of the terrorists - just "protesters." I could write a whole book about why today's biased mainstream media is one of Israel's biggest enemies. The media should be ashamed of their slanted reporting, and for trying to deceive their ignorant audiences to believe their biased narrative. They always portray Israel as the "bad guy," and the Palestinian terrorists as the "good guys." Exactly what kind of alternate reality do these liberal media journalists live in anyway?

The term gets tossed around a lot today, but when it comes to reporting on the Israeli-Palestinian conflict, the mainstream media is full of *fake news*. Besides the nations I have already mentioned, Israel is preparing for possible wars with every bordering nation. I've already addressed Hamas on the South-Southwest border in Gaza. They are in league with another Palestinian terrorist group known as Islamic Jihad. On the Northern border, there is Lebanon - home to the Iran-backed Hezbollah terror group. In 2006, they fired around 4,000 rockets into the Jewish State. On the Northeast border, there is Syria and ISIS - and neither of them are fond of Israel. On the Eastern border, there is Jordan. The country's King, Abdullah, is anti-Semitic and anti-Israel to the core.

The tiny Jewish Nation is surrounded by much larger hostile enemies on every side. Yet, those nations have never succeeded in their quests to destroy Israel. And the number one reason for their constant failure is that Almighty God dwells *in the midst of* Israel, as their eternal Defender (Joel 2:27). In the end, though virtually the whole world comes against them, *Israel wins*. They will win, because *God wins*. The LORD's always been, still is, and forever will be, fighting on their behalf. HalleluYah to the God of Israel!

AND IT SHALL COME TO PASS IN THAT DAY, THAT I WILL SEEK TO DESTROY ALL THE NATIONS THAT COME AGAINST JERUSALEM, SAITH THE LORD.

- ZECHARIAH 12:9

CHAPTER SEVEN

SIGNS IN THE HEAVENS

I WILL SHEW WONDERS IN THE HEAVENS... THE SUN SHALL BE
TURNED INTO DARKNESS, AND THE MOON INTO BLOOD,
BEFORE THE GREAT AND NOTABLE DAY OF THE LORD COME.

- ACTS 2:19-20 & JOEL 2:30-31

OUR GENERATION HAS SEEN, quite possibly, far more signs in the heavens than any other since Christ ascended into Heaven about 2,000 years ago. It's undeniable that God has been trying to get our attention. Between 2014-2018, we observed an abundance of extremely rare and historic occurrences in the Sun, the Moon, and our skies in general. After reading this compelling chapter, it is my hope that you'll find it very difficult to not be enthusiastic about the coming Rapture of the Church.

During the years 2014-2015, we had witnessed the very rare occurrence of a *Blood Moon Tetrad*. Four Blood Moons had risen directly on Biblical Feast Days. Try chalking that up to just mere coincidence. Two years in a row, we'd observed 2 of them rise on the Feast of Passover; while the other 2 occurred during the Feast of Tabernacles. If a pair of Blood Moons transpired during God's Holy Feasts in one year, that would be intriguing enough in itself. The fact that this happened two years in a row is unprecedented, and it is beyond fascinating.

That's not all though... 2 of the 4 Blood Moons occurred in the Biblical *Shemitah Year*. The Shemitah Year only occurs once every seven years. Moreover, that particular Shemitah was what is known as a *Super Shemitah* - meaning it was the 7th Shemitah in a cycle of seven! How can even the most hardened Bible skeptics write off, as a coincidence, Blood Moons rising on Biblical Holy Days AND during the all-important 7th Shemitah in a set of 7?! The Biblical Year which followed the Super Shemitah was known as the *Jubilee Year*. The Jubilee only comes around once every 50 years! We had seen the final Blood Moon of the Tetrad rise in the Jubilee Year of 2015.

All of this is so extremely important, concerning the return of Jesus Christ, because it has all taken place in the generation that witnessed the rebirth of Israel. As I've explained in the "Fig Tree" chapter, none of the "Last Days" signs given in the Bible could mean anything until the Nation of Israel was reestablished. While there've always been Blood Moons, Total Solar Eclipses, or other signs in the heavens throughout history, they have had nothing to do with End Times Prophecy. Those occurring in our generation have absolutely *everything* to do with it.

If I ended this chapter here, I believe this should be enough to strengthen the faith of even the most backslidden of believers; but I am far from done. In 2016, again on the Feast of Tabernacles, God had ushered in His Holy Week with a sign in the heavens. A Supermoon had risen. The celestial event occurs when the Moon makes its closest approach to Earth. 2016's Supermoon had come to its second nearest position to Planet Earth since 1948 (222,365 miles), behind only the Supermoon to fall just a month later. One night earlier, on the eve of the Biblical Feast, a *Super Blood Moon* rose! Remember the significance of 1948? Keep the year in mind as we go further, as it is beyond important prophetically.

The second Supermoon of 2016 was the closest the Moon has been to Earth in this *century*. It will not be that close again until the fall of 2034. The closest Full Moon of the 21st century will not rise until the winter of 2052! The year in which we witnessed the two historic Supermoons, while being 2016 on our Gregorian calendar, was the year 5777 on the Hebrew calendar. In the "Fig Tree" chapter, I'd explained why 777 is the number of Almighty God (YHWH) - the God of Israel. Speaking of Israel, the reason I told you to remember the year 1948 was because it was the year that the Nation of Israel was officially reborn! So, the Supermoon of 5777 was the largest and the brightest it has ever been since the fulfilled prophecy of the Jewish State's rebirth.

If you are not saying WOW yet, you aren't paying attention. In chapter 4, I had also mentioned that God "appointed the Moon for seasons." Given all of the recent signs in the Moon, I believe we are living in *the season* of something historic prophetically. Could it really be the Rapture? Maybe a Biblical War? A historic disaster? Global government? All I know for certain is that the LORD is using the Moon to alert us to something coming; and as I've previously said, I wholeheartedly believe that the *something* is really a *Someone*.

In Luke, Chapter 21 and verse 25, Lord Jesus prophesied that "There shall be signs in the Sun, and the Moon, and the stars." In verse 27, He said, *"Then* shall they see the Son of man coming in a cloud with power and great glory." Notice He also mentioned the Sun. Most Biblical prophecies about the Sun reveal it "will be darkened." This, to me, signifies a *Total Solar Eclipse*. Now, yes, there've been thousands of Eclipses throughout history. Because of this, some people tend to ignore the prophetic significance of Total Solar Eclipses. They are wrong to do so. As I have already explained, no signs could mean anything until 1948. That began the time frame to start paying closer attention to the heavens.

Just last year, America had experienced its first coast-to-coast Total Solar Eclipse in 99 years. That is extremely significant, as it would be the first our nation has seen since the Jews reclaimed their ancient Holy Land. It was also the first Total Eclipse of the Sun since 1979. I wasn't even born yet! So, it has definitely been awhile. To say that it was a rare occurrence of the Sun would be an understatement. On August 21st of 2017, in the middle of the day, skies were darkened from one American coast to the other. The Moon passed between the Sun and Earth, blocking the face of the Sun and leaving only its corona visible in the sky. All of North America had experienced at least a partial Eclipse.

The difference between a full and a partial Eclipse is literally the difference between night and day. During a Total Eclipse, the temps drop and the horizon is ringed by colors of sunset. The sky becomes a twilight blue, and stars and planets become visible in the middle of the day. The Eclipse moved over a dozen States, occurring at the end of the Biblical month of Av - right before the start of Elul, which is known as the "month of repentance." What is even more important, is it occurred in the significant year 5777.

I had found it thought-provoking that the path of the Eclipse had drawn a line directly through the *heartland* of America. This is noteworthy; because President Donald Trump, at the time, was following in the Obama administration's footsteps in attempting to forge a Peace Deal between the Israelis and Palestinians. Any deal between the two parties would unquestionably divide up the Holy Land of Israel (the *Heartland* of God). In previous chapters, I mentioned that the division of Israel's God-given Land is what causes the LORD to pour out His Wrath upon the nations (Joel 3:2). If our country has any role in the division of the Holy Land, we can be sure that God will *divide America.*

So, it was no surprise that as President Trump was pushing hard for Israel to give up "Land-for-peace" to Palestine, God used the Eclipse to *literally* draw a line through the *heart* of America. It was no coincidence that this warning to America came during the 50th Anniversary of Israel reunifying Jerusalem. In virtually every Land-for-Peace Deal that U.S. Presidents have drawn up for

Israel and Palestine, chunks of Jerusalem have been on the table. This absolutely infuriates the LORD.

I was fascinated when I found that the Eclipse had more than a few connections to the Holy City. I had discovered that the first major American city to witness the Total Eclipse was the Capital of Oregon, which is SALEM. For those of you who are unaware, Salem is the original Biblical Name for Jerusalem. God's beloved City was first known as Salem in the days of Melchizedek, and it was first referred to in Genesis, Chapter 14. In another instance that was hardly coincidence, there were 14 States in the totality line of the Eclipse. Genesis 14 and 14 States. Pretty awesome if you ask me! Also, out of the 14 States that could view the Eclipse in totality, 13 of them had cities named *Salem*. Google it to see I am not just cooking this stuff up in my head.

Those 13 States were Georgia, Idaho, Illinois, Iowa, Kansas, Kentucky, Missouri, Montana, Nebraska, North Carolina, Oregon, South Carolina, and Tennessee. The only State that did not have a city named Salem was Wyoming, but there is a city in Wyoming named *Homa Hills*; and there is a Hill in Israel named *Har Homa*. Israel's Har Homa just so happens to be located in JERUSALEM. Also, seven years from 2017's Eclipse, another Total Eclipse will pass over the United States (in 2024). The 2024 Eclipse will cross directly over the line of the previous Eclipse's path, forming an X. When two Eclipse paths cross, there is only one singular point on Earth where both centerlines meet. So, literally, X marks the spot.

The centerlines of the two Eclipses will meet near the eastern shore of Cedar Lake in Illinois. If you were to zoom in on a map, you will get goosebumps. Believe it or not, the closest road to the point where the two Eclipses intersect is SALEM Road. What are the odds?! It's also important to note that two Total Solar Eclipses occurring exactly seven years apart is really rare. A Total Solar Eclipse can only be seen from the same place on Earth once every

375 years. I think God is sending a message to U.S. leadership through the Eclipse, saying, "Hands off My Holy Land!"

Sadly, Trump's administration seemed to ignore the warning, and continued forcing Israel back to the negotiating table with the Palestinians. In the month following the Eclipse, the President's son-in-law, Jared Kushner, flew to Israel to meet with the Israeli and Palestinian leaders to discuss a Peace Deal. In the same hours that he did, one of the most powerful hurricanes to ever strike the USA - Harvey - devastated the Southeast.

In January of 2018, for the first time since March of 1866, an extraordinarily rare *Blue Super Blood Moon* had appeared in the heavens. The trifecta event combined a Blue Moon, a Supermoon, and Blood Moon (Total Lunar Eclipse) all-in-one. The old saying, "once in a Blue Moon," may imply that it's rare, but a Blue Moon is actually quite common. What is extremely uncommon is when it's combined with a Blood Moon *and* Supermoon. To put it into perspective, the last time that these three celestial events occurred in conjunction with one another was two centuries ago!

Besides these rare occurrences in the heavenly bodies, there's been another sign taking place in the skies above - trumpet-like sounds and mysterious booms have emanated from the skies for much of the past decade. The unexplained noises have been heard all over the world. They purportedly began in 2008, but became more widespread in 2011. The sounds have baffled governments, local authorities, meteorologists, geologists, and even NASA. The trumpet sounds have become a global phenomenon. I've watched many videos chronicling them, from across the globe, and they all sound exactly like a shofar being blown.

For those not aware, a shofar is a ram's horn that was used by ancient Israel to call assemblies, prepare for battle, or to signal a Holy Feast beginning. The shofar is referred to as a trumpet in the Bible. The trumpet sounds coming from our skies should be an obvious "Last Days" sign for believers everywhere. There are so many verses in God's Word that declare the sounding of heavenly trumpets as a precursor to the Rapture and as heralding judgments during the 7-year Tribulation. Trumpets are mentioned numerous times in the Book of Revelation. The fact they are mysteriously being heard from the heavens, all around this world, should have believers shaping up, looking up, and packing up, because I truly believe that we will be *going up* real soon. Maranatha!

AND HE SHALL SEND HIS ANGELS WITH A GREAT SOUND OF A TRUMPET, AND THEY SHALL GATHER TOGETHER HIS ELECT... FROM ONE END OF HEAVEN TO THE OTHER.

- MATTHEW 24:31

CHAPTER EIGHT

EARTHQUAKES & EXTREME WEATHER

THERE SHALL BE GREAT EARTHQUAKES IN DIVERS PLACES.

- LUKE 21:11/MATTHEW 24:7/MARK 13:8

THERE ARE MANY SCOFFERS of the Holy Bible, and of Bible Prophecy in particular, who love to say that "we have *always* had powerful earthquakes." What they fail to realize, as I have pointed out in the previous chapters, is that none of the world's strongest quakes could have meant anything regarding End Times Prophecy until 1948. That, of course, was the year that the Nation of Israel reappeared on the world scene. The existence of the Jewish State is absolutely central to the return of Christ. With that in mind, I'm sure the scoffers would be surprised to learn that 7 out of the 10 most powerful earthquakes of the past 400 years have come *after* 1948. 70% occurred in *our generation*.

On top of that, 5 out of the 7 magnitude 9.0 or higher quakes have occurred after 1948. Again… over 70%. I think it is obvious that this generation has seen an uptick in powerful earthquakes. The largest temblor ever recorded, a 9.5 on the Richter scale, had devastated Chile in 1960. So, the most powerful quake on record shook the earth *after 1948*. Also, the top 5 most massive quakes had all come after '48 - Chile (9.5 in 1960), Alaska (9.2 in 1964), Sumatra (9.1 in 2004), Kamchatka (9.0 in 1952), and Japan (9.0

93

in 2011). One year before the historic Japan quake and tsunami, Chile had been rocked by a destructive 8.8 magnitude temblor.

Since the year 2000, there have been about 275 earthquakes of magnitude 7.0 or higher. Earthquakes above 6.0 magnitude are considered "strong," while those at or above the 7.0 threshold are dubbed "powerful." Obviously, anything above an 8.0 is referred to as "great." Since 1948, this world has experienced over 50 of those quakes that Jesus prophesied would occur in the *Last Days* leading up to His imminent return.

In the last chapter, I had written about the Supermoon of the Century. On the eve of that historic sign in the heavens, there was a massive 7.8 magnitude quake that rocked New Zealand. In the news reports, the New Zealand city dominating the headlines was CHRISTCHURCH. Students of Bible Prophecy strongly believe that the Rapture of Christ's Church is ever on the horizon. That's the reason I am writing this! God may have been giving sleeping believers a wake-up call. In the Hebrew Year 5777, on the eve of the historic Supermoon, "ChristChurch" topped the headlines of every major news source in the world! How can we not be eagerly looking up, and listening for our Lord to say "come up hither"?!

Now, before I address the hurricanes, I would be remiss not to mention California when speaking about great earthquakes. In recent years, there has been an increase of quake activity along America's West Coast. This has many believing that the next "Big One" in the world may very well strike the USA. A recent study had concluded that, in the very near future, the 800-mile-long San Andreas fault could unzip all at once. The fault runs the length of California, where the Pacific and North American plates meet. It was long thought that it could only rupture in isolated sections. But the study by federal, state, and academic researchers showed much of the fault could rupture all at once - which would unleash a devastating historic catastrophe.

Top geological experts all believe the fault is way overdue for a *massive* earthquake. If you're a believer in Cali, I'd be praying for the Lord's protection over your property and family. If you are anywhere near the San Andreas fault, I would highly recommend that you *move*. California is one of the most Godless States in our union today, so they're due for judgment, and believers should get out while they can. Speaking of judgment, I'd now like to focus on the historic hurricanes that the world has experienced in recent memory and how they relate to Scripture.

Like earthquakes, wildfires, tornado outbreaks, and economic collapse, I believe hurricanes are a form of God's judgment upon a nation. The biggest reason for His Wrath being poured out upon the nations is the mistreatment of Israel. That mistreatment entails leaders of a nation pressuring the Jewish State to give up some of their eternal God-given Land for potential peace with their hostile neighbors in Palestine. In this chapter, I will connect some of the strongest, costliest, most destructive, and deadliest hurricanes in American history to our leaders attempting to broker the division of Israel's Holy Land. While there've indeed been many reasons throughout the past few decades that the USA has given God to judge our nation, forcing Israel into lopsided Peace Deals in favor of the terrorist Palestinians takes the cake.

Some other big reasons for incurring His wrath are: removing Him from government and public square, widespread blasphemy, legalization of sins (such as Gay Marriage), moral decay, and the holocaust of babies through abortion. 21st century America has given God *far too many* reasons. Our country was founded as a Judeo-Christian Nation; and there can be no argument that when this country departs from its Godly foundation, it certainly suffers the devastating consequences.

The list of names for the 2018 Atlantic Hurricane Season was recently released, and I'd advised fellow believers to take note of them. Now, let me be clear, I don't claim to be a prophet. I simply observe the signs of the times occurring all around us through a Biblical lens. I do not follow a majority of the world in attributing the record-breaking weather events to random climate change or global warming. The connections of so many U.S. disasters to the mistreatment of Israel, alone, should convince the most hardened skeptics that the Hand of our God is truly at work in the weather.

The reason I tell believers to pay close attention to the names of hurricanes is because the LORD is well aware of the names on every year's list. If history is any proof, I believe He specifically uses Biblically-named storms to leave no doubt that they are His judgments. After I observed the 2018 List, I counted five Biblical names, and they were:

1. Debby (*Deborah*)
2. Isaac
3. Michael
4. Rafael (*Raphael*)
5. Sara (*Sarah/Sarai*)

Anyone familiar with their Bible will clearly recognize these names. Michael and Raphael are Archangels, and the other three are well-known Old Testament names. To prove the significance of Biblically-named hurricanes, I researched the list of all retired U.S. hurricanes. In 1953, storms began being named. Originally, only female names were used for tropical cyclones. The World Meteorological Organization had added the male names in 1979. Storms causing the most devastation had been deemed significant enough to have their names retired. It is no coincidence that the first male hurricane name to ever be retired was a *Biblical* one. That 1979 hurricane was named DAVID, which was the name of God's beloved King of ancient Israel.

David was a historic Category 5 hurricane. With winds of 175 mph, the storm had left widespread damage in its wake - costing

$320-million (nearly one-*billion* dollars today). It was the first - and last - use of the name David, being immediately retired after the storm because of its devastation and high death toll. What I'd found extremely interesting, while viewing an image of the storm making landfall in the United States, was that it looked to me like a map of the modern-day Nation of Israel. Sure enough, after I'd downloaded a map of Israel and superimposed the image over it, it fit almost perfectly. Coincidence? I do not think you can believe in coincidence or chance, while also believing in God. Everything happens for a reason with Him.

The fact that the first ever male-named hurricane to be retired was David (King of Israel), and the storm had actually mirrored the shape of the modern-day State of Israel, is beyond captivating. Prepare to be fascinated even more by the connection between the hurricane and the U.S. brokering a deal in which Israel had been pressured to give up "Land-for-peace" to their hostile neighbors. On March 26th, 1979, a Peace Treaty was signed between Israel and Egypt *on American soil*. It was witnessed by U.S. President Jimmy Carter in Washington. The treaty required the "complete withdrawal by Israel from the Sinai Peninsula," which the Jewish State captured during the Six-Day War of 1967.

On August 25th, 1979, the eve of the 6-month anniversary of the treaty signing, Hurricane David formed. This was one of the first of many examples showing God's extreme displeasure with America pushing Israel to give up chunks of their Promised Land for so-called "peace." The first retired Biblically-named female hurricane I discovered, that was also associated with Israel, was BEULAH. While David was an obvious Biblical name that even unbelievers are familiar with, Beulah is a name familiar only to well-studied Bible students. The name is used in Isaiah, Chapter 6 and verse 4, where God says the Jews will reinhabit their ancient God-given Land. He tells them that they are *married* to the Land of Israel. Beulah, in the Hebrew, means "married."

It is extremely interesting to note that Hurricane Beulah had struck America in the year 1967. Beulah formed exactly 3 months *to-the-day* of June 5th, which just so happened to be the start of Israel's 6-Day War with their aggressive Muslim neighbors. That was the miraculous war in which Israel defeated the many Arab nations coming against the Jewish State to destroy her, and when they had reclaimed much of their ancient Homeland. Two of the most important pieces of the Promised Land that Israel reacquired in the war were Eastern Jerusalem and Judea. So, the LORD had fulfilled the ancient Biblical prophecy of Isaiah, that contained the name "Beulah," three months to-the-day of the storm forming!

Also, it is important to note that leading up to the Six-Day War, American leadership had refused Israeli requests for military aid. The U.S. also refused to approve an Israeli preemptive attack on Egypt, even though the Jewish State's enemies were preparing to launch an attack against her on all sides. Could Beulah have been Almighty God's rebuke to the USA for not defending His chosen Nation? I can't possibly be the first one to ever notice this, can I?! This was nothing short of the Hand of God at work.

Beulah was the strongest, and the only, major hurricane of the 1967 Atlantic Hurricane Season. It, like David, was a devastating Category 5 storm. It spawned 115 tornadoes across Texas, which had established a new record for the highest amount of tornadoes ever produced by a tropical cyclone. Due to slow movement over Texas, Beulah led to significant flooding and the total damage had reached $235-million (that is over $800-million dollars today). It is greatly symbolic that Texas was the State which God chose to bring His wrath upon, as it's called the "Lone Star State." There is another place known as a *Lone Star State* in the world today, and that would be the Nation of ISRAEL.

The next retired Biblical name I came across was ANDREW, who was one of our Lord Jesus' disciples. For those of you not well-studied in the disciples, Andrew and his brother Peter were the two whom Jesus said that He would make "fishers of men." In August 1992, Andrew became a disastrous Category 5 hurricane. It was the most powerful hurricane to ever hit the State of Florida until 2017's Irma. It was also the costliest hurricane to ever make landfall in America until Katrina in 2005. It is the 7th costliest hurricane in U.S. history, and caused over $27-*billion* in damage. I am sure you're wondering if Andrew was also connected to the mistreatment of Israel? The answer would be yes.

On the 23rd of August, President George H.W. Bush held his second Madrid Conference which had pressured Israel to give up "Land-for-peace" to Palestinians. On the very *same day*, Andrew made landfall in Florida. At that time, the hurricane was the worst natural disaster to ever hit America. Just a few years ago, another disciple made the list of Biblically-named retired hurricanes - and that was MATTHEW. Hurricane Matthew was the first Category 5 Atlantic hurricane since Felix in 2007. The destructive storm had caused widespread damage in Haiti, and in the Southeastern United States. It was the deadliest Atlantic hurricane since Stan in 2005. In Florida, over one-million homes lost power, and damage from Matthew across the United States reached about $10-*billion*.

The storm made landfall in the U.S. during the *same week* of the Feast of Trumpets, also known as Rosh Hashana. Moreover, the hurricane formed in the Atlantic on September 24th. That's so Biblically significant. Matthew's Gospel, Chapter 24, is regarded among Prophecy buffs as one of the most important portions of Scripture pertaining to signs of Jesus Christ's return. Aside from Revelation, Mark (Chapter 13), and Luke (Chapter 21), Matthew 24 gives us Jesus' firsthand account of the signs we are to watch for pointing to the Rapture and His Second Coming. The fact that Matthew had formed on the 24th, during the *High Holy Days*, is not just interesting... but it is simply *incredible*.

The final and most recent Biblically-named retired hurricane you should all be very familiar with, as it occurred in 2017. It was

MARIA, the 3rd most costliest Atlantic hurricane in U.S. history. For those unaware, Maria is the translation in many languages for the name of *Mary*. Everyone on planet Earth should know Mary was the Virgin Mother of our Lord Jesus. Just like the hurricane bearing the name of globally recognizable King David, the storm bearing Mary's name will be remembered for a long time. Maria, also a powerful Category 5, had become the worst natural disaster on record in Dominica and Puerto Rico - and 10th most intense Atlantic hurricane ever recorded. Total damages are estimated to be close to $100-*billion*.

Much like the other historic Cat-5 hurricanes that have struck the U.S., Maria was connected to our leadership demanding that Israelis give up some of their Land for "peace" with Palestinians. The devastating storm had made landfall in the U.S. territory of Puerto Rico on the eve of the Feast of Trumpets (also New Year's Day in Israel). It was the third and final major hurricane to strike real estate of the USA in only a month's time - following Harvey and Irma. The three Category 4 and 5 storms striking that close together was unprecedented. Even more astounding, all three of the back-to-back-to-back devastating hurricanes struck at the end of the Hebrew year 5777. All three had made the list of the Top 5 Costliest U.S. Hurricanes on record.

I also believe that the three of them hitting in close succession symbolized the Trinity (the Father, Son, and Holy Spirit) warning U.S. leadership to "*back off Israel.*" I say this, because the trifecta of hurricanes struck our nation immediately following the Trump administration restarting the Israeli-Palestinian Peace Process. It was in the same day - even the *same hours* - that their delegation had met with Israeli Prime Minister Netanyahu and Palestinian President Abbas to renew the Mideast Peace Talks, when the first major hurricane to hit Texas in twelve years had formed; and that record-shattering hurricane was known as Harvey.

It was the longest a Texas hurricane remained a named storm after landfall since 1971. The storm would pour out the greatest amount of rain ever recorded in the Lower 48 States from a single storm. Nearly 30-*trillion* gallons of rain had fallen on Texas and Louisiana over a six-day period - enough to fill Texas' Houston Astrodome 85,000 times. In less than a week! WOW. Think about that. Harvey became the 2nd most expensive storm in American history, at around $125-*billion*, behind only Katrina. Harvey was also the first Cat-4 storm to make landfall in the U.S. in almost 15 years. While the hurricane was still wreaking havoc on the Lone Star State, and its surrounding States, another monster storm was forming in the Atlantic - Irma.

Sadly, the POTUS did not learn from Harvey to stop pushing "Land-for-Peace" on Israel. Trump would meet with Netanyahu and Abbas on the sidelines of the UN General Assembly in New York. His administration had said that the meetings would focus specifically on "laying a foundation" for the Peace Process, which would include Israeli Land on the negotiating table. Irma, another Category 4 hurricane, made landfall in the U.S. on the first day of the week that Trump held the meetings. Irma became one of the strongest storms ever recorded, packing 185 mph winds before it struck America. It was the first storm ever observed, in any ocean, to sustain winds of 185 mph for more than 24 hours. Irma had maintained 185 mph for 37 straight hours.

The storm's arrival in Florida, following Harvey, marked the first time on record that two Category 4 hurricanes made landfall in the USA during the same year. Hurricane Irma had generated enough accumulated cyclone energy to meet NOAA's definition of a *full* Atlantic Hurricane Season. Also, by itself, Irma had been more powerful than 18 of 51 full Hurricane Seasons since 1966. That mammoth storm blanketed the entire State of Florida, and had impacted surrounding States with hurricane-force winds and record flooding. There have also been some other historic storms and hurricanes striking the USA, connected to our leaders forcing Israel into Land-for-Peace Deals, that were not Biblically-named.

Back on October 31st of 1991, George H.W. Bush promoted his first Madrid Peace Conference - in which he sought to divide up the Land of Israel in exchange for peace with the Palestinians. On the very *next day*, what would become known as "the Perfect Storm" had formed in the Atlantic. The rare storm moved east to west, as opposed to a natural track from west to east. The storm was so unusual that a book and a movie had been made about it. President Bush's home and his vacation compound were severely damaged by the storm. Waves as high as his 3-story home filled the house with sea water, and had caused extensive damage.

On September 13th of 1993, President Bill Clinton signed the "Oslo Accord," labeled a "Land-for-Peace" accord that demanded Israel give away some of their Holy Land to the Palestinians. The very *next day*, Hurricane Emily would slam into the United States with winds up to 115 miles per hour.

On September 28th, 1998, while Secretary of State Albright was finishing up final details of an agreement that required Israel surrender 13% of Judea and Samaria to the Palestinians, President Clinton met with Palestinian President Yasser Arafat and Israeli Prime Minister Benjamin Netanyahu at the White House. As he briefed them on the agreement, Hurricane George had blasted the Gulf Coast with 110 mph winds and gusts up to 175 mph. The storm caused $1-*billion* in damage. It was at the exact time when Arafat departed U.S. soil that the storm began to dissipate.

In 2005, Hurricane Katrina formed on the *same exact day* that Israel was being forced by President George W. Bush, through his *Roadmap to Peace,* to finalize forcibly evacuating thousands of Jews from their homes in the Gaza Strip. In a mirror image, at the *same time* that the Jews were being forced out of their homes in Gaza, thousands of Americans in the South were being evacuated from their cities and towns due to Katrina's flooding.

Back to present-day... It was announced in early 2018 that the Trump Peace Plan would be unveiled after the Embassy move to Israel's Capital of Jerusalem. The Embassy event took place on May 14th, the 70th Anniversary of Israel's rebirth. There've been reports (and I pray they are false) that the President's upcoming plan would call for Israel to hand over 40% of Judea and Samaria to the Palestinians. Not to mention, parts of Jerusalem. There are some reports indicating that the Old City of Jerusalem could be internationalized! That sounds like something the United Nations has been calling for, and it would *not* sit well with our God.

Hurricanes are not the only extreme weather that the world has been contending with in recent years. There has been extreme heat across the globe. 2016 was the warmest year on record since record-keeping began in the 1800s. The heat record was recently broken 3 years in a row, according to NOAA (National Oceanic and Atmospheric Administration). 16 of the 17 hottest years have occurred since the year 2000, and 2017 was the third hottest year on record. As many of you know, the Godless liberals have been pushing the "global warming" theory - that *man* is responsible for the increase in temperature instead of God controlling it. As with theories of evolution and the Big Bang, global warming theorists desire to eliminate God from the picture.

Newsflash to everyone reading this: "man" has no power over the weather. Our actions cannot influence it in any way except for *one*. The only way we can ever influence the conditions on Earth is through our *sin*. Hear what God says in Isaiah, Chapter 24 and verses 5-6 -

"THE EARTH IS DEFILED UNDER THE INHABITANTS THEREOF; BECAUSE THEY HAVE TRANSGRESSED THE LAWS, CHANGED THE ORDINANCE, BROKEN THE EVERLASTING COVENANT. THEREFORE HATH THE CURSE DEVOURED THE EARTH, AND THEY THAT DWELL THEREIN ARE DESOLATE: THEREFORE THE INHABITANTS OF EARTH ARE BURNED, AND FEW MEN LEFT."

The LORD says that our sins bring a curse upon the earth, and one of the effects of that is inhabitants of Earth being burned with "great heat" (Revelation 16:9). Also, for the theory of global warming to be true, Earth would have to continue to get hotter year after year. That was not the case in 2018. We went from the 3rd hottest year on record in 2017, to one of the coldest winters in over a century. In Southern Michigan, where I'm from, only the winter of 2000-01 had been colder than the 2017-18 season over the course of the past century. Enduring such a miserable freezing winter, which was also the longest since the 1800s, has led me to believe we're experiencing *global cooling* - not global warming!

Michigan wasn't alone, as hundreds of millions of Americans had suffered under record-low temperatures this past winter. 2017 saw the coldest first week of any winter on record for dozens of cities in the East. The New Year's Eve ball drop in NYC's Times Square took place amid the coldest weather in half-a-century. The midnight temp was only 10 degrees above zero, with a wind chill of -5 to -20 degrees below zero. Numerous record lows had been set across the United States all throughout December and January, and wind chills in the 50s below zero were recorded. The deep freeze wasn't just occurring in the U.S. either. In my research, I discovered that Bangladesh, Russia, South Korea, and the UK had endured record-cold temperatures during the winter of 2017-18.

Rollercoaster weather changes, from extreme hot to extreme cold, can only ever be explained by Someone controlling it. The theories of global warming and climate change cannot explain the seesaw weather we've recently been experiencing. The only thing that has ever made sense of it, for thousands of years, is the Word of God. Why is it so far-fetched to believe that the Creator of the Universe, Creator of everything that is seen and unseen, controls our weather? His Word is clear that He does. Every verse I found pertaining to weather starts with the words "He brings, He causes, He commands, He creates, He gives, He makes, and He sends."

Notice that *not once* does the Holy Bible ever use the phrases "man causes" or "man makes" when speaking of weather on the earth. This means the theory of climate change is incompatible with Almighty God's Word. No Christian or Jew should embrace the theory, which is forcefully pushed upon the world as truth. It most certainly is not. The climate change/global warming agenda discourages belief in the *real* truth, which is God's Eternal Word. Men and women of influence, like former U.S. President Obama, uber-liberal Pope Francis, Al Gore, and atheist scientist Bill Nye, all push the false narrative that "man can make the weather" - and that man can take steps to "change the weather." This widely held belief denies our God, by replacing the Creator with the creation.

This fulfills a "Last Days" prophecy of Saint Paul in Romans, Chapter 1 and verse 25 –

"THEY CHANGED THE TRUTH OF GOD INTO A LIE, AND WORSHIPPED AND SERVED THE CREATION MORE THAN THE CREATOR, WHO IS BLESSED FOREVER."

I believe this verse also condemns those worshiping the earth, spending their whole lives trying to *save it* - while the Holy Bible is clear that God will fix it in the end. If this generation actually read their Bibles, they'd know that. We must focus our short time in this world on getting *souls* saved. Let God take care of saving Earth, because only *He* can. Proverbs 11:30 teaches that "He that winneth souls is wise." Yet, the far-left Scientific community and our day and age's *thinkers* call climate change deniers uneducated simpletons whose beliefs are archaic. Well, I would much rather believe, teach, and do the things that God says are wise, than go along with the crowd so I could be celebrated as a "progressive" man of this world.

I'll never apologize, nor be shamed by anyone, for believing the word of our Maker over *opinions* of sinful men. For thousands upon thousands of years, the Bible's been the only book in human history that has always proven true - and has *never* been proven false. In our Holy Book, Jesus prophesied that extreme weather, hurricanes, tsunamis, and great earthquakes would be birth pangs to usher in the end of the age. So, the next time you see "breaking news" headlines about historic disasters and extreme weather, are you going to believe a liberal newscaster explaining it all away as a result of climate change... or will you believe JESUS? Will you believe YHWH? Will you heed His warnings, repent of sins, and spread the word that His Son is coming back soon?

With two diametrically opposed accounts of what is causing the disasters in the world and the extreme weather, whose account are you going to trust? Will you trust the Word of our all-knowing God, or take a chance on opinions of imperfect men? Whenever severe weather strikes anywhere near my home, I find comfort in the fact that I pray to the LORD who can divert it away from my property and loved ones. I find absolutely *no* comfort whatsoever in other men telling me that the severe weather is just "random"; and that if I'm lucky, it might just pass me by. Who are *you* going to put *your* faith in? God or man? I have made my choice. Now, it is time to make yours. Choose wisely.

JESUS SAID, UPON THE EARTH (THERE SHALL BE) DISTRESS OF NATIONS, WITH PERPLEXITY; THE SEA AND THE WAVES ROARING; MEN'S HEARTS FAILING THEM FOR FEAR, AND FOR LOOKING AFTER THOSE THINGS WHICH ARE COMING ON THE EARTH: FOR THE POWERS OF HEAVEN SHALL BE SHAKEN.

- LUKE 21:25-26

CHAPTER NINE

ABORTION

BEFORE I FORMED THEE IN THE BELLY I KNEW THEE; AND
BEFORE THOU CAMEST FORTH OUT OF THE WOMB I
SANCTIFIED THEE, SAITH THE LORD.

- JEREMIAH 1:4-5

ABORTION IS MURDER... PERIOD. Human beings should not be entitled to the *choice* of murdering other humans. While many liberal women today shout "my body - my choice," they couldn't be more wrong. If the LORD has chosen to place a baby inside of your womb, then it's your responsibility to bring it into the world. God's Will always trumps your *feelings*.

There's only ever been one woman in human history who has ever conceived outside of sexual relations, and that was the Virgin Mother of our Lord Jesus Christ. This means that virtually every single woman on this planet, who has ever become pregnant, has made a choice to bring a child into this world (with the exception of rape and forced incest). Everyone knows that sex can result in pregnancy. If you're going to sleep with someone before marriage - especially unprotected - then you're fully aware of the potential results of your actions. The day that you become pregnant with a human life inside of your womb, you should not be afforded the luxury of *choice* again. You have already made your choice, and with choices come consequences.

Now, if a teenager is not mature enough or does not have the financial means to care for a baby - or in cases of rape and incest - there are plenty of women who can and will mother the child. There are over two-million women, in America alone, who cannot bear children. They'd gladly care for the baby. So abortion should *never* be an option. Obviously, if the life of a mother is in danger, then that's a different story - but that is a *very rare* occurrence. Dr. Landrum Shettles said, "Less than 1% of abortions are performed to save the mother's life." This means that 99% of abortions are *not* done to save the life of the mother. So much for that argument by abortion advocates!

As for cases of rape and incest, which are also rare, I know that not allowing an abortion under those circumstances may be hard to understand and may even sound like cruel punishment to victims; but if you view the dilemma from a Biblical standpoint, you can see why abortion is wrong in *every instance*. In the Bible, whenever a child was conceived through rape or incest, God had always reaped out punishment for the rapists and perpetrators of incest. They never went unpunished. Also, He *never* punished the baby. He allowed babies of such horrendous crimes to live their lives. We must do the same. One victim of such tragedies should be enough. Why make two victims?! That, my friends, would be the *real* cruel punishment. The unborn baby committed no crime.

Unfortunately, there are a whole lot of abortions being done today - especially through the murderous organization known as Planned Parenthood. Their latest Annual Report revealed that the Nation's largest abortion peddler had received about $550-million from American taxpayers in the 2016-2017 fiscal year. For every adoption referral that PP had made last year, they performed over 80 abortions. They performed a total of 321,384 abortions in the most recent fiscal year. Over 300,000! That's almost 900 *per-day*.

It has been calculated that if PP were to do abortion procedures around the clock, for an entire year, they would have to abort 37 babies per-hour - equaling a dead baby *every 98 seconds* in order to reach their annual total.

Think about that... in one year, a child of God lost their life every minute and a half. What a disgrace and bloody stain on this nation. That is why it's great news to hear States are beginning to defund the abortion giant, and that over 30 Planned Parenthoods had closed their doors in 2017. Yet, the $543-million which they received from our government was a staggering 61% more than what they received a decade ago. That is one big reason why we need to defund Planned Parenthood, but I can give 7-*million* more reasons. In just 50 years, the lives of over 7-million babies have been senselessly ended by PP. Since the Supreme Court's *Roe V. Wade* ruling in 1973, legalizing abortion-on-demand nationwide, over 60-*million* babies have been murdered.

PP has been the nation's largest abortion provider since that abominable SCOTUS decision. There is no other national group that comes close. PP propagates the lie that they are a "women's health" organization that does more than abortions, but statistics tell a different story. 20 years ago, PP did over 165,000 abortions in a year. 15 years ago, they did over 230,000. 10 years ago, they cut short the lives of over 305,000 babies. Since then, they have been responsible for murdering around 320,000 infants *every year* - equaling over 3-*million* murdered babies in the past 10 years.

If murdering babies was not enough to withdraw the taxpayer funding from PP (which it should be), the crooked organization has been exposed in recent years for the illegal trafficking of baby body parts - covering up child abuse and sex-trafficking - as well as promoting sex to children. Planned Parenthood is, no doubt, *of the devil*. I am sure that statement will draw criticism from fellow Americans who support the organization, but it is 100% truth.

Satan was "a murderer from the beginning" (John 8:44), and Jesus said that anyone who commits murder is a child of Satan. What Planned Parenthood is doing through abortion is ending the life of an innocent human, and murder in the Bible is defined as "shedding innocent blood." So, Biblically, PP fits the description of a "murderer" in God's Sight. Like it or not.

Something else that has long bugged me about the demonic organization is that calling themselves "Planned Parenthood" has got to be the biggest oxymoron in the entire world. How can they call themselves "Planned" Parenthood, while they do everything that they possibly can to *prevent* parenthood?! PP should be sued for false advertising. They only "plan" for how mothers murder their children - never for how to raise them. Their slogan is "Care. No matter what." It should be "MURDER. No matter what."

No human being on Earth should ever be able to take the life of another human being legally. The only exceptions should be self-defense and capital punishment. If someone had committed a crime that was beyond heinous, would forever remain a threat to themself and to others, and could not be rehabilitated, then God gives us authority to end that life. All other lives are precious in His Sight. Especially *innocent* life. And you cannot get any more innocent, or pure, than a baby who has not even exited the womb. Yet, PP is murdering over 300,000 of them every single year.

Abortion today is equivalent to false god worship of ancient times. In the Bible, we read of children being sacrificed unto false gods like Baal and Molech. While children aren't being sacrificed to these or other pagan gods today, specifically, the murder of this generation's babies is just as abominable as child sacrifices of Old Testament times. The blood of innocents is being spilled, and that warrants God's Wrath. Read verses 37 and 38 of Psalm 106 with abortion in mind, and then tell me these verses don't describe our baby-killing Planned Parenthood society perfectly -

"THEY SACRIFICED THEIR SONS AND THEIR DAUGHTERS TO
THE DEMONS; THEY POURED OUT INNOCENT BLOOD, THE
BLOOD OF THEIR SONS AND DAUGHTERS... AND THE LAND
WAS POLLUTED WITH BLOOD."

Without question, our land is being polluted with the blood of innocents. God warns of the consequences for shedding innocent blood in Exodus 23:7, Proverbs 6:17, Jeremiah 22:17, Isaiah 59:7, Matthew 18:6, Mark 9:42, and Luke 17:2. Jesus said it would be better for you to have a cinderblock tied around your neck, and to be thrown into the deepest sea, than to incur the wrath of God for harming one of His "little ones."

The number one reason why the LORD detests the crime of abortion, so very much, is because He has plans for us *before* He forms us in the womb" (Jeremiah 1:5). So, it does not matter how many days, weeks, or months, that a fetus has been forming in a woman's womb. Before it even becomes a fetus, it already has *life* in God's Eyes. That is exactly why we pro-lifers defend life from the womb. We must stop arguing with unbelievers about *when* a fetus *becomes* human, and start telling them when our *God says* it does - and that is *the second* it appears in the mother's womb. If none of what I have said sways any pro-choicers from supporting Planned Parenthood, then hopefully horrific accounts of botched abortions will convince you. At least they should!

Dr. Kermit Gosnell was an abortionist convicted of murdering at least three infants who had been "born alive" during attempted abortion procedures. In 2011, he and his employees of Women's Medical Society Clinic, in Pennsylvania, were charged with eight murder counts, 24 felonies, and 227 misdemeanors. There were seven newborns killed, when their spinal cords were severed with scissors, after being born alive. Sadly, it was not an isolated case. An undercover sting into PP exposed abortionists who had openly admitted they would "let a baby die" if a live birth were to occur in spite of an attempted abortion.

According to research by *Live Action*, and statistics that were recorded by Centers for Disease Control and Prevention (CDC), at least 500 babies will be born alive following a botched abortion every year. The statistics also show that a majority of them will be "left to die." What amazes me is that the same liberal activists who support Planned Parenthood are also pushing for stricter gun control laws to prevent mass shootings in American schools. How can you say that you care for the lives of innocent children, while at the same time, supporting the organization which specializes in murdering the most innocent of them all?!

Planned Parenthood is responsible for taking *150-times more* innocent lives, each year, than mass shootings have in the past 50 years! Since the 1960s, less than 2,000 people have been killed in mass shootings. Less than 10% of victims were children or teens. About 200 kids have been murdered by mass shooters in the past 50 years, while PP murdered 320,000 babies in the previous year *alone*. If you are outraged over school shootings but also support Planned Parenthood, then you are a *hypocrite* - plain and simple.

God has said that the fruit of the womb is His *"gift"* (Psalms 127:3). Sadly, many women are quick to throw His precious gifts in the trash - literally. To all women who've had an abortion in the past, but now regret the error of your ways: God wants to forgive you, but you need to do your part by repenting of your sins and asking to get washed in the sin-cleansing Blood of Jesus. He will cleanse you not just of your sins, but of all your guilt, shame, and regret. Only then will you live in that incomparable peace of God, which comes through forgiveness *in Christ*. Take comfort that *all* babies, everywhere, in the womb or out of it, will go to Heaven at the moment of death. So, while you may not have mothered your child on Earth, you will meet and mother them someday!

On the flipside of that coin, to all women who are unrepentant after abortions, or who even shamelessly promote the abominable procedure to others: you really must be "pro-choice," because you have freely chosen Hell over Heaven for your eternal home. Heed my words while you still can, and REPENT.

I would like to close this chapter with something to meditate on. Did you know that the first human being to physically rejoice upon the news of Jesus' birth was an unborn baby? In Luke 1:41, we read that John the Baptist leaped inside of his mother's womb. He wasn't some clump of cells. He had LIFE with a soul, just like all babies in the womb. So, don't end them. Don't abandon them.

LO, CHILDREN ARE AN HERITAGE OF THE LORD: AND THE FRUIT OF THE WOMB IS HIS REWARD.

- PSALMS 127:3

CHAPTER TEN

LGBT PRIDE

WOMEN DID CHANGE THE NATURAL USE INTO THAT WHICH
IS AGAINST NATURE: AND LIKEWISE ALSO THE MEN, LEAVING
THE NATURAL USE OF THE WOMAN, BURNED IN THEIR LUST
ONE TOWARD ANOTHER; MEN WITH MEN WORKING THAT
WHICH IS UNSEEMLY, AND RECEIVING IN THEMSELVES THAT
RECOMPENCE OF THEIR ERROR WHICH WAS MEET. AND EVEN
AS THEY DID NOT LIKE TO RETAIN GOD IN THEIR
KNOWLEDGE, GOD GAVE THEM OVER TO A REPROBATE MIND,
TO DO THOSE THINGS WHICH ARE NOT CONVENIENT.

- ROMANS 1:26-28

RIGHT OFF THE BAT, so that I am not immediately condemned as being a "hateful bigot" before people even take the time to read this chapter, let me be crystal clear that I don't "hate gays." In this life, I've had close friends and colleagues who are homosexuals. Some have been as close to me as family, and I have loved them like family. So, how in the world could I possibly *hate* gays? I do not. Just as I don't hate Muslims, even though I staunchly oppose Islam. I do, however, stand against everything that is against God. Therefore, I oppose the LGBT agenda and *pride*; while I see the LGBT *people* as confused sinners who have yet to come to full knowledge of the truth.

LGBT activism, like Islam, is an anti-God religion. Yes, that's right, I called the LGBT movement a *religion*. Because, just like the Muslims or climate change activists, they hold strong beliefs which they *force* others to accept and support. That's exactly why Christianity is not a religion, but the *truth*. We don't need to force our beliefs on anyone. We simply present others with what God's Word says, and then allow them to either accept or reject it.

The Godless movements I have mentioned, on the other hand, don't afford you any such choice. For instance, with the Islamists, it is "convert or die." Climate change activists say that denial of their theory should be "criminalized." And the LGBT community says "support us - or else." Isn't it funny how the vocal adherents to these movements all accuse us Christians of forcing our beliefs upon others? In reality, it is so obviously the other way around.

I am not afraid to say that I stand uncompromisingly against the pride of the homosexual community. Pride is of Satan. Lucifer fell from Heaven because of his "pride" (Ezekiel 28). In Proverbs 8:13, we read that "the fear of the Lord is to hate evil: pride, and arrogancy, and the evil way, and perverse mouth, do I hate." Take notice of the words "pride" is grouped with - arrogancy, evil, and perverse. Pride is not something to be celebrated, by any means.

Do I *hate* the pride, evil ways, and perverseness of the LGBT community? You'd best believe I do. But do I hate LGBT *people?* Of course not. I'm sure you've heard it said a thousand times (and you should, because it's true) that "God hates sin - not the sinner." He wills for all poor sinners to repent and to turn to Him through His Son, our Lord Jesus Christ. My friends, the Benham Brothers, say it best - "God loves all people, but He *does not* love all ideas." That's how I try to live my life. I love everyone, but don't always support their actions and beliefs. I hate sin, with a passion, but at the same time I have compassion toward the people stuck in sin. I tell all sinners that God doesn't approve of their behavior, but also that it is never too late to turn from their wicked ways.

For those who may not know my backstory, I wasn't always a Holy Bible thumper. A decade ago, I was the worst sinner on the block. I'd committed virtually every sin under the Sun, and still... *God loved me.* He had pulled me out of the deep dark waters of sin, and now I try to love others as He has loved me. He gave me a new life. He gave me a second chance. I was truly *reborn* as a new creation. We all can be. We all *must be,* in order to reach His Holy Heaven. You cannot dwell in unrepentant sin, and still call yourself a Christian. You must turn and flee from sin wherever it rears its ugly head in your life. And We ALL sin. *No one* has ever been perfect except for Christ Jesus, and thus we will all fall short of God's Glory (Romans 3:23).

Still, as long as you repent of your sin and regret committing it, you can receive God's forgiveness and mercy every single day *through Christ.* Without repenting, you'll receive no forgiveness. You'll receive no mercy. That is the reason I despise LGBT Pride; because there is absolutely *no repentance* found in the movement. Instead, they're *celebrating* their sin - not regretting it. Christians need to start viewing the issues of this world through the Biblical Lens. Until we all do, this nation will remain in a sinful mess.

Think about it... what other sin, mentioned in God's Word, is *celebrated* by our society? Is blasphemy celebrated? What about dishonoring parents? Theft? Murder? Coveting? Lust? Adultery? Gossip? Lying? Drunkenness? The answer is NO to all the above. Not one of these sins is celebrated in our society, because they are recognized for what they are: SIN. Why is homosexuality treated differently from all other sins mentioned in the Bible? I am pretty sure there are far more liars, gossipers, drunkards, adulterers, and thieves in the world than homosexuals. Why not celebrate them?

If you don't think that it is right to do so, and you believe it is inherently wrong for those sinners to be *proud* of their lifestyles, then why would you support Gay Pride? Why wouldn't you stand with the other sinners in their trespasses against God too? If you are going to say one sin is okay, then you might as well support them all. Otherwise, you are a *hypocrite*.

What exactly are gays so "proud" of in the first place? Have any of you ever pondered that? Are they proud of being what the LORD dubs "a sinner"? It sure seems like it. They don't want to repent of an abominable lifestyle, because they don't see anything wrong with it. They could care less what Almighty *God* thinks. They believe that He needs to "get with the times," because they refuse to change their ways. Sodom and Gomorrah had thought the same way. How did they turn out? The Pride movement today flaunts their debaucherous sin in the same way as the inhabitants of the depraved cities of old. They've even gone so far as to take God's ancient symbol of His Covenant with mankind, a Rainbow, and make it the symbol for their rebellion against Him!

Yet, there sure are a whole lot of Christians who seem to have no problem "standing with" the LGBT movement or in declaring support for their *pride*. Shame on you all. I said "a whole lot of" you because for the first time in the history of our Judeo-Christian Nation, a majority of Christians in this country now *support* Gay Marriage. Around 60% of so-called "Bible believers" to be exact, according to recent polls. Amongst all Americans, about 65% say same-sex marriage should be legal, and support for homosexual relationships has climbed to 72%. God forgive us for not putting His Word first in this once-God-fearing country.

When asked whether gay sex (sodomy) was normal, 60% of Americans said they believe it is "morally acceptable - while only 37% percent said it is "morally wrong." Apparently, the morals of the USA are no longer derived from the moral Laws of Almighty God. The only thing I'll ever be personally *proud* of in this life is that I'm a part of the 28% of Americans still standing with GOD, and *against* LGBT Pride. I consider it a badge of honor when I'm labeled a "conservative Christian extremist." I am about as far to the right politically as you can get; because I believe that is where our God is standing. Many claim to be conservatives, but are also supporting Gay Marriage. They seem to forget that we were once dubbed the "Religious Right" *for a reason*.

It is because we stood firmly on and faithfully for the Word of God, without compromise. To all of you so-called conservatives who support Gay Marriage: you need to look up the definition of *conservative* in the dictionary. When you do, you are gonna find out that you most certainly *are not one*. To fellow believers, who support the LGBT community in their pride: you need to repent and get right with God about as much as they do! Because when you stand with them, you endorse their sins against the LORD. This is just as bad as committing their sins yourself. Think about just who you're standing with, by meditating on Psalms 10:4 -

"IN THEIR PRIDE THE WICKED MEN DO NOT SEEK HIM; IN ALL THEIR THOUGHTS THERE IS NO ROOM FOR GOD."

Still, many of you are making *plenty of room* for "equality" in this nation today. While I agree that we're all *equally* poor sinners in God's sight, and should all be treated equally as human beings, all lifestyles and beliefs are not equal. In the adoption of a young boy, two 50-year-old men in leather chaps should not be viewed as "equal" to a Bible-based husband and wife when selecting the parents. As far as homosexual relationships go, do whatever you want in your personal life - just as I live my life how I choose to. God has given us all free will. So, I'm not telling you how to live. I am simply telling you how God says *not* to live! And as for Gay Marriage, I oppose it 110% - because it's an affront to the sanctity of the LORD's Plan for mankind.

Sadly, it appears that many of my brothers and sisters in the Faith today have accepted that Gay Marriage is here to stay. They think the radical LGBT agenda is just too powerful to defeat, and so they surrender and adopt the "if you can't beat 'em - join 'em" mentality. My friends, the fight will never be over in the battle of good versus evil as long as we have lifebreath. As Bible believers, we cannot stand with the LGBT Pride movement *and* with God Almighty. It is just not possible. You can love the sinner, but you better be careful about allying with an anti-God faction. Because there is absolutely no "on the fence" with the LORD.

You cannot stand in the middle. You can't be half in and half out. You're either with Him or you're against Him. You are either in Him or in the world. Take your pick. There is right and wrong, good and evil, holy and unholy, moral and immoral, or righteous and wicked. There's absolutely no gray area with Almighty God. There never has been, and never will be. It may not be politically correct, but it is Biblically-direct, to say that the LORD is *against* the LGBT Pride movement. Does He love the people? Absolutely. He forever hopes that they will repent and turn to Him. Sadly, in their pride, the majority refuse to do so.

The Bible is dubbed by much of the homosexual community as an outdated book, with archaic laws, that needs to be revised. They say that God needs to "evolve" into the 21st century. What they fail to realize is that God is *"the same yesterday, today, and forever"* (Malachi 3:6 & Hebrews 13:8). Unfortunately, even most Christians have forgotten this timeless truth. They believe Satan's lie which says that if a majority of this generation believes God is wrong on any issue, then He *must change* His stance - in order to *adapt* to the current culture. All I can say to that is... don't hold your breath! God has never been, He is not, and He never will be, wrong on any subject. He is GOD for God's sake!

It is us poor sinners that need to change our ways, in order to adapt to *Him*. I promise you that it is not the other way around. If the LORD called something a "sin" yesterday, then it is *still* a sin today. If He had called something an "abomination" thousands of years ago, then I assure you that it is *still* an abomination today! He is God, and so He gets to make the rules - whether this sinful generation likes it or not. There are a lot of people today who like to ignore the fact that Sodom and Gomorrah's biggest sins were homosexuality and sodomy. Yet, the U.S. Supreme Court deemed these sins perfectly normal in this nation just a few years ago.

Don't think for one second that just because this is the good ol' US of A that the LORD would treat us any differently than the rebellious nations of old. It does not matter to Him how big, rich, prosperous, or powerful a nation is. Once any nation departs from Him, He departs from them. Psalms 9:17 couldn't be more clear -

"THE WICKED SHALL BE TURNED INTO HELL, AND ALL THE NATIONS THAT FORGET GOD."

When our nation departs from its Judeo-Christian foundation, we believers must speak up. When Gay Marriage was essentially made a "law of the land" by the Godless Supreme Court in 2015, those who fear God had refused to accept that abominable ruling. #WeWillNotObey had become our battle cry across social media. Normally, Christians are the most obedient to laws of this or any country. Since the dawn of this nation, our laws have been rooted in the Law of the LORD God Almighty, so they've been easy to follow. But when any law of the USA comes into conflict with the Laws of God, that national law becomes *null and void*. We cannot obey. As Jesus' first followers boldly proclaimed in Acts 5:29 -

"WE MUST OBEY GOD, RATHER THAN MEN."

Believers who actually support Gay Marriage would counter my Biblical take on the matter with verses from Romans 13 and Matthew 22:21. These verses of Scripture command us to obey the laws of a nation, but surely *do not apply* to unGodly laws. The laws which Christ and Paul had referred to in those verses did not come into conflict with our God's Law. To any Christian using the

Romans and Matthew verses to argue that the LORD approves of His children observing unGodly laws of this world: I ask you to answer one simple question... If the law of Rome (or any nation) ever commanded that Jews and Christians must *burn* their Torahs and Bibles, do you think Jesus and Paul would say that "You need to obey your government"?

Sorry, but I don't believe that our Lord or Saint Paul would be lighting that match. No one can read the entirety of the Bible and argue that God would ever allow us to obey worldly laws which are directly opposed to His Laws. Do you remember the Biblical prophet Daniel and what he did when he was faced with either obeying the "law of the land" or the Law of God? In Chapter 6 of Daniel, we find him living in an unGodly nation. The King there passed a law stating that no one but the King could offer prayers in the land. So, what did Daniel do? Verse 10 tells us -

"WHEN DANIEL KNEW THAT THE DECREE WAS SIGNED, HE WENT INTO HIS HOUSE; AND HIS WINDOWS BEING OPEN IN HIS CHAMBER TOWARD JERUSALEM, HE KNEELED UPON HIS KNEES THREE TIMES A DAY, AND PRAYED, AND GAVE THANKS BEFORE HIS GOD, AS HE HAD ALWAYS DONE IN THE PAST."

So, we find that Daniel "knew" of the king's law - and that he blatantly *disobeyed* it. Wow, how could a man of God ever break a national law?! It is simple... the worldly law was antithetical to God's Law. Why then is it different for believers today? Over the past decade, America has become just as unGodly, perverted, and rebellious as Babylon was. Would our God (Who was the God of Daniel) expect us to sacrifice our Faith, in order to obey laws that violate *His* Law? I don't believe for one second that He would. I believe that He is looking for faithful Daniels in a world full of backsliders and "religious" cowards.

Putting your faith on the backburner, in order to *fit in* with the world, is extremely displeasing to the LORD. Ignoring His Word, in order to *evolve* with society, is a disgrace to Him. Violating His Commandments, in order to adhere to man's laws, is abomination in His Sight. Forgetting His Moral Law, in order to be a friend of a wicked immoral world, makes you His *enemy* (James 4:4). God is clear that we are not to be conformed to the ways of this world (2nd Corinthians 6:17). We know, full well, that the entire world is under the influence of the devil (John 12:31 & 2nd Corinthians 4:4). That is precisely why Lord Jesus said, "The *world* hates Me, because I testify of it, that the works thereof are *evil*" (John 7:7).

Our Lord did not mince words when teaching that we would not be accepted in a society that's hostile to the Word of God. He prophesied that true Christians, in the Last Days, would be hated - falsely accused - persecuted - imprisoned - and that our beliefs would bring us into conflict with the worldly rulers and *their* laws (John 15, Mark 13, Luke 21, Matthew 5 & 24). In our day and age, these prophecies have been (and are being) fulfilled. Since the 2015 Gay Marriage ruling by the SCOTUS, uncompromising Bible-believers in America have been mocked - shunned - hated - sued - persecuted - attacked - and, yes, even imprisoned.

If you are a Christian or Jew who is not being labeled a hater, a bigot, discriminatory, or Bible-thumping looney-tune, regarding your stances on the hot button issues of our day, then you are not reading God's Word right. *Read it again.* If you have read it, front to back, you are probably cherry-picking parts of the Bible that suit *your* worldview - not God's. You can't pick and choose what you want to believe, and discard the rest. You cannot render some of God's Word untrue, simply because you disagree with it. The Word of the LORD will not be popular in an evil, perverted, and rebellious generation. You can't expect to be loved by all, holding a Biblical worldview. Turn on your TV and watch God's Word be mocked, attacked, and blasphemed, without remorse 24-7.

Along with not believing all of the Bible, there are Christians who use Biblical verses out of context in order to justify support for the LGBT agenda. "We all sin and fall short of the Glory of God," and "Judge not," are the most widely used verses to defend same-sex relationships. Well, I'd like to counter those arguments once and for all. As I stated earlier, it is 100% true that "we *all sin*"; but that is also why we *all need* Jesus. That's why God calls us *all* to repentance. Is the gay community repenting? Are they kneeling at the Cross of Christ, acknowledging a need for Him? If they have been, I must have missed it. The fact is that they have not repented, because they don't believe they're sinners. So, while we *all* sin, sadly, we do not *all* repent.

As to the "judge not" verse, which unbelievers all across the world have memorized to justify just about every sin in the Book, have you ever read the verse, "Show my people *their sins*"? When you make someone aware that they're sinning against the LORD, you are *not* "judging." What Jesus meant (in context) was for us to not go around being critical of everyone else's sins, while we ourselves are laden with them. I personally repent daily; because I acknowledge I sin every day, whether I realize it or not. If I were to go around claiming I am "holier than thou," while condemning the sins of everybody else, *then* I'd be judging. To make someone (who does not know God) aware that their lifestyle is against His Word is not judging them, but rather *loving* them.

I do not want to see anyone end up in Hell at the end of the road. Apparently, the "judge not" Christians will have no problem watching them burn. When believers err on the side of political correctness, refusing to condemn celebration of LGBT lifestyles, we push confused souls further into Satan's hands. We are called to be light in this dark world, and God expects us to be the moral compass. If we aren't being either of these things, then we might be judged as harshly as the unrepentant sinners. For the LORD is not willing that any perish, but that *all* would come to repentance (2nd Peter 3:8). All means ALL.

If you are telling the gay community that they are "all good," have nothing to worry about, and that our God loves them just the way they are, they will not come to repentance - and will perish in Hell. God isn't willing that they should, but apparently you are okay with it. The demonic forces possessing the gay community can only be cast out and defeated by the sinless holy Blood of the Lamb of God, Christ *JESUS*. Homosexuals will never approach the Saviour of the world if they do not believe there is anything they need to be *saved from*. They will never repent if Christians don't have the cojones to tell them that they are wrong. So, do not be afraid to speak up and show them their sins! Their eternal lives very well may depend on it.

I can't finish this chapter without addressing the Transgender insanity that is sweeping across our nation and the world. Call me old-fashioned, but I still see things the way that God created them to be. When I was growing up in the 80's and 90's, boys still liked girls and girls still liked boys. Boys were still boys and girls were still girls. Today, you never know what someone is half the time. People are calling themselves transgender, pangender, cisgender, gender-fluid, genderqueer, even *genderless*. It's utterly ridiculous.

Modern society has been making war (virtually unopposed by the Church) on every truth of God's Word, and I mean *every* truth - including the most basic truth of all, that "In the Beginning, God created them *male* and *female*." This verse is pretty plain and to the point. There is no wiggle room for other interpretations. God made man, and then God made woman. He said to be fruitful and multiply, and so they had sexual relations and made babies. That is the reason why all of us are here today! If Adam decided one day that he wanted to be the woman, or if Eve decided that she wore the pants in the garden, there would've never been an Abel, Seth, Enoch, Noah, Shem, Abraham, Isaac, Jacob (Israel), Judah, Joseph, Moses, David, Elijah, Daniel, nor a Lord Jesus Christ!

The human race would have died out 6,000 years ago if they thought like today's society. Since the dawn of Earth, as we know it, there have been only two genders - male and female. Period. First, God created man, and then He created the woman *for* man. If God thought that it was okay for Adam to lay with other men, then God would have created another man. He didn't. He created Eve. The LORD also calls for a union of marriage - for a husband to take a wife, and for them to cleave together and become "one flesh." He created men and women with their distinct body parts that come together to produce offspring. You cannot produce kids with two male parts or two female parts. Basic human biology!

In 2012, the American Psychiatric Association had referred to "gender identity disorder" as a mental health problem. In the eyes of God, it most certainly is. While society tells you to encourage your kids to find their own *identity*, Almighty God already gave them one at birth. The Book of Proverbs, Chapter 22 and verse 6, commands us to "Train up a child in the way they should go; and when they are old, they will not depart from it." Christian parents must be more active in the lives of their children than ever before; because if you're not raising them, be sure that someone else *will*.

I personally could care less if a man or woman gets offended when I call them what God created them to be, which is a *man* or a *woman*. If their feelings are hurt because I don't refer to them by another pronoun, then they should take it up with their Creator - not me. His language was not vague when He said that men and women shouldn't live in a fantasyland, nor play make-believe, by dressing up like the opposite sex. In Deuteronomy 22:5, He said -

"THE WOMAN SHALL NOT WEAR THAT WHICH PERTAINETH UNTO A MAN, NEITHER SHALL A MAN PUT ON A WOMAN'S GARMENT: FOR ALL THAT DO SO ARE ABOMINATION UNTO THE LORD THY GOD."

ABOMINATION. Get it?! We believers cannot tiptoe around Biblical truth, in order to not offend somebody. I do not care how many sex changes someone like Bruce Jenner has had or will ever have. He can call himself "Caitlyn" all day long, but he'll always be Bruce *the man* to me. That is what he will forever be in God's Sight. It has gotten so bad today that we're actually debating over Transgender Bathroom Bills to decide whether or not grown men should be allowed in the same restroom as little girls. Craziness! There should be no debate. If you were born with male parts, then you use the men's room. If you were born with female parts, then you use the ladies' room. Period. End of story!

Besides transgenderism, there is another fallacy running wild in America and across the world, and that's "preferred pronouns." Instead of the pronouns we've used to describe men and women from the beginning of time, this generation has created at least 7 pronouns to describe a human being. In reality, a man is a he/him and a woman is she/her. A group would be they/them. Now, a guy can "identify" as a she/her, or they/them, or even ze/zie (whatever that is). I won't name all of the other nonsensical pronouns in this book. They are a waste of paper and your time. LGBT groups say, "you should never refer to a person as he or she." They say these pronouns are *offensive* to trans and non-conforming individuals. Sorry, but make-believe time ends when you become an adult!

If you were born a boy, then you're he/him. If you were born a girl, then you are she/her. Those have been your pronouns since you entered this world. You can't change them because you "feel" like you are something else. Do we call our cats "dogs," or dogs "cats"? I've never met anyone who does. So, why is it okay for us to mislabel other human beings as something we know darn well they are not? Male is male and female is female – just as the sun is hot, black is black, white is white, and 2+2=4. I'd prefer winter to be warm like summer, but that doesn't change the fact that it is and has always been COLD. You can pretend all you would like, put on a bikini or pair of shorts, and lay out in your backyard to get a tan in January. The only thing you're gonna get is frostbite.

God-fearing people in America and all across this world need to stand up and say ENOUGH IS ENOUGH to this insanity. If we do not speak out against it, then who will? In this generation, full of lies and confusion, we must boldly declare the truth - no matter what the lamestream narrative is, or how many people oppose us for speaking it. Always remember this wise quote from the film, *God's NOT Dead 2*: "I'd rather stand with God and be judged by the world than stand with the world and be judged by GOD."

THOU SHALT NOT LIE WITH MANKIND, AS WITH
WOMANKIND: IT IS ABOMINATION.

- LEVITICUS 18:22

CHAPTER ELEVEN

FALLING AWAY FROM THE FAITH

NOW THE SPIRIT SPEAKETH EXPRESSLY, THAT IN THE LATTER
TIMES SOME SHALL DEPART FROM THE FAITH, GIVING HEED
TO SEDUCING SPIRITS, AND DOCTRINES OF DEVILS.

- 1ST TIMOTHY 4:1

JUST OVER A DECADE ago, in 2007, there were approximately
227-million adults in the United States. Nearly 80% of them had
identified as Christian. Between 2007 and 2014, while the overall
size of this country's population grew by about 20-million, those
who identified as Christians shrunk to around 70% - about a 10%
decline, and a net decline of roughly 5-million.

Today, 70% of millennials (aged 18-33) believe Christianity
is alienating young adults by being too "judgmental" about LGBT
issues. 31% of them, who've been raised in Christian households,
say they're now unbelievers because of negative Biblical teaching
about gay and lesbian people. Half (45%) of young Evangelicals
(aged 18-29) actually *support* Gay Marriage. They are professing
Christians, mind you, not unbelievers. While they may profess the
Faith, and are churchgoers, they are obviously not being reared in
Godly homes. If they were, then their parents would instruct them
in the Biblical truth and teach them to fear God. If nearly half of

this generation's young Evangelicals endorse same-sex Marriage, then their parents should be ashamed.

Recent statistics revealed that about 7 in 10 American seniors (67%) are Christians, while only 3 in 10 (29%) young adults are. Evangelicals made up 22% of the population in 1988. 20 years later, they had remained strong at 21% (in 2008). As of 2015, that number rapidly dropped to 17%. This means there was only a 1% drop in two decades, and nearly a 5% drop in just a 7-year period! While there are many reasons for the massive falling away from the Faith which we have seen in America (and this world at large) throughout the past decade, the biggest reason is former President Obama's radical transformation of America.

During his tenure, the United States devolved into a cesspool of Biblically-hostile attitudes and beliefs. Islam was celebrated, while Christianity was targeted as "hateful" and "bigoted." Israel was treated like an enemy, as opposed to our greatest Ally. The schools forced the Godless theories like evolution, Big Bang, and climate change on America's youth. Our culture was flooded with blasphemy, violence, sex, legalization of mind-altering drugs, and LGBT propaganda. Add the cowardly backslidden Church to the mix, and we had a recipe for disaster. Worldly pastors were afraid (and most still are) to preach Biblical truth. They were afraid of losing liberal congregants in their pews, being targeted by Obama for discrimination, or threatened by Islamists and LGBT bullies.

Too many churches in our once-God-fearing Nation did not, and will not, preach on *sin*. The reason we're supposed to come to Jesus and go to church, in the first place, is because we're all poor sinners! Once you stop teaching what sin is, why we must repent of it, and why we need a Saviour because of it, there would be no need for Christianity. Unfortunately, our Faith today is not about Lord Jesus dying on the Cross to reconcile the sinful world to the Father in Heaven. Instead, it has become about entertainment and "feel good" time for so-called believers.

Honestly, you don't even need to be a Holy Bible believer to attend church these days. You are more likely to see a secularized concert, a few skits, and hear a poem from the pastor, as opposed to getting taught the Word of God. This is because, in the early 2000's, Rick Warren (who's wrongly dubbed "America's Pastor") had influenced Christian leaders all across this nation to join his *"Purpose Driven Church"* movement. His sinner-friendly plan for churches, which was meant to help pastors gain larger audiences and appeal to more unbelievers, set forth a list of do's and don'ts.

Some of the most troubling suggestions that Warren laid out were: *don't* mention sin - *don't* say "saved" or "unsaved," but use the words "churched" and "unchurched" instead - *don't* mention Hell - *don't* give altar calls to "accept Jesus as Saviour" - *remodel* churches to resemble venues like nightclubs or casinos, in order to be more inviting to sinners - allow coffee and snacks in pews with no dress code - and have hip music (such as hard rock, hip hop, or heavy metal) to attract the youth. I am sure that every one of you has a church doing one (or all) of these things in your local area, as we speak. I can name quite a few in my area.

Though I disagree with everything on Warren's list, the two that hurt the Church the most are not preaching on sin or Hell. If there is NO sin, where is the need for a *Saviour*? If NO Hell, then what are any of us trying to live good lives for in the first place? If we are all going to Heaven, then we might as well *live it up*. Any pastors not preaching on either one of these all-important Biblical issues will be guilty of their flocks ending up in the Hell that they conveniently fail to mention. At least their church memberships will continue to grow in the meantime! It's sickening. This is one of the biggest reasons why our society is laden with sin more so than ever before in American history.

Christian "leaders" today who've been given a charge by God to "cry aloud, and spare not to show the people their *sins*" (Isaiah 58:1), are doing the exact opposite. They're saying that sin is OK, because "we all do it, so why judge"? They ignore the reality that, from the beginning, sin *kills*. Saint Paul said, "the wages of sin is death" (Romans 6:23); and for the disease of sin there is but *one* remedy: JESUS. If today's churches are not teaching this central truth of our Faith, then it does not matter how many "Christians" are sitting in our houses of worship. None are getting saved, and they are going to be unpleasantly surprised when they don't meet God at the end of the road.

Also, because of not being taught Biblical truth in churches today, more and more believers are embracing false doctrines like the Big Bang theory, evolution, and Replacement Theology. Some "Christians" no longer accept that Jesus Christ is the Only Way to Heaven, though God's Word emphatically states that *He is* around 1,000 times. If they were actually being taught the Bible in their churches, they would know that. Instead, it's become acceptable in some Christian circles to say that Muslims, Buddhists, Hindus, witches, and other false god worshippers are going to the "same Heaven" that we are in the end. That statement may be politically correct, but it is 100% Biblically incorrect.

A 2017 survey found only 25% of American Christians feel that they have a personal responsibility to share the Gospel with others, and only 40% believe that the Holy Bible is truly the *Word of God*. If this were just a study of all Americans, it'd be sad but not surprising. But since only professing Christians participated in the survey, it is extremely alarming. How can anyone ever call themself Christian, and say they have no obligation to preach the Gospel to others? Are we reading the same Holy Bible?! Are we worshipping the same Christ? The Jesus who said to "Go into all the world and proclaim the Gospel to the *whole creation*" in Mark 16:15 and Matthew 28:19-20?

What is worse than believers not sharing the Gospel message is that the study also revealed that only 1 in 4 pastors say they feel a responsibility to share it. Apparently, Warren's "purpose driven" pastors are still thriving. It seems their only purpose is to fill seats and sell self-help books. They're focusing on being friends of *the world*, rather than desiring to hear "well done, good and faithful servant" from our Lord someday. It is no wonder this generation's Christians are so Biblically ignorant! Even the pastors don't truly know the Word of God.

I can understand some Christians not being able to recite the Ten Commandments, not being able to name a few of the 16 Old Testament prophets, or even not being able to explain the Trinity or the Rapture. What I cannot possibly begin to grasp is how 3/4 of American believers and pastors don't understand that the basic preaching of the Gospel to the lost is the *heart* of Christianity. If they don't believe in evangelism, then they are in the wrong Faith. Christianity is all about taking the Good News of what Christ did for us at Calvary, and sharing it with everyone we can in this life. Jesus taught this so many times. There's no way you could miss it if you are a true believer.

Read the "Parable of the talents," or when Jesus had taught of not hiding a lamp under a bushel, or when He said that the Gospel must be preached to *all nations* before He would return. Our Lord couldn't have stressed strongly enough that we're not to keep our salvation to ourselves. We've been called to share the message of God's Grace with the entire world. I love the saying, "we are not saved to be silent." It is so very true. It is so very Biblical. Too many Christians, these days, want to accept the Gift of God, but then selfishly keep it all to themselves - keeping the life-changing Gospel message confined to their own homes or church.

Sharing the Gospel with others is one of the primary duties of a Christian in this life. The only two duties that ever come before it are repentance of sins, and acceptance of Jesus as our personal Lord and Saviour. And since 3/4 of Christians today don't believe in sharing the Gospel, I'd bet that most American believers do not even know what it is. It is simple, and Paul laid it out in detail in 1st Corinthians, Chapter 15 and verses 1-4 –

"I DECLARE UNTO YOU THE GOSPEL WHICH I PREACHED UNTO YOU, WHICH YOU HAVE RECEIVED... HOW THAT CHRIST DIED FOR OUR SINS ACCORDING TO THE SCRIPTURES; AND THAT HE WAS BURIED, AND THAT HE ROSE AGAIN THE THIRD DAY ACCORDING TO THE SCRIPTURES."

If you don't want to share this message with others, then you are no Christian at all. You need to truly *get saved*, because you quite obviously are not. I don't mean to come across being harsh with fellow believers, but I don't think you can call yourself a true believer if you don't feel the need to bring others to Christ.

Nearly 20% of Christians (not unbelievers) today believe that "men" wrote the Bible - not the Holy Spirit of God. Only 40% of American Christians say that the Bible is the Word of Almighty God. What a disgrace! 37% of Christians say reading the Bible is *"not essential"* to being a believer. So, the Book which led you to become a Christian, in the first place, is no longer important once you *are one*? How ridiculous! Today's wishy washy, don't offend anyone, PC, unBiblical Christianity is the reason why our nation's been cursed for decades. All of the Christians not doing their job of preaching God's Word to the heathen are leading the rest of the country straight to Hell in a handbasket.

Instead of preaching truth to their congregations, churches are *rewriting it*. The confusion of the Gender-fluid movement, which has been sweeping the world, has found its way into Christianity. As far-fetched as it sounds, prepare to be shocked as to just how much this fallacy has been embraced in the mainstream Christian institutions and churches across this world.

There are so many churches today, like the Church of Sweden and Episcopal Church of Washington, DC, who urge their clergy to stop referring to the LORD as "Male." Though all of the Books in Jewish and Christian Scriptures leave no doubt that He is, some churches have decided they no longer want to worship the God of the Bible. They'd rather cower to the demands of our backslidden society, reinvent God, and sacrifice eternal truth, so that they can appease sinners with a politically correct delusion. The Bible has never minced words about God being Male.

1st Corinthians, Chapter 8 and verse 6, states, "There is but One God, the *Father*, from whom all things came and for whom we live; and there is but One *Lord*, Jesus Christ, through whom all things came and through whom we live." All throughout the entirety of both Old and New Testaments, YHWH God is referred to as our Father in Heaven and as "He" or "Him." And Lord Jesus was not some made up character in a fable or fairytale. Historical records outside of the Bible prove HE was a real, living, breathing *Man* on Earth. So, how could any believer or entire denomination approve of publicly denying these facts? Even worse, how could they approve of replacing the facts with something that they know darn well to be a flat-out LIE?

Many backslidden churches today are using "Gender-neutral" language to replace instances of "Lord - He - His - Him" in their services. Some do not even utter the holy names of YHWH, Jesus Christ, or the Spirit any longer - diverting to using the generic word "God." Also, "The Father, the Son, and the Holy Spirit" is being replaced in churches with "God and the Holy Trinity." This destroys the Doctrine that the Christian Church is supposed to be teaching the world. How can they say God *and* the Holy Trinity? The Father, Son, and Holy Spirit ARE God. This new language implies that there is *another* God besides the Holy Trinity. This is blasphemy and heresy.

Modern churches are filled with false prophets. Christ Jesus prophesied that a sign of His return would be a world full of false prophets and "wolves in sheep's clothing" (Matthew 7 & 24). He said they'd deceive and lead believers astray in the Last Days, and countless believers today have no doubt been led astray with this gender-neutral nonsense! It has even found its way into popular new translations of the Bible. In 2016, the SBC (Southern Baptist Convention) published their Christian Standard Bible (CSB); and to the surprise of many, a number of the gender-neutral elements which the SBC long condemned were inserted into its translation.

The CSB translated "anthropos," a Greek word for "man," in gender-neutral form more than 150 times - rendering it "human" or "people" instead. Concerning Jesus' incarnation, the "likeness of men" became "likeness of humanity." Also, "Adelphoi" (Greek for "brother") appears in the gender-neutral form over 100 times. "Men" is replaced with "humans, humanity, humankind, people, or persons" about 250 times. There were many other instances of gender-neutral replacements for masculine terminology found all throughout CSB. YHWH warned in Deuteronomy 4:2, and Jesus repeated the warning in Revelation 22:18-19, that there is a severe eternal punishment that awaits anyone who is adding to or taking away from the words of the Holy Bible.

Unfortunately, there's so much of this occurring all across our world; and the gender-neutral craze has been playing a huge role in it. Whether done through ignorance, or with full knowledge of breaking the LORD's commands, every guilty party has to repent. Some are deceived by Satan to think that by being more inclusive they are leading more people to God. On the contrary, by ignoring or rewriting key verses of the Bible, and hiding the truth to avoid offending someone, they're leading their converts straight to Hell.

There are even mainline Christian denominations today who are turning their backs on God's beloved Nation of Israel. There is no nation that is mentioned more within the pages of our Holy Bibles; and the LORD could not be any more clear, in the Holiest Book on Planet Earth, that He is forever the "God of Israel." Still, Presbyterians, Methodists, Episcopalians, and others, have joined the anti-Israel BDS movement - which calls for the destruction of the Jewish State. What Bible are these denominations reading? It is not my version, and not any legitimate version that I'm familiar with for that matter.

On top of all this, for the very first time in Judeo-Christian America's history, a majority of Christians support Gay Marriage. 55% of so-called Bible believers, to be exact, according to recent polling. Many churches perform same-sex marriage ceremonies, and even ordain homosexual or transgender priests and pastors. Some have held "Gay Pride" events inside of their church! Along with the Methodist Church, United Church of Christ, Presbyterian Church USA, and the Episcopal Church, about 30 denominations now endorse the LGBT agenda. These are supposed to be Houses of God, but they have shamefully become dens of sin!

Finally, no chapter about backslidden churches and Christian leaders would be complete without mention of uber-liberal Pope Francis. The current Pope of the Roman Catholic Church has told his flock that "the Quran, and the spiritual teachings contained in it, is just as valid as the Holy Bible." NO. It most certainly is not. It is a book that is filled with brutality, cruelty, ruthlessness, and bloodshed; while our Book's a Love Story between God and man. It is filled with grace, forgiveness, mercy, and peace. How can the Pope, who is so ignorant to the polar opposites of Christianity and Islam, be the leader of billions of Christians globally?!

In 2015, Francis was the first Pope, in all of world history, to hold Islamic prayers in Vatican square and to allow reading of the Quran in church services. If this Pope really believed the Bible, then he would acknowledge that the teachings of Islam's Quran are antithetical to our Holy Book's teachings. The Quran denies that Jesus is the Christ and the Son of God, and that Muhammad (the warmonger pedophile false prophet of Islam) is "greater than Jesus." The Quran says that Jesus returns "as a Muslim," destroys every Cross, and murders every Christian and Jew who refuses to convert to Islam. On top of that, Islam's "messiah" (the Mahdi) is said to do everything that the Antichrist is prophesied to do! Our sacred Books, and our Gods, are most definitely *not the same*.

There have been some other red flags raised about the Pope's sincerity to Biblical doctrine, such as his stance toward the Nation of Israel. Since assuming power, Francis has been much more of a friend to Israel's terrorist neighbors in Palestine than he's been to God's Nation. And, if all of this was not troubling enough, the Pope has spoken out *in favor of* evolution and the Big Bang. He has said, "When we read about Creation in Genesis, we run the risk of imagining God was a magician, with a magic wand able to do everything, but that is not so." Wow. The blasphemous words that you just read were not spoken by atheist Bill Maher, nor by Creation-mocker Bill Nye, but by a man revered by so many - the world over - as the "mouthpiece of God."

He has also said that "Evolution in nature is not inconsistent with the notion of Creation." Evolution is *completely* inconsistent with the Creation account. God says that He created man in *His Image*, not in the image of a monkey! Christian belief in evolution is a slap in the Face of Almighty God, and is nothing but a bunch of monkey business. This "progressive" Pope has even urged the Vatican's Bishops to ease the language on same-sex unions, and has said that atheists can get to Heaven by *good deeds*. Our Holy Bible says that we are "not saved" by any of "our own deeds," but by Faith in Christ *alone*.

I truly believe that Francis could be the "False Prophet" of the Last Days, whom we read about in Revelation (Chapter 13). That leader, who rises to power in the season of the Antichrist, will be a globally-influential Christian leader. He'll visibly represent the Church on Earth, but through words and deeds he will destroy it. He also ushers in a One-World-Religion; and given Pope Francis' ignorant comments on Islam, this appears to be something that he would be in favor of. Many of you may not be aware that when Francis (Jorge Bergoglio) was announced as new Pope on global television, the exact time was 7:06 pm in Rome (66 minutes past 6:00) - 6:66! Just something for my Catholic friends to ponder.

Please understand that this is not an attack on all Catholics. I have family members and friends who are. I am just warning you all to not be led astray by the current leader of the global Church of Rome. I suspect he will be responsible for numerous Christians *falling away* from the Faith, so do not be deceived! There are too many believers who are. There are also too many self-proclaimed Christians today who "know of" Jesus Christ, but have never truly "known" Him. As someone who has walked with Jesus, for over a decade, I don't think you can walk away from Him after enjoying a personal relationship with Him. Christians who have departed, are departing, or will depart, from the Faith - turning their backs on Christ - were *never* truly saved in the first place. End of story.

LET NO MAN DECEIVE YOU BY ANY MEANS: FOR THAT DAY (OF CHRIST'S COMING) SHALL NOT COME, EXCEPT THERE COME A FALLING AWAY FIRST, AND THAT MAN OF SIN BE REVEALED, THE SON OF PERDITION.

- 2ND THESSALONIANS 2:3

CHAPTER TWELVE

FAITHLESS GENERATION

JESUS SAID, O FAITHLESS AND PERVERSE GENERATION, HOW
LONG SHALL I BE WITH YOU? HOW LONG SHALL I SUFFER
(PUT UP WITH) YOU?

- MATTHEW 17:17/MARK 9:19/LUKE 9:41

A 2017 STUDY BY the Barna Group discovered that Generation
Z is the *"least Christian Generation"* in American history. Gen-Z
is made up of those born between the years 1999-2015. It is very
fitting that the generation is labeled "Z," since the letter signifies
the end. After reading the past eleven chapters, I think you would
have a hard time arguing that we are not living in the End Times
described in the Holy Bible. I also find it very interesting that this
current generation of teenagers began in 1999, which happens to
be three upside down sixes. The infamous 6-6-6 of Revelation 13
is associated with the "Mark of the Beast" of the Antichrist.

To be perfectly clear, I am not saying that every child born in
'99 is a child of the devil. There are plenty of fine young people
that are actually being raised right in this generation. I'm also not
saying that the entire generation is "of Satan." What I am saying,
which is backed up by the recent Barna Study, is that Generation
Z is more prone to following after him than any other generation
in our nation's history. The Bible prophesies that a majority of the

"Last Days" generation will worship Antichrist and that there will be a great falling away from God during a perverse, faithless, and demonically-influenced final generation. You'd be hard-pressed to argue that those adjectives do not apply perfectly to the society in which we currently live.

In the "Generation Z Research Project," Barna conducted a total of four focus groups with U.S. teenagers between the ages of 14 and 17, and had also conducted two national surveys. The first survey, conducted in November of 2016, interviewed about 1,500 teens aged 13 to 18. The second survey was conducted in July of 2017, and interviewed just over 500 teens of the same age group. Barna's research had revealed that only 4 out of 100 teens hold a Biblical worldview. 4%! That is scary. Also, more teens than ever before identify as atheists. The study indicated that 35% of teens consider themselves atheist, agnostic, or not religiously affiliated. That is close to *half* of this generation!

Barna's findings also showed that almost twice as many teens in Gen-Z claimed to be atheists than Millennials: 13% compared to 7%; and less than 60% of Gen-Z teens consider themselves as Christian - compared to 65% of Millennials, and 75% of the Baby Boomers. While you would think that it is a small positive (in a research study full of negatives) that nearly 6 in 10 Gen-Z teens identified as Christians, remember that only 4% of them actually hold the Biblical worldview. They most likely only check off the religion box as "Christian" because that is what their parents are, but they themselves do not live or believe the Faith which they claim to be a part of. Sadly, Barna's study had exposed a lack of Biblical faith among all age groups in America today.

Using a classification of Faith based on the widely accepted orthodox Christian beliefs, Barna developed a set of theological criteria that each respondent had to meet in order to be classified as holding the Biblical worldview. The percentage of Americans whose beliefs qualified them for the worldview declines in each successively younger generation: 10% of Baby Boomers, 7% of Gen-X, and 6% of Millennials see this world through the Biblical lens - compared to only 4% of Gen-Z.

The research also found that only 60% of "churched teens" agreed that the Bible is "totally accurate" in all the principles that it teaches. This means that nearly half of American teens, who are raised in Christian homes, don't believe what they've been taught. I suspect much of that has to do with the utter lack of Biblical faith among their peers. When a majority of their friends and this generation mock God, it must be extremely difficult for the young impressionable minds to stay true to Him. As I said at the start of this chapter, Satan wants to claim this generation as his own; and, unfortunately, he appears to be achieving his goal.

After a decade of false religions being forced into our country (while Christ was forced out), national embrace of homosexuality and transgenderism, and a demonic mainstream media forcing sex - violence - drugs - and Godless music down the throats of kids on a daily basis, it is no wonder Gen-Z doesn't want to know the God with a *moral* Law. Satan's loving every minute of it. He's the author of confusion after all.

One thing the devil's succeeded in confusing this generation about is their gender. Instead of saying, "I was born a boy, so I'm a boy," like every other generation in history, Satan has so many lost souls thinking that they're *anything but* what they had entered into this world as. Barna found 12% of Gen-Z identified sexually as something other than heterosexual. 7% said they are bisexual. These are *kids,* mind you! David Kinnaman, who is the President of Barna, said this was "the highest percentage of self-identified non-heterosexuals ever seen in *any* generation."

Sadly, it is not just the middle and high school crowd that the devil has been confusing, deceiving, and manipulating. He is also infiltrating this country's colleges through atheist professors who attack God, belittle the Bible, and teach the Big Bang, evolution, and climate change as unquestionable "truth." All these theories are designed to pull us away from faith in our Creator, and they appear to be succeeding with a large portion of our population.

A 2016 *LifeWay* study revealed that over 50% of Americans rarely or *never* read the Holy Bible, and that only 1 in 10 hold a Biblical worldview. 25% of 18-24 year olds in America admitted that they have *never* read the Bible at all. No, haven't even picked it up off of the shelf. Only a minuscule 2% of this age group said they've read "most of the Bible." 2 percent! God help us. 52% of Americans believe that the Holy Bible is simply a "good source of morals," 37% feel it's just "helpful," only 36% believe it to be "true," 34% call it just "a story," and 14% say that it is "outdated." That all sure explains a lot about why this nation has been in such a sad state, and seems to only be getting worse year after year.

This isn't just happening in America either, as there are other historically-Christian nations that are falling away from the Faith as well. In 2017, it was reported that the Church of England has been facing a catastrophic decline in the proportion of their young adults who describe themselves as Christian. Data shows a rapid acceleration toward a secular society. For the first time in history, more than half of the population of the United Kingdom say that they have "no religion"; and only 8% of UK adults (under age 24) describe themselves as a form of Christian. A whopping 75% of 18-24 year-olds say that they have "no Faith at all."

I believe that much of the decline in Biblical belief has had to do with the influence of God-hating mainstream media. Whether it be television, movies, music, the internet, or dirt rag magazines, people are inundated daily with demonic messaging - perversion - celebration of sin - and blatant blasphemy. The popular magazine, *GQ*, made headlines in 2018 when its writers placed the Bible on a list of "*21 Books You Don't Have to Read.*" That sure puts *GQ* at the top of the list for magazines Christians should never read!

The editors of the magazine all chose their own books for the list, writing in the introduction: "We've been told all our lives that we can only call ourselves well-read once we have read the Great Books. We tried... We realized that not all the Great Books have aged well. Some are racist and some are sexist, but most are just really, really boring." Writer Jesse Ball was the ignoramus who'd added the Holy Bible to the list. He said that the Bible is "foolish, repetitive, and contradictory," and also that "the Bible's rated very highly by people who supposedly live by it, but who in actuality have not read it... Those who have read it know there are some good parts, but overall it is certainly not the finest thing that man has ever produced."

He is right in one tiny aspect of his inaccurate criticism, and that is when he said it was "not the finest thing that *man* has ever produced." He is right, because "man" didn't write the Holy Bible - *God did*. So, it truly is the finest thing ever produced on Planet Earth - by GOD. Holy men of God penned the Bible through the inspiration of His Holy Spirit (2nd Peter 1:21). Had Ball actually read the Holiest Book on Earth, then he'd know that. For those unfamiliar with him (as I was), Ball apparently penned around 15 books. How many of them have you heard of? As for me, *not one*. I am sure you all can say the same.

I guess it is some kind of inferiority complex that Ball and other critics of the Bible struggle with. As a failing author, he has to resort to attacking the greatest Author of all-time to be able to garner some attention. He did accomplish the goal of getting his otherwise unheard-of name out there. Heck, I had to take the time to mention him in this book. At what cost did he make his name known though? His attack on the Holy Bible garnered far more negative press than positive, and he unfortunately sold his soul for 15 minutes of fame (more like 15 seconds). Sadly, we're living in an age where lamestream media pushes boundaries to gain more followers; and not even blasphemy is out of bounds today.

Ball and many other critics of God's Word love to argue that there are errors and contradictions. Though, they can never point out even one solid example. I have personally read the Holy Bible front-to-back at least seven times, throughout the past decade, and I've never found one error nor contradiction. If God's Word really was "foolish" and "contradictory," like Ball claims, how is it the Best-selling Book of *all-time*? It sells at least 100-million copies annually. I am curious as to how many copies of Ball's books, or *GQ*, have been sold? Yet, they seem to think that they know what is better for the world than the LORD does. It is the blasphemous content, which they and a majority of the media promote, that is turning some people downright demonic these days.

It's one thing to not believe in God, but there are far too many atheists who flat-out hate Him and His Word with a passion. At a Louisiana Town Hall in 2017, hosted by Republican Senator Bill Cassidy, a group of raucous Democrat protesters erupted in anger during the opening Prayer. The second that the Chaplain, Michael Sprague, announced that he would open the event with a Prayer, the crowd became unruly and began shouting him down. Childish hecklers yelled, "Prayer?! Pray on your own time. It is our time!" or "Separation of Church and State!" Not even a few seconds into the prayer, one attendee had rudely shouted, "Amen! We're done. Shut up!" A woman shouted, "Lucifer" (original name of Satan), when the Chaplain mentioned God.

When he closed the prayer "in the Name of Jesus," the room of rowdy Democrats had erupted in riotous anger and booed him. Immediately following that Town Hall, Cassidy said to reporters, "Wow, they booed the Name of *Jesus*." And Sprague said, "I have never been shouted down throughout a time of Prayer like that. I've never been in a situation like that. It's sad there wasn't honor and respect for God." It is beyond sad, disgusting, and alarming that human beings like this exist in our once-God-fearing nation.

Though shocking, on so many levels, this wasn't the first time the Democrats were publicly enraged at the mere mention of God.

During the 2012 Election, while drafting the Party's platform for Obama's second term, the Democrat leaders had removed *all* references to GOD - along with any pro-Israel language. They did not ignorantly forget to mention God either. The leaders came to the conscious decision to *remove Him*. When the absence of God in the platform was discovered, it became headline news. Dems realized that they would need to put God back into the picture, or else risk losing Christian votes for Obama. So, an amendment to the platform was placed on the Democratic Convention's agenda. The amendment would serve to restore the mention of God to the platform, but the Dems would find that it wouldn't be an easy fix.

The Democrat Party, under 4 years of Obama, had moved so far away from God that the delegates of their Convention actually opposed the amendment and loudly *booed* the restoration of God into the platform. Besides booing or shouting down the Names of Jesus or God, there are also many Democrat politicians who want absolutely nothing to do with the LORD. The former President, Barack Hussein Obama, put our Heavenly Father and Lord on the backburner for eight long years. At the same time, he uplifted the god of Islam and other false gods of foreign religions.

At a Georgetown University Speech, in 2009, Obama ordered the Name of Jesus to be covered up with a black drape while he spoke there. He had also deliberately omitted the word "Creator" many times when quoting the Declaration of Independence in his public speeches. Obama's administration made numerous public apologies for Qurans being burned by the U.S. military in 2012; but when it was revealed that his military had burned Bibles in the Middle East, his administration had given several reasons why it was "the right thing to do." I could go on and on about how he had publicly mocked the Bible, and disrespected our God, but that would be a whole 'nother book in itself.

I believe the Biblically-hostile 44th President, and the popular liberal celebrities of our day, have emboldened God-haters to take blasphemy to alarming new heights in America. During the 2017 Women's Day March, the abortion advocates carried placards that depicted Mary (the Virgin Mother of our Lord Jesus) as a bloody vagina. One disgusting sign read, "If Mary had an abortion then we wouldn't be in this mess." The *Huffington Post* has published many blasphemous articles over the years, but a piece by Suzanne Dewitt Hall may have taken the cake as the worst yet. She penned an article claiming that Mary was a "transgender," and that Jesus was the "first transgender man." Un-freakin-believable!

20 years ago, blasphemous content like that would have been blacklisted, the writer would be shamed, and publications printing such garbage would end up in the trash bin of history where they belong. Sadly, in today's day and age, that kind of filth is not only acceptable, but it's become commonplace in society. Things have gotten so bad that Nativity scenes and 10 Commandments statues at State Capitols have been taken down, and replaced with Satanic monuments! No joke. After complaints from atheists that Judaism and Christianity have long taken precedence over other faiths on government property (which they should, given National history), States like Oklahoma, Florida, and Michigan all displayed Satanic monuments on their Capitol lawns.

On top of that, something that would have been unheard of a decade ago, places of Satanic worship are springing up all across this country. The Satanic Temple currently has over 20 chapters in the USA, in States like California, New York, Texas, and sadly (again) in my State of Michigan. So, not only has faith in our God been dwindling in this nation, but Satanism is filling the void. The Holy Bible is clear that, in the Last Days, society will depart from the LORD and be "led astray" by fables - witchcraft - sorcery - false gods - and doctrines of demons. We are no doubt seeing all of these prophecies come to pass before our eyes, in a generation that knoweth not God.

While that sad realization would bring an end to this book, it would be irresponsible of me (as an ambassador for the LORD) to leave you without hope for change. While the world appears to be in the worst shape spiritually that it's ever been in, since Christ ascended into Heaven, what can we believers possibly do to turn the tide? Number one: Keep preaching God's Word and standing up for His truth in a world filled with Satan's lies. Number two: Train up your children to know the Lord. That way, when they go out on their own into this Godless society, they will draw closer to Him - as opposed to pull away. Number three: Make the Holy Bible available to *everyone*.

I suspect the reason so many people mock, criticize, or attack the Bible is because (as studies I have shared revealed) they have obviously never read it in the first place. This is what inspired me to head to my local dollar store one day and buy a couple dozen Bibles. I believe that until a majority of homes in America have a Bible in them, things can never get any better. Whenever I am at my day job, or in a particular place besides home for an extended period of time, I place a box of Bibles on my car or somewhere nearby with heavy foot traffic. I write the invitation on the box to "Please TAKE ONE." I've done this for a while now, and I hope that my idea will catch on and become a habit for other believers.

I don't think that people truly hate God. They just don't know Him. If given the chance to get to know Him, I think most would be inclined to want to do so. The problem is, in a society where belief in God and the Bible is becoming more and more frowned upon, most people won't purposely head out to purchase the Holy Book. Sadly, most of this generation avoid church at all costs. So, how then do we reach the "least Christian generation in American history"? We must get God's Word into their hands.

Yes, there are street evangelists who preach, and others who hand out Bible tracts, but most teenagers tend to avoid them. By leaving the Bibles out in the open with no one forcing it on them, I believe they'll be more inclined to take one. This way, it is only between them and God. No one else has to know that they took a Bible. This is especially important for youngsters reared in atheist homes, who'd never be allowed to purchase the Bible. Lord Jesus commanded us to take the Gospel to *all* creation, not just to other believers. We must take God's Word to *everyone*. By distributing free Bibles, you are planting a seed for everyone around you to be able to know God. Most dollar stores sell Bibles, and I am sure you all can spare at least five dollars to do God's Work.

As many signs of our times are pointing to the Rapture in our generation, we should strive to get as many souls up there with us as we can. The unfortunate souls that are left behind are going to endure the worst tribulation this world has ever seen. I sure don't want to be responsible for anyone going through that, because of me not doing my part to tell them about our Lord. So, I'm issuing a call to my brothers and sisters in Christ who are fed up with the absence of God in this world, and in the hearts of its people - *put God's Word into their hands*.

Buy 3, 7, 10, 12, or even 20 Bibles. Put them in public where unbelievers can easily find them. You may never meet those who accept your gifts, but every soul that your Bible reaches will most likely reach another - and another - and another - and so on and so on. Maybe they will start leaving Bibles for others to find! Can you imagine the chain reaction across this nation, and revival that could be sparked, by making the Bible as available to people as a daily newspaper? This nation desperately needs the Word of God more so than ever before in our history; and if we don't give it to America, then who else will?

I say we start giving it freely right now, one Bible at a time to one soul at a time. If we would all do this, we could change one neighborhood at a time - one town at a time - one city at a time - one county at a time - and one State at a time - until this country again becomes "One Nation under God" *all the time*. I pray this book proved to you that Jesus is coming back soon. Now don't be caught sleeping on the job when He arrives! Our time is running out, so we believers must GET TO WORK. The King is coming! Our King is coming! Keep looking up.

THE FOOL HATH SAID IN HIS HEART, THERE IS NO GOD.

- PSALMS 14:1 & 53:1

ACKNOWLEDGMENTS

TO THE BENHAM BROTHERS - You two are the most genuine, humble, and kind souls I've ever known. When you had become household names, after being fired from HGTV because of your faith, I was immediately drawn to your mutually bold spirits for God. Everything you've preached, stood for, and written, is on the same page with my beliefs. Even when making the rounds on just about every news network, to tell the story of not sacrificing your faith for a hit TV show, you still took the time to respond to my messages. I have never known anyone else in the spotlight that's ever been as warm and approachable as you guys. You are both perfect examples of humility.

When I was still an amateur writer (at best), and my website was still just a blog with a couple hundred visitors, you'd granted me an interview to post there. Since then, you have always taken time out of your very busy schedules to be a part of the annual Christmas Special every year. On top of that, you have blessed me with the honor of being able to share your articles on the website. I believe the LORD has truly blessed the website, and has taken it to heights I'd never dreamed possible. I also believe that it would not have come as far as it has, in just a few short years, without your constant presence on it.

Though we've never met in person, you guys are like family to me. Definitely brothers from another mother! While I'd always been bold for our Lord since I began my walk with Him, because of the great mercy He had shown this poor sinner when He saved me, you have been the only guys who've *increased* that boldness and inspired me to take an even stronger stand for Him each new day. The way you live your lives, lead your families, and run your businesses, is an inspiration. Your Bible studies have taught me so many valuable lessons, and have revealed new truths that I'd yet to discover on my own. I believe the LORD brought you two into my life for a reason, and I will eternally be thankful that He did.

Jason, you've always taken the time to sit down and respond to every email that I've ever sent your way. Whether it be for an interview request, guidance, prayer, or just to get your opinion on an article for the website, you've always been there. You are more of a blessing than you'll ever know. You're the man brother.

David, I haven't always reached out to you as much as I have your brother; but whenever I have, just like him, you have always responded. Your contributions to the website and your advice are always appreciated so much. I am so glad that I finally get to tell the whole world just how #Ossum the Benham Brothers truly are.

May God bless you and yours always Bros.

NOTES

CHAPTER ONE: ANTI-SEMITISM

1. "BDS IS NOTHING BUT BS": Anti-Israel Movement Fueling Anti-Semitism," BiblicalSigns.com, September 6, 2016, https://biblicalsignsintheheadlines.com/2016/09/06/bds-is-nothing-but-bs-anti-israel-movement-fueling-anti-semitism-in-colleges/
2. "DEFEND THE JEWS: We Must NEVER FORGET the Holocaust," BiblicalSigns.com, January 27, 2017, https://biblicalsignsintheheadlines.com/2017/01/27/defend-the-jews-we-must-never-forget-the-holocaust/

CHAPTER TWO: CHRISTIAN PERSECUTION

1. "50 MOST DANGEROUS COUNTRIES FOR CHRISTIANS: Over 200 Million Experience 'High-Level' Persecution," BiblicalSigns.com, January 12, 2018, https://biblicalsignsintheheadlines.com/2018/01/12/50-most-dangerous-countries-for-christians-over-200-million-experience-high-level-persecution/
2. "WORST YEAR YET: Global Persecution of Christians Hits Another All-Time High," BiblicalSigns.com, November 15, 2017, https://biblicalsignsintheheadlines.com/2017/11/15/worst-year-yet-global-persecution-of-christians-hits-another-all-time-high/
3. "MARTYRED EVERY 6 MINUTES: Christians Were Most Persecuted Group in 2016," BiblicalSigns.com, January 3, 2017, https://biblicalsignsintheheadlines.com/2017/01/03/martyred-every-6-minutes-christians-were-most-persecuted-group-in-2016/
4. "COPTIC CRISIS CONTINUES: Christian Persecution in Egypt Escalates," BiblicalSigns.com, June 21, 2016,

https://biblicalsignsintheheadlines.com/2016/06/21/coptic-crisis-continues-christian-persecution-in-egypt-escalates/

5. "EGYPT'S EXTERMINATION OF CHRISTIANS CONTINUES: Islamists Massacre Nearly 30 More Coptic Christians," BiblicalSigns.com, May 27, 2017, https://biblicalsignsintheheadlines.com/2017/05/27/egypts-extermination-of-christians-continues-islamists-massacre-nearly-30-more-coptic-christians/

6. "BIBLE BAN: China's Crackdown on Christianity Continues as Word of God Pulled from All Online Retailers," BiblicalSigns.com, April 13, 2018, https://biblicalsignsintheheadlines.com/2018/04/13/bible-ban-chinas-crackdown-on-christianity-continues-as-word-of-god-pulled-from-all-online-retailers/

7. "LIBERAL HYPOCRISY: Kneeling in Prayer is Ridiculed, But Kneeling in Protest Revered," BiblicalSigns.com, October 1, 2017, https://biblicalsignsintheheadlines.com/2017/10/01/liberal-hypocrisy-kneeling-in-prayer-is-ridiculed-but-kneeling-in-protest-is-revered/

8. "WE CAN'T BAKE THE CAKE: Why We Refuse to Participate in Gay Weddings," BiblicalSigns.com, February 9, 2018, https://biblicalsignsintheheadlines.com/2018/02/09/we-cant-bake-the-cake-why-christians-refuse-to-participate-in-gay-weddings/

9. "LGBT WAR ON CHRISTIANS RAMPS UP: How We Can Fight Back," BiblicalSigns.com, March 30, 2016, https://biblicalsignsintheheadlines.com/2016/03/30/lgbt-war-on-christians-ramps-up-how-we-can-fight-back/

10. "LGBT MAFIA TARGETS ANOTHER PAIR OF CHRISTIANS ON HGTV: It's Time for Believers to Turn the Tables," BiblicalSigns.com, December 1, 2016, https://biblicalsignsintheheadlines.com/2016/12/01/lgbt-mafia-targets-another-pair-of-christians-on-hgtv-its-time-for-believers-to-turn-the-tables/

11. "COLLEGES PURGING CHRISTIANITY: Secular Universities Kicking Out Christians in Name of Inclusiveness," BiblicalSigns.com, March 16, 2018, https://biblicalsignsintheheadlines.com/2018/03/16/colleges-purgi

ng-christianity-secular-universities-kicking-out-christians-in-na
me-of-inclusiveness/

12. "IMMORAL INSTITUTIONS: Schools Persecuting, Sullying and Alienating Christians," BiblicalSigns.com, April 21, 2017, https://biblicalsignsintheheadlines.com/2017/04/21/immoral-insti tutions-public-schools-persecuting-sullying-and-alienating-christ ians/

13. "CANADA'S WAR ON CHRISTIANS: Holy Bible CENSORED, and Biblical Beliefs CRIMINALIZED," BiblicalSigns.com, June 16, 2017, https://biblicalsignsintheheadlines.com/2017/06/16/canadas-war- on-christians-holy-bible-censored-and-biblical-beliefs-criminaliz ed/

CHAPTER THREE: TERRORISM

1. "AS THE DAYS OF NOAH WERE: Worldwide Terrorism Reaches ALL-TIME HIGH," BiblicalSigns.com, June 1, 2017, https://biblicalsignsintheheadlines.com/2017/06/01/as-the-days-of -noah-were-worldwide-terrorism-reaches-all-time-high/

2. "WE ARE NOT AT WAR WITH ISIS: WE ARE AT WAR WITH ISLAM," BiblicalSigns.com, July 15, 2016, https://biblicalsignsintheheadlines.com/2016/07/15/we-are-not-at -war-with-isis-we-are-at-war-with-islam/

3. "ISLAMIC TERROR IS ISLAM: The Quran Says So," BiblicalSigns.com, December 7, 2015, https://biblicalsignsintheheadlines.com/2015/12/07/islamic-terror -is-islam-the-quran-says-so/

4. "EXPOSING ISLAM: The Anti-GOD Religion," BiblicalSigns.com, October 30, 2015, https://biblicalsignsintheheadlines.com/2015/10/30/exposing-isla m-the-anti-god-religion/

CHAPTER FOUR: THE FIG TREE

1. "THIS GENERATION?: 70th Anniversary of Israel's Rebirth Heralds Christ's Return," BiblicalSigns.com, November 10, 2017,

https://biblicalsignsintheheadlines.com/2017/11/10/this-generatio
n-70th-anniversary-of-israels-rebirth-could-herald-christs-return

2.   "MAY 14th, 1948: The REBIRTH of Israel," BiblicalSigns.com,
     May 11, 2016,
     https://biblicalsignsintheheadlines.com/2016/05/11/may-14th-1948
     -the-rebirth-of-israel/

3.   "5777: YEAR OF THE RAPTURE?," BiblicalSigns.com,
     September 9, 2016,
     https://biblicalsignsintheheadlines.com/2016/09/09/5777-are-you-
     rapture-ready/

4.   1948 Math, http://www.alphanewsdaily.com/mathprophecy2.html

CHAPTER FIVE: JERUSALEM

1.   "FINALLY!: Trump Keeps Promise to Move Embassy as He
     Recognizes Jerusalem as Israel's Capital," BiblicalSigns.com,
     December 7, 2017,
     https://biblicalsignsintheheadlines.com/2017/12/07/finally-trump-
     keeps-promise-to-move-embassy-as-he-recognizes-jerusalem-as-is
     raels-capital/

2.   "MIRACLE OF 1967: 50th Anniversary of Israel's Victory in Six
     Day War and Reunification of JERUSALEM," BiblicalSigns.com,
     June 6, 2017,
     https://biblicalsignsintheheadlines.com/2017/06/06/miracle-of-19
     67-50th-anniversary-of-israels-victory-in-six-day-war-and-reunifi
     cation-of-jerusalem/

3.   "IT'S TIME TO CALL OUT THE REAL "OCCUPIERS" IN
     THE MIDDLE EAST (And Israel Isn't One of Them),"
     BiblicalSigns.com, May 6, 2018,
     https://biblicalsignsintheheadlines.com/2018/05/06/its-time-to-ca
     ll-out-the-real-occupiers-in-the-middle-east-and-israel-isnt-one-o
     f-them/

4.   "THE HISTORY OF JERUSALEM: Israel's Capital is An Eternal
     GOD-GIVEN Possession," BiblicalSigns.com, December 9, 2017,
     https://biblicalsignsintheheadlines.com/2017/12/09/the-history-of
     -jerusalem-israels-capital-is-an-eternal-god-given-possession/

CHAPTER SIX: THE ENEMIES OF ISRAEL

1. "NATIONS GATHERED AGAINST JERUSALEM: Anti-Israel Vote At UN Fulfills Biblical Prophecy," BiblicalSigns.com, December 22, 2017, https://biblicalsignsintheheadlines.com/2017/12/22/nations-gathered-against-jerusalem-anti-israel-vote-at-un-fulfills-biblical-prophecy/

2. "ALLIED AGAINST ISRAEL: Is the Gog-Magog War At the Door?," BiblicalSigns.com, February 14, 2018, https://biblicalsignsintheheadlines.com/2018/02/14/allied-against-israel-is-the-gog-magog-war-at-the-door/

3. "DEFUND THE UN: America Must Stop Financing United Nations' War On Israel," BiblicalSigns.com, March 25, 2017, https://biblicalsignsintheheadlines.com/2017/03/25/defund-the-un-america-must-stop-financing-united-nations-war-on-israel/

4. "UNITED NATIONS CONTENDING WITH GOD: Anti-Israel Resolution Rewrites History of Jerusalem," BiblicalSigns.com, October 13, 2016, https://biblicalsignsintheheadlines.com/2016/10/13/united-nations-contending-with-god-anti-israel-resolution-rewrites-history-of-jerusalem/

5. "LAST DAYS' ENEMIES OF ISRAEL ON THE MARCH," BiblicalSigns.com, October 28, 2015, https://biblicalsignsintheheadlines.com/2015/10/28/last-days-enemies-of-israel-on-the-march/

6. "THE MOST ANTI-ISRAEL PRESIDENT OF ALL-TIME," BiblicalSigns.com, November 1, 2015, https://biblicalsignsintheheadlines.com/2015/11/01/the-most-anti-israel-president-of-all-time/

7. "REAL 'FAKE NEWS'": As Palestinians Terrorized Israel, Lamestream News Media Portrayed Them As VICTIMS," BiblicalSigns.com, May 17, 2018, https://biblicalsignsintheheadlines.com/2018/05/17/real-fake-news-as-palestinians-terrorized-israel-lamestream-news-media-reported-exact-opposite/

Chapter Seven: Signs in the Heavens

1. "SIGNS IN THE HEAVENS CONTINUE: Supermoon Rises On Feast of Tabernacles," BiblicalSigns.com, October 16, 2016, https://biblicalsignsintheheadlines.com/2016/10/16/signs-in-the-h eavens-continue-supermoon-rises-on-feast-of-tabernacles/

2. "SUPERMOON OF THE CENTURY: Largest Moon Since Israel's Rebirth Rises Next Week," BiblicalSigns.com, November 12, 2016, https://biblicalsignsintheheadlines.com/2016/11/12/supermoon-of- the-century-largest-moon-since-israels-rebirth-rises-next-week/

3. "WILL GOD DIVIDE AMERICA?: Once-In-A-Century Total Solar Eclipse Could Be A Final Warning," BiblicalSigns.com, June 22, 2017, https://biblicalsignsintheheadlines.com/2017/06/22/will-god-divi de-america-once-in-a-century-total-solar-eclipse-could-be-a-final -warning/

4. "AMERICA'S ECLIPSE AND JERUSALEM: The Remarkable Connection Amplifies God's Warning," BiblicalSigns.com, August 18, 2017, https://biblicalsignsintheheadlines.com/2017/08/18/americas-ecli pse-and-jerusalem-the-remarkable-connection-amplifies-gods-wa rning/

5. "ONCE IN A BLUE SUPER BLOOD MOON," BiblicalSigns.com, January 27, 2018, https://biblicalsignsintheheadlines.com/2018/01/27/once-in-a-blu e-super-blood-moon-rare-heavenly-event-has-not-occurred-in-ov er-150-years/

6. "MYSTERIOUS GLOBAL PHENOMENA IN THE HEAVENS," BiblicalSigns.com, November 24, 2017, https://biblicalsignsintheheadlines.com/2017/11/24/mysterious-glo bal-phenomena-in-the-heavens-loud-booms-and-trumpet-sounds -baffle-scientific-community/

Chapter Eight: Earthquakes & Extreme Weather

1. "SIGN OF THE TIMES: Powerful Earthquakes," BiblicalSigns.com, April 15, 2016, https://biblicalsignsintheheadlines.com/2016/04/15/sign-of-the-times-powerful-earthquakes/

2. "MASSIVE EARTHQUAKE ON EVE OF HISTORIC SUPERMOON: 7.8 Magnitude Quake Strikes Near Christchurch, NZ," BiblicalSigns.com, November 13, 2016, https://biblicalsignsintheheadlines.com/2016/11/13/massive-earthquake-on-eve-of-historic-supermoon-7-8-magnitude-quake-strikes-near-christchurch-new-zealand/

3. "AFTERSHOCKS: Looking Back At 2016's Powerful Earthquakes, And Looking Ahead To A BIG ONE in 2017," BiblicalSigns.com, December 10, 2016, https://biblicalsignsintheheadlines.com/2016/12/10/aftershocks-looking-back-at-2016s-powerful-earthquakes-and-looking-ahead-to-a-big-one-in-2017/

4. "TRACKING THE TROPICS: Pay Close Attention To Biblically-Named Hurricanes," BiblicalSigns.com, May 25, 2018, https://biblicalsignsintheheadlines.com/2018/05/25/tracking-the-tropics-pay-close-attention-to-biblically-named-hurricanes

5. "1st JUDGMENT FALLS: On Same Day Trump Renews Israeli-Palestinian Peace Push, U.S. Hurricane Forms," BiblicalSigns.com, August 25, 2017, https://biblicalsignsintheheadlines.com/2017/08/25/1st-judgment-falls-on-same-day-trump-renews-israeli-palestinian-peace-push-u-s-hurricane-forms/

6. "2nd JUDGMENT: In Same Week of Trump's UNGA "Land-for-Peace" Push, Another Big Hurricane Targets USA," BiblicalSigns.com, September 8, 2017, https://biblicalsignsintheheadlines.com/2017/09/08/2nd-judgment-in-same-week-of-trumps-unga-land-for-peace-push-another-big-hurricane-targets-usa/

7. "THE CASE AGAINST CLIMATE CHANGE: Combating the Theory That DENIES God," BiblicalSigns.com, May 10, 2017, https://biblicalsignsintheheadlines.com/2017/05/10/the-case-against-climate-change-combating-the-theory-that-denies-god/

8. "GLOBAL WARMING? MORE LIKE GLOBAL COOLING: Who Withstands His Cold?," BiblicalSigns.com, January 19, 2018, https://biblicalsignsintheheadlines.com/2018/01/19/global-warming-more-like-global-cooling-who-can-withstand-his-cold/

9. "UNNATURAL: Rare Weather Events Are Not Result of Climate Change, But Harbingers of Climactic Change," BiblicalSigns.com, April 20, 2018, https://biblicalsignsintheheadlines.com/2018/04/20/unnatural-rare-weather-events-are-not-result-of-climate-change-but-harbingers-of-climactic-change/

CHAPTER NINE: ABORTION

1. "DEFUND PLANNED PARENTHOOD: Over 7 Million Reasons Why It Must Be Done," BiblicalSigns.com, January 5, 2018, https://biblicalsignsintheheadlines.com/2018/01/05/defund-planned-parenthood-over-7-million-reasons-why-it-must-be-done-in-2018/

2. "BENHAM BROS: "Sex Ed Sit Out" – Let's Take A Stand for Our Kids," BiblicalSigns.com, April 22, 2018, https://biblicalsignsintheheadlines.com/2018/04/22/benham-bros-sex-ed-sit-out-lets-take-a-stand-for-our-kids/

3. "AMERICA'S JUDGMENT COMING: Our Supreme Lawgiver Is Not A Court," BiblicalSigns.com, June 28, 2016, https://biblicalsignsintheheadlines.com/2016/06/28/judgment-coming-our-supreme-authority-is-not-a-court/

CHAPTER TEN: LGBT PRIDE

1. "I STAND AGAINST PRIDE: Christians Cannot Stand With God AND the LGBT Movement (So Pick A Side)," BiblicalSigns.com, June 10, 2017, http://biblicalsignsintheheadlines.com/2017/06/10/i-stand-against-pride-christians-cannot-stand-with-god-and-the-lgbt-movement-so-pick-a-side/

2. "WE CAN'T BAKE THE CAKE: Why We Refuse To Participate in Gay Weddings," BiblicalSigns.com, February 9, 2018,

http://biblicalsignsintheheadlines.com/2018/02/09/we-cant-bake-the-cake-why-christians-refuse-to-participate-in-gay-weddings/

3. "TRANSGENDER INSANITY: God Created Male and Female .. PERIOD," BiblicalSigns.com, July 4, 2017, http://biblicalsignsintheheadlines.com/2017/07/04/transgender-insanity-god-created-male-and-female-period/

CHAPTER ELEVEN: FALLING AWAY FROM THE FAITH

1. "FAITHLESS GENERATION: Belief in Holy Bible Dwindling, Being Mocked, And Even Criminalized in America," BiblicalSigns.com, April 26, 2018, https://biblicalsignsintheheadlines.com/2018/04/26/faithless-generation-belief-in-holy-bible-dwindling-being-mocked-and-even-criminalized-in-america/

2. "DISTURBING DISREGARD FOR THE TRUTH: Studies Reveal Lack of Biblical Knowledge in America," BiblicalSigns.com, April 29, 2016, https://biblicalsignsintheheadlines.com/2017/04/29/disturbing-disregard-for-the-truth-studies-reveal-americans-lack-of-biblical-knowledge/

3. "THE POPE'S LOVE AFFAIR WITH ISLAM: Is Francis Revelation's "False Prophet"?," BiblicalSigns.com, August 1, 2016, https://biblicalsignsintheheadlines.com/2016/08/01/the-popes-love-affair-with-islam-is-francis-revelations-false-prophet/

4. "EMASCULATING THE LORD: Liberal Churches And Bible Translators Adapt "Gender-Neutral" Pronouns for God," BiblicalSigns.com, December 2, 2017, https://biblicalsignsintheheadlines.com/2017/12/02/emasculating-the-lord-liberal-churches-and-bible-translators-adapt-gender-neutral-pronouns-for-god/

5. "GENDER-NEUTRAL NONSENSE: Episcopal Church of D.C. Will No Longer Acknowledge GOD As Masculine," BiblicalSigns.com, February 1, 2018, https://biblicalsignsintheheadlines.com/2018/02/01/gender-neutra

l-nonsense-episcopal-church-of-d-c-will-no-longer-acknowledge-god-as-masculine/

6. "SIN: The Word Nobody Wants To Hear, But SHOULD," BiblicalSigns.com, November 10, 2015, https://biblicalsignsintheheadlines.com/2015/11/10/society-of-sin-why-stopping-it-starts-with-us/

CHAPTER TWELVE: FAITHLESS GENERATION

1. "DEGENERATION: New Study Finds "Generation Z" Is the Least Christian Generation in American History," BiblicalSigns.com, January 25, 2018, https://biblicalsignsintheheadlines.com/2018/01/25/degeneration-new-study-finds-generation-z-is-the-least-christian-generation-in-american-history/

2. "FAITHLESS GENERATION: Belief in Holy Bible Dwindling, Being Mocked, and Even Criminalized in America," BiblicalSigns.com, April 26, 2018, https://biblicalsigns.com/2018/04/26/faithless-generation-belief-in-holy-bible-dwindling-being-mocked-and-even-criminalized-in-america/

3. "DOWNRIGHT DEMONIC DEMOCRATS: Town Hall Protesters Erupt in Anger At the Name of Jesus," BiblicalSigns.com, February 28, 2017, https://biblicalsigns.com/2017/02/28/downright-demonic-democrats-town-hall-protesters-erupt-in-anger-at-the-name-of-jesus/

4. "SATANIC WORSHIP ON THE RISE IN AMERICA," BiblicalSigns.com, November 3, 2015, https://biblicalsignsintheheadlines.com/2015/11/03/satanic-worship-on-the-rise-in-america/

EVEN MORE

SIGNS OF

OUR TIMES

MORE BIBLICAL REASONS WHY THIS COULD BE

THE GENERATION OF THE RAPTURE

Even More
SIGNS OF OUR TIMES

EVEN MORE
SIGNS OF OUR TIMES

MORE BIBLICAL REASONS WHY THIS COULD BE THE GENERATION OF THE RAPTURE

MICHAEL SAWDY

**BIBLICAL SIGNS
PUBLISHING**

TO LORD JESUS:

Thank You for every blessing that I have ever received from the Father in this life through You. I especially give You thanks for my parents, brother, Jacob, and entire family. Thank You for Your Heavenly gifts of grace, mercy, wisdom, and salvation. Thank You, above all, for Your Holy Spirit and Word - which guide me daily on the right path. Thank You for using me to spread the good news of Your return to all nations of the world. I am forever humbled and grateful for all that You do in me and through me. Glory to You and to our Father in Heaven always my Lord. I love You forever.

CONTENTS

INTRODUCTION

THE RAPTURE

FOR THE LORD HIMSELF SHALL DESCEND FROM HEAVEN WITH A SHOUT, WITH THE VOICE OF THE ARCHANGEL, AND WITH THE TRUMP OF GOD: AND THE DEAD IN CHRIST SHALL RISE FIRST: THEN WE WHICH ARE ALIVE AND REMAIN SHALL BE CAUGHT UP TOGETHER WITH THEM IN THE CLOUDS, TO MEET THE LORD IN THE AIR: AND SO SHALL WE EVER BE WITH THE LORD... COMFORT ONE ANOTHER WITH THESE WORDS.

- 1ST THESSALONIANS 4:16-18

COMFORT... THAT IS WHAT hope in the long-awaited Rapture of the faithful is meant to bring. How can we instill that hope in those around us, so that we may truly "*comfort* one another," in a generation plagued by despair, evil, hatred, and violence? Exactly as Saint Paul told us to... "*with these words.*" With the words that describe Lord Jesus' descent from Heaven to rescue us from this wicked world, both the dead and living of His Church, before all hell breaks loose on Planet Earth. This message brings a believer lasting peace and serenity in an ever troubled world that is filled with chaos. It reminds us - in the midst of rampant evil - that the worse things get, the closer we draw to that glorious day.

That day when our corruptible mortal bodies are transformed into incorruptible immortal bodies, and when we'll finally get to see our Lord face to face. How could anyone not be comforted with that thought? Unfortunately, today, there appears to be a lot of believers who do not ascribe to the doctrine of the Rapture - who believe we will endure every plague and judgment foretold in the Book of Revelation. They obviously don't know the God of the Book they claim to believe. Our LORD is a just, faithful, and merciful God. He delights in the righteous, and He rewards those who diligently heed His Word and seek His Face.

When He first destroyed the wicked from off the face of the earth in the Flood of Noah's days, notice how He preserved Noah and his family on the Ark - keeping them *out of* global judgment. Remember the two words "out of" going forward, because they're key to understanding the Rapture. Noah did not endure the wrath of God along with the wicked. Also, think back to the judgment of Sodom and Gomorrah, and how the LORD delivered Lot and his family *out of* it for Abraham's sake. Lot did not endure God's punishment along with the wicked.

So, why then are there some believers who think that we will be going through the worst tribulation the world has ever seen - along with the wicked? It doesn't make sense that God would all of a sudden change the way that He deals with the righteous and the wicked. His Word is clear that He's the same yesterday, today, and forever (Hebrews 13:8). He tells us that He will never change (Malachi 3:6). The advocates of a Post-Tribulation Rapture have obviously never read the words of Lord Jesus in Revelation -

"BECAUSE YOU HAVE KEPT THE WORD OF MY PATIENCE, I ALSO WILL KEEP YOU FROM THE HOUR OF TEMPTATION, WHICH SHALL COME UPON ALL THE WORLD, TO TRY THEM THAT DWELL UPON THE EARTH." - REVELATION 3:10

I said to remember the words "out of," because (in English translations of the Holy Bible) we read "keep you *from* the hour" in that verse of Revelation. The word "from" in the Greek is "ek," which means "*out of.*" So, contrary to the thinking of my brothers and sisters who expect to go through the seven-year Tribulation, Jesus didn't mince words when promising that He would keep us *out of* it altogether. Instead of us boarding an Ark like Noah, or fleeing to another place like Lot, the Lord Himself comes down to evacuate us from Earth before God's judgments are poured out. I don't understand how some Christians can read their Bibles from front to back, and believe the LORD would somehow allow us to endure the worst tribulation in human history. He will not.

Besides Christians who think that we'll be going through the Tribulation, there is also a group of so-called believers who mock the idea of the Rapture and Christ's imminent return altogether. This group believes we shouldn't be concerned about the Rapture or Jesus' return at all, because they say every generation before us believed that they would experience these events and did not. Oh, how I wish that this backslidden group of Christians would read my previous book. In it, I give many irrefutable reasons why our generation is the *first* in world history to see specific prophecies related to the Lord's return being fulfilled.

I explained why no generation before 1948 could have had any hope of seeing Christ return, because there had to be a Nation of Israel on Earth for the "Last Days" signs of the Bible to mean anything. Until the spring of '48, there was no Israel on the map. There hadn't been for thousands of years. If you haven't yet, read *The Signs of Our Times.* I go into great detail as to why a reborn Israel is central to Jesus' Second Coming. Don't listen to Rapture scoffers. They're too comfortable in this sinful world. Thus, they don't want to see our Lord return in this day and age. They are actually *fulfilling* a "Last Days" sign -

"THERE SHALL COME IN THE LAST DAYS SCOFFERS, WALKING AFTER THEIR OWN LUSTS, SAYING, WHERE IS THE PROMISE OF HIS COMING? SINCE THE FATHERS FELL ASLEEP, ALL THINGS

CONTINUE AS THEY WERE FROM THE BEGINNING OF THE
CREATION." - 2ND PETER 3:3-4

There are also Christians believing that a Rapture of Christ's
Church already occurred, that Jesus has already returned to Earth
(spiritually - not physically), and that the Book of Revelation has
already been fulfilled. None of these beliefs make one bit of sense
whatsoever. Christians believing these things, known as Preterists,
have obviously never studied Biblical Prophecy.

First off, millions of believers would go missing all over this
world simultaneously during the Rapture. When in world history
has that ever happened? The answer is *never*. Second, the Bible is
clear that Jesus' Second Coming - like His First Coming - would
be in the flesh, and that *every eye* would see Him (Revelation 1:7,
Zechariah 14:4, Matthew 16:27 and 24:30 & 25:31, Mark 13:26,
Luke 21:27, Acts 1:11, and John 14:3). It will not be an invisible
"spiritual" return. If it were to be, God would have told us so. He
did not. Instead, He was clear that Christ's *literal* feet will hit the
literal Mount of Olives in Jerusalem upon His return to the earth.
Read all of the Biblical verses that I listed above, and you'll find
there can be no logical argument for an *invisible* return to Earth.

Finally, I cannot understand how anyone ascribes to the view
that Revelation has already been fulfilled. That's nonsense. When
in history has ⅓ of the earth and ⅓ of mankind been destroyed?
When have all men and women of the earth ever worshipped the
AntiChrist - as he sat in Jerusalem's Temple, declaring himself to
be God? When did the inhabitants of Earth ever receive the Mark
of the Beast in their right hands or foreheads, in order to buy and
sell goods? When did all nations of the world come against Israel
in an attempt to destroy the Jewish State? When did Christ and
His Armies come down to save Israel from certain destruction?
When did the Jews of the world look upon Jesus and realize that
He was truly their Messiah all along?

When was Satan cast into the bottomless pit? When did "New Jerusalem" descend from Heaven? When was Christ's Kingdom ever set up on Earth, and when did believers of the world rule and reign with Him from the Holy Land of Israel? Can anyone, who believes the nonsensical theory that the Book of Revelation has already been fulfilled, point to a time in history when those events have occurred? Obviously, you cannot - because those prophecies have never been fulfilled! The groups of backslidden Christians that I've addressed are ignoring the numerous "Last Days" signs occurring all around them. Whether due to fear of prophesied End Times events taking place, or due to living unrepentant lives, they do not want to witness our Lord return anytime soon.

They are of the crowd in today's Church that loves to quote Matthew 24:36, in which Jesus said, "Of that day and hour knows no man, no, not the angels of Heaven, but My Father only." They use this verse as an excuse to not be looking for, or recognizing, the Latter-Day signs happening all around us. This is dangerous for a Christian to do. Yes, Jesus said that we would not know the "day or hour," but He also taught that we *would know* the season. Back up just a few verses in Chapter 24 - to verse 33 - and notice how Jesus said, "When you shall see all these things, *know that I Am near*, even at the doors."

He also said, in the Book of Luke, "When these things begin to come to pass, then look up, and lift up your heads; for your redemption draweth near... So likewise you, when you see these things come to pass, *know you* that the Kingdom of God is near at hand" (Luke 21:28-31). What *things* was He referring to exactly? The *signs* of His return. If we are not to be concerned with His return, because "no one" knows the day or hour, then why'd He ever bother giving us signs to watch for in the first place?

The reason why He said no one would know the exact day or hour of His return is because days and hours differ all around the globe. 3:00 am in Israel is 8:00 pm in the northeastern U.S., 7:00

pm in parts of the southern U.S., 5:00 pm in the western U.S., and 1:00 pm in Britain. Due to different time zones across the world, days and hours can never be the same. So, there is no way anyone could ever predict the exact date and time of the Second Coming. They would have to give multiple days and hours in order to fit their prediction into every time zone. That is why Lord Jesus has commanded us to be ready at *all times*, especially when the signs that He gave begin to occur - and they have undoubtedly begun.

This is why I believe the Spirit called me to write these books - because the time of our redemption draweth near, and sleeping Christians need a *wake-up call*. I pray that my books will sound an alarm in the hearts, souls, and minds of all believers. It is high time to awake out of sleep, to give heed unto the Word of God, to listen attentively to His Holy Spirit, and to look up, because the King is coming! Our King is coming! ARE YOU READY?

BEHOLD, I SHEW YOU A MYSTERY; WE SHALL NOT ALL SLEEP, BUT WE SHALL ALL BE CHANGED, IN A MOMENT, IN THE TWINKLING OF AN EYE, AT THE LAST TRUMP: FOR THE TRUMPET SHALL SOUND, AND THE DEAD SHALL BE RAISED INCORRUPTIBLE, AND WE SHALL BE CHANGED.

- 1ST CORINTHIANS 15:51-52

CHAPTER ONE

THE SIGNS OF OUR TIMES CONTINUE

As He sat upon the Mount of Olives, the disciples
came unto Jesus privately, saying, Tell us, when shall
these things be? And what shall be the sign of thy
coming, and of the end of the age?

- MATTHEW 24:3

IN MY FIRST BOOK, *The Signs of Our Times*, I covered twelve
specific Latter-Day signs that may be heralding the Rapture in our
generation. This Sequel will pick up where that book had left off,
covering *Even More* Signs occurring in our lifetimes. But before I
delve into them, there've been many new developments regarding
the signs that I previously addressed; and so, therefore, in the first
few chapters, I am going to revisit them...

ANTI-SEMITISM

The Anti-Defamation League (ADL) reported that the number of
anti-Semitic incidents in the United States was nearly 60% higher
in 2017 than in 2016, which was the largest single-year increase
on record. A 2018 EU (European Union) poll found that 90% of
Europe's Jews felt anti-Semitism increased exponentially over the

previous five years. Also last year, France saw a 75% increase in anti-Semitic crimes; and there had been a 60% rise in Canada. In October 2018, the worst anti-Semitic attack in American history occurred. A demonic psychopath carried out the deadliest attack ever on U.S. Jews, opening fire on the congregation of the Tree of Life Synagogue in Pennsylvania, murdering 11.

Since the shooter was an unrepentant Jew-hater, I refuse to mention his name. Anti-Semites are of the devil, and their names must be erased from history - never to be spoken again. The only time I'll ever name anti-Semites in my books is when I expose or warn against those who are in positions of power and influence. That is exactly what the Harvard Law School professor emeritus, Alan Dershowitz, has been doing. Though he has been a lifelong Democrat, he recently chastised his party for turning a blind eye to the alarming rise of anti-Semitism within its ranks. He points specifically to a growing anti-Israel animus of the Left, especially regarding their support for the wicked BDS (Boycott, Divestment, and Sanctions) movement.

This new breed of Dems that Dershowitz has alluded to are namely the Muslim Congresswomen Ilhan Omar (Minnesota) and Rashida Tlaib (Michigan), Muslim DNC Deputy Chairman Keith Ellison, and Muslim leader of the United States' Women's March, Linda Sarsour. Dershowitz, himself, does not hold a personal bias against Muslims; but there is no denying that the religion of Islam teaches a bitter hatred of the Jews and Israel. I go into great detail about Islamic disdain for God's people in my previous book.

Dershowitz rightly accuses Dems of tolerating anti-Semitism. He's said, "The Democrat Party, itself, isn't anti-Semitic; but they tolerate anti-Semitism on the hard-left part of their base, because they don't want to alienate their base. And so Keith Ellison gets elected Deputy Chairman of the Democratic National Party, while he had close associations with Louis Farrakhan and falsely denied them." For those not familiar, Farrakhan is leader of the Nation of Islam who has called the Jews "Satanic" and "termites."

Dershowitz says many members of the Congressional Black Caucus have had associations with Louis Farrakhan. Even former President Obama had closely allied himself with the self-avowed Jew-hater. Dershowitz (a Jewish man) said of a Obama-Farrakhan photo from 2005, that was suppressed by the mainstream media, "If I had known that the President posed, smiling with Farrakhan, when he was a Senator, I wouldn't have campaigned for Obama." Being friends with a man like Farrakhan may explain the former President's hostility toward Israel.

While both parties today - Republican and Democrat - have problems with anti-Semites, from the alt-right and hard-left, it is clear that only one of the two parties is propping them up unto positions of power. Dershowitz says the Republican Party does a good job in condemning anti-Semites on the alt-right, and that the Democrats must do a better job of condemning anti-Semites on the hard-left. Dershowitz is concerned about the future of Jews and their treatment in the Democrat Party. With Jew-haters, such as Omar, Tlaib, and Sarsour, being poster children for the Dems, he has good reason for his concern. All three women promote the BDS campaign, which publicly calls for the destruction of Israel.

Sarsour has proudly admitted that her family in Palestine has committed terror attacks against Israelis, and refuses to condemn them or apologize for it. Her husband has expressed support for the Palestinian terror group Hamas, while Linda has held events to raise money for them and the Muslim Brotherhood. She also advocates strongly for Sharia Law, while claiming to be a "liberal feminist." If that is not an oxymoron, then I don't know what is! Democrats need to do some serious soul-searching, or else they'll find that many souls in their party have already been sold; and I'll give you one guess as to who the buyer is. Here's a hint: his name starts with an "S," and ends with "ATAN."

CHRISTIAN PERSECUTION

Believers are still facing extreme persecution all across the world. The current Top 10 worst offenders are North Korea, Afghanistan, Somalia, Libya, Pakistan, Sudan, Eritrea, Yemen, Iran, and India. The deadliest country for Christ's followers in 2018 was Nigeria. It has been reported that over 6,000 Christians were murdered for their faith in just the first half of 2018. The Christian Association of Nigeria warns that "Christianity is on the brink of extinction" there, due to the rapid spread of Islamic ideology in the country. A report released in 2018 by Aid to the Church in Need (ACN), on "Religious Freedom in the World," revealed that half a billion Christians today face persecution across the globe. ACN reports Religious Freedom is declining in 1 out of 5 nations of the world.

Outside of North Korea, India, and the Islamic nations (which account for 8 of the top 10), China is becoming one of the most dangerous places on Earth for a Christian to live. Reverend Bob Fu, a prominent Chinese Religious Freedom activist, told the U.S. Congress in 2018 that China's government was preparing a 5-year plan to conform Christianity to Socialism. He said that their intent was to essentially "rewrite the Holy Bible." Under the leadership of the Communist President, Xi Jinping, the Chinese government regularly arrests Christians, destroys Crosses (tens of thousands), raids and closes churches, and even *burns* Bibles. They also force Christians in the country to sign papers renouncing their faith.

Here in the United States, even though the Supreme Court is becoming more conservative and friendly toward Bible believers, anti-Christian liberals continue to take believers to trial before the highest court in the land. They are targeting Christians who refuse to bow to their Godless agenda. Case in point, after he had won his SCOTUS case upholding his right to refuse to bake cakes for gay weddings, Colorado baker Jack Phillips is being sued *again*. This time, because he'd objected to making a cake that celebrated transgenderism. The Court had previously ruled 7-2 in his favor, arguing that - as a Christian - he was targeted by Colorado's Civil Rights Commission due to his beliefs. Apparently, the liberals in Colorado did not get the Supreme Court's memo.

Just a few weeks after the SCOTUS decision, the State ruled Phillips "violated the law by refusing to make a cake celebrating a gender transition." In 2017, a transgender lawyer asked Phillips to make the "transition celebration" cake. When he had declined on religious grounds, he was swiftly sued. It is important to note that Jack had also turned down requests to make cakes celebrating the devil, drugs, witchcraft, and sexually explicit images. So, contrary to what the lamestream media says, he doesn't single out anyone for discrimination. He opposes celebrating *anything* that the Bible has dubbed sinful. It's also telling that many of the cake requests I mentioned had come from the *same* lawyer who is suing Phillips.

Many believers across this country have come under attack by the lunatic left for not embracing the transgender revolution that's been sweeping across America. Last year, Nicholas Meriwether, a professor at an Ohio college, was punished by his university for refusing to refer to a transgender student by their preferred gender pronoun. Meriwether, an Evangelical Christian who is a 22-year employee of Shawnee State University, answered a male student's question with "Yes, sir." His response was directed to a biological male who now *identifies* as female. The student, Alena Bruening, approached Meriwether after class and demanded that he refer to him using only feminine pronouns. Meriwether refused.

Bruening then promised to get him fired and used derogatory language toward him. Meriwether says he has always referred to every student as either sir, ma'am, mister, or miss. Due to SSU's anti-Christian "non-discrimination policy," the acting Dean of the college charged Meriwether with causing "a hostile environment" in his classroom for refusing to violate his beliefs. The professor submitted a grievance request to his union, arguing that SSU had violated his freedom of expression. When he met with a school administrator and a union representative to explain how he felt his Religious Freedom was being attacked, they "openly laughed" at his convictions and denied his grievance request.

In 2018, anti-Christian posters started popping up near trash cans across New York City. The posters featured two images - a white man wearing a "Make America Great Again" hat, holding a Chick-Fil-A cup; and a white woman, also wearing a MAGA hat, holding a Bible. The posters read: "Keep NYC trash-free." Hatred of President Donald Trump is nothing new, and we all know how dirty politics can get. So, attacks against his "MAGA" slogan and his supporters are not surprising. What *is surprising*, and deeply disturbing, is that Christians are being dubbed as "trash" in NYC. Worse, the lamestream media barely reported on it. I am sure that if the posters featured Muslims, instead of us Christians, it would have been around-the-clock headline news.

TERRORISM

Islamic terrorism is still the greatest threat to Christians globally. Suicide attacks in churches, schools, hotels, and markets continue to claim the lives of hundreds of believers at a time. Due to great progress that's been made by the Trump administration in its war on ISIS, terrorists have been brainstorming new methods to harm American citizens. In the upcoming chapters on "Pestilences" and "Wars and Rumours of Wars," you'll learn why bioterrorism and power-grid attacks are at the top of their list.

THE ENEMIES OF ISRAEL

Recent clashes between Israel and Hamas terrorists in Gaza have Middle East experts believing another war, like the battle of 2014, is ever on the horizon. In that war, Hamas fired over 4,000 rockets into the Jewish State. In July of 2017, the Palestinian terror group launched nearly 200 rockets into Israeli communities in *one day*. A month later, they fired another 220. In the fall of 2018, Hamas bombarded Israel with 300+ rockets - in less than 5 hours. In the spring of 2019, Hamas and Islamic Jihad terrorists fired *over 700 rockets* into southern Israel. Another war is inevitable.

SIGNS IN THE HEAVENS

In 2013, an asteroid entered Earth's atmosphere over Russia as a fireball and exploded above the city of Chelyabinsk. Over 7,000 buildings, across six cities, were damaged due to the shock wave from the explosion. About 1,500 people were injured. It had been the largest recorded object to encounter Earth in over a century. In 2018, another meteor struck the earth - actually exploding in my local area of Michigan. It sparked a small earthquake in the Metro Detroit area. I actually witnessed the jaw-dropping event, as I saw a huge burst of light in my backyard around 8:00 pm. After hours of trying to figure out what I had seen, the local news confirmed a meteorite had fallen nearby. I believe these events were a preview of Revelation 6:13, when the stars of heaven fall unto the earth.

Another rare event, occurring in 2018, happened a few weeks after publication of my first book; and that was the longest Blood Moon of the 21st Century. A Total Lunar Eclipse of such length won't appear in the skies again until 2123. I think it is safe to say that we will not be around for the next one!

EARTHQUAKES

Indonesia was rocked by a massive 7.5 magnitude earthquake in late 2018, and a devastating tsunami followed. Just over a month later, both the ground and residents of Alaska were rattled by a powerful 7.0 earthquake. The major temblor had violently shook buildings, damaged roads, and knocked out power in Anchorage - Alaska's most populated city. The quake was felt up to 400 miles outside of the city. There were several reports of serious damage. Walls had been cracked, ceiling tiles fell, contents of store shelves were littered across floors, and an onramp to a freeway collapsed. One resident of Palmer, Alaska, said that it was "the most violent earthquake" she ever experienced in her 37 years as a resident.

At least four airports closed in the State following the quake, and Alaska's Governor issued a disaster declaration. Nearly 2,000 aftershocks shook the region within three days. Jesus prophesied that, in the *Last Days* leading up to His imminent return, there'd be "powerful earthquakes" around the world. In my first book, I explained that quakes over 7.0 magnitude are dubbed "powerful." Since the year 2000, there've been about 300 earthquakes that fall into this category. That's an average of over 15 per year. I believe the Alaska quake may have been a forerunner for more powerful earthquakes coming to the USA in the very near future.

EXTREME WEATHER

The 2018 Hurricane season was officially the most active season ever recorded, and the most memorable name of that season was my namesake - MICHAEL. In *The Signs of Our Times*, I had told readers to keep an eye on the upcoming Biblically-named storms - especially Michael. As I predicted, the historic storm that bore the name of God's most powerful Archangel was added to the list of retired hurricanes bearing Biblical names. Catching forecasters off guard, by strengthening to a Category 4 within just three days, Michael had made landfall in the Florida Panhandle as the most powerful hurricane on record to ever strike that area of the Gulf Coast. Packing 155 mph winds, with 175 mph gusts, it had been the first Category 5 to strike Florida in almost 3 decades!

There had been States of Emergency declared in the Sunshine State, Georgia, and Alabama. About 3-million people were under evacuation orders, and 3.7-million were under hurricane watches or warnings as Michael approached. The storm had made landfall in Mexico Beach, Florida, and absolutely destroyed the oceanside city. The hurricane also devastated Panama City Beach. Michael remained a hurricane for twelve hours after landfall. Describing the damage, a police officer said, "it looked *like the Apocalypse*."

In the "Extreme Weather" chapter of my previous book, I had documented connections between many Biblically-named storms and America's mistreatment of Israel. While not all such storms in our nation's history were associated with the U.S. doing Israel wrong, there can be no question that a majority were. This time around, I don't believe that Michael was connected to U.S.-Israeli relations. I couldn't find American leadership doing anything that could be considered anti-Israel during Michael's life cycle. But I still firmly believe it was a judgment sent by the LORD upon this backslidden nation. As I stated in my previous book, America has given Him far too many reasons to pour out His Wrath upon this rebellious people.

Besides mistreatment of His beloved Israel, there are at least seven national abominations that I can think of which provoke the LORD to anger. They are...

1. Removing Him from the public square
2. National decline in Biblical belief
3. Widespread blasphemy and moral decay
4. False god worship
5. Legalizing SIN – such as same-sex marriage
6. Sexual rebellion against God
7. Holocaust of America's babies through abortion

Going down this list, do you think that our nation is deserving of God's judgments? I think America is more than deserving. If it weren't for His merciful and patient nature, the USA would have been wiped out a long time ago - especially under the previous President's administration. So if it wasn't connected to Israel, was Hurricane Michael connected to any of the abominations that I've listed above? I think it was. Michael formed in the Caribbean as Tropical Depression #14 on October 6th. In my research, I had discovered that a God-provoking SCOTUS decision occurred on that *exact same date*.

On October 6th, 2014, Barack Obama's left-leaning Supreme Court paved the way for nationwide legalization of Gay Marriage (coming 9 months later, in June 2015). Exactly 4 years *to the day* of Michael's formation, the Court declined to hear appeals from States seeking to uphold bans on same-sex marriage. The Court slamming the door on those cases, and all future appeals, cleared the way for Gay Marriage to expand to well over 30 States and, ultimately, all 50 States by the next year. Michael forming on the anniversary of that **2014** decision and also being the **14**th Tropical Depression was surely no coincidence.

Archangel Michael is God's Warrior who fights against evil. He makes war on anything that is against our God. The Bible tells us that he was the one who battled Lucifer (the devil) and sent him falling from Heaven. Thus, it is fitting that the judgment for a history-changing wicked decision - by what was a Supreme Court majority under the influence of Satan - bore the name of God's Angel who wars against all that is evil.

In my previous book, I also wrote about how God destroyed the theory of "man-made" global warming when he had brought a historically cold winter in 2017-2018. Well, He would do it again - and then some - during the 2018-2019 season. In late January, tens of millions of Americans experienced unbearable temps of 30 degrees below zero (or lower) during the "Polar Vortex." Some areas within the northern U.S. saw temps fall as low as 60 degrees below zero! In my area of southeast Michigan, the freezing temps had the ability to cause frostbite within 5-10 minutes throughout a 48-hour period. Also in the Metro-Detroit area, 99-year-old low temperature records had been shattered.

In nearby Illinois, Chicago broke records as well - registering temps nearly 50 degrees below zero with the windchill; and a new record low temperature for the State of Illinois was set during the Vortex. Alabama, Illinois, Michigan, Mississippi, and Wisconsin all declared States of Emergency. Illinois and Wisconsin had been among six States recording temps as low as the South Pole. The other four were the Dakotas, Minnesota, and Iowa. And speaking of Minnesota and Iowa, Minneapolis had recorded 14 consecutive hours of "Real Feel" temps of 50 degrees below zero; and in Des Moines, Iowa, the temperature fell to nearly 60 below!

Sometimes I really wish the "global warming" theorists were right, because the record-breaking cold's absolutely miserable for those of us who live in the North. I believe the Polar Vortex was meant to be miserable for the Northeast, especially for New York, being a judgment of the LORD. The "once-in-a-generation" deep freeze began on January 29th - exactly 7 days after New York's abominable abortion-on-demand bill had become State law. In the Book of Revelation, the number seven is synonymous with God's judgments upon a rebellious world.

The record-shattering cold put God-denying global warming advocates on their heels, and they had tried to come up with every explanation as to why the global cooling was *the result* of global warming. There's just one logical explanation for the Polar Vortex of 2019: a God who *controls weather* on the earth. Every other explanation falls flat, and any other theory falls apart.

JESUS SAID, WHEN THESE THINGS BEGIN TO COME TO PASS, THEN LOOK UP, AND LIFT UP YOUR HEADS; FOR YOUR REDEMPTION DRAWETH NIGH.

- LUKE 21:28

CHAPTER TWO

MORE SIGNS CONTINUE

JESUS ANSWERED AND SAID UNTO THEM, WHEN IT IS
EVENING, YE SAY, IT WILL BE FAIR WEATHER: FOR THE SKY IS
RED. AND IN THE MORNING, IT WILL BE FOUL WEATHER TO
DAY: FOR THE SKY IS RED AND LOWERING. O YE HYPOCRITES,
YE CAN DISCERN THE FACE OF THE SKY; BUT CAN YE NOT
DISCERN THE SIGNS OF THE TIMES?

- MATTHEW 16:2-3

ABORTION

IN 2018, MORE PEOPLE had died from abortions than any other cause of death in the world - approximately 42-million. There is also a new President at Planned Parenthood, Dr. Leana Wen, who replaced Cecile Richards as head of the nation's largest abortion business. She told *People* magazine that she viewed abortion as "a basic human right." So, much like her predecessor, Wen believes that murdering your child is the "right" of every American.

In 2019, on the 46th Anniversary of the abominable Roe V. Wade SCOTUS decision, New York's Democrat-controlled State legislature and Governor passed a law to enshrine a "fundamental right" to abortion in the State's Constitution. The abominable law wiped out all restrictions on abortions, allowing the procedure to be performed up to birth! It's a license to murder babies without consequence. Other Dem-controlled States followed suit, passing similar bills soon after. Many Dems now embrace *infanticide*.

Under the New York law, non-physicians and midwives can perform abortions - and protections for babies surviving abortion procedures ("born alive") are removed. This means that they can be "left to die" after birth. Not only did the Democrats and their pro-choice supporters express absolutely no remorse, but on the day that the bill was signed into law they publicly *celebrated* it. I warned in my first book that California was at the top of the list to receive judgments from the LORD for many reasons, and later in this book you will read how those judgments have begun to fall. New York is now at the top of the list as well. You cannot shed innocent blood on this earth - let alone *celebrate* shedding it - and expect to escape the consequences of provoking the LORD.

A month after the New York law was passed, 44 Democrat Senators voted against the Born Alive Act. Essentially, they voted to let a baby DIE if born alive after a botched abortion. That is nothing short of Satanic. Also, for the first time in over 150 years, abortion became free and legal in Ireland in 2019. Irish legislature voted to allow a woman to have an abortion into the 12th week of pregnancy. A member of the Irish Parliament, Bríd Smith, said it was "one of those rare moments in life when you feel such joy - the sheer joy of beating back the Church's agenda, really beating it back for once." WOW. Someone taking such delight in making war on the people of God is downright demonic. It is the Book of Revelation playing out before our eyes -

"AND THE DRAGON (SATAN) WAS WROTH WITH THE WOMAN, AND WENT TO MAKE WAR WITH THE REMNANT OF HER SEED (CHRIST), WHICH KEEP THE COMMANDMENTS OF GOD, AND HAVE THE TESTIMONY OF JESUS CHRIST." - REVELATION 12:17

LGBT PRIDE

Since the days of Obama's administration, there have been public libraries across America hosting what is known as "Drag Queen Story Time." During the events, men dressed in drag (even demon costumes) read "Trans" books to young children. As if that were not bad enough, Planned Parenthood and left-wing Human Rights Campaign (HRC) push initiatives in schools that teach kids about masturbation, crossdressing, gay sex, transgenderism, and BDSM in Sex-Ed programs all across the country.

LifeSiteNews recently reported that attacks on Christians by LGBT activists in Canada have significantly escalated. In Alberta, Education Minister David Eggen is threatening to defund or shut down religious schools not accepting Gay-Straight Alliance clubs. The Supreme Court of Canada recently ruled against a Christian university in British Columbia, forbidding that private institution from having students agree to a lifestyle contract when enrolling.

In 2018, Canada's government had forced employers to sign a document indicating they support transgender rights and abortion. If business owners refused, which most (hopefully all) Christians did, then they were denied Canadian Summer Jobs grants. While the Christian-owned organizations were being shut out of the Jobs program, there had been nearly $100,000 in grants awarded to the Canadian organizations affiliated with Planned Parenthood.

Feeling emboldened under their liberal leader, Justin Trudeau, Canada's LGBT activists are now targeting churches - demanding the government strip charitable status from churches disagreeing with their radical ideology. Obviously, *true* Christian churches do (or should). Canadian pro-life activist, Jonathon Van Maren, has warned that the radicals in the LGBT crowd will soon be saying, "Any good that these churches do is vastly outweighed by their fundamental bigotry."

In other shocking news from 2018, it was reported that there was a 4000% increase in kids who identify as transgender. Kids! God help us. That's an ominous sign of the Tribulation coming in the very near future, during which Christians all across the world will be hated even more so than we are now. We will be murdered for our Faith, and thrown into prison, just for believing the Word of God over the opinions and feelings of modern society. Belief in basic human biology - that God created "male and female" - will most likely be a criminal offense. We're not yet in the Tribulation, and transgender activists are already threatening the lives of those refusing to embrace their ideology.

In December of 2018, LGBT radicals threatened the life of a professor in England because she refused to bow to their agenda. *BBC News* reported that a University of Reading professor, Rosa Freedman, received threats of murder and rape. She said that she endured constant online abuse and that her office door had been covered in urine. The threats and hostility started after Freedman publicly discussed a government program that would aid people wanting to change their gender. She opposes the idea that people can choose their gender, believing the Bible's truth that we are all born as one particular gender.

When she had made her way to an event, where she'd discuss proposed changes to the Gender Recognition Act, she was forced to hide in bushes to avoid menacing activists who were following her. Seriously?! It's insane that this can happen in a so-called civil society. A woman is forced to hide from a mob of men because she won't submit to their radical agenda. Where is the #MeToo movement in this case? Does it not count when men making the threats advocate for the LGBT agenda? The Left are hypocrites, and should be ashamed of their egregious double standards.

What's interesting about the modern mob mentality of LGBT activists is that homosexuals we read about in the Bible behaved in the *exact same way*. In Sodom, a mob of them stormed Lot's home in an effort to get their way -

"THE MEN OF THE CITY, EVEN THE MEN OF SODOM, COMPASSED THE HOUSE ROUND, BOTH OLD AND YOUNG, ALL THE PEOPLE FROM EVERY QUARTER: AND THEY CALLED UNTO LOT, AND SAID UNTO HIM, WHERE ARE THE MEN WHICH CAME IN TO YOU THIS NIGHT? BRING THEM OUT UNTO US, THAT WE MAY KNOW (LAY WITH) THEM. AND LOT WENT OUT AT THE DOOR UNTO THEM, AND SHUT THE DOOR AFTER HIM, AND SAID, I PRAY YOU, BRETHREN, DO NOT SO WICKEDLY. BEHOLD NOW, I HAVE TWO DAUGHTERS WHICH HAVE NOT KNOWN MAN; LET ME, I PRAY YOU, BRING THEM OUT UNTO YOU, AND DO YOU TO THEM AS IS GOOD IN YOUR EYES: ONLY UNTO THESE MEN DO NOTHING; FOR THEREFORE CAME THEY UNDER THE SHADOW OF MY ROOF. AND THEY SAID, STAND BACK. AND THEY SAID AGAIN, THIS ONE FELLOW CAME IN TO SOJOURN, AND HE HAS BECOME A JUDGE: NOW WILL WE DEAL WORSE WITH YOU, THAN WITH THEM. AND THEY PRESSED SORE UPON THE MAN, EVEN LOT, AND CAME NEAR TO BREAK THE DOOR. BUT THE MEN (ANGELS) PUT FORTH THEIR HAND, AND PULLED LOT INTO THE HOUSE TO THEM, AND SHUT TO THE DOOR. AND THEY SMOTE THE MEN THAT WERE AT THE DOOR OF THE HOUSE WITH BLINDNESS, BOTH SMALL AND GREAT: SO THEY WEARIED THEMSELVES TO FIND THE DOOR." - GENESIS 19:4-11

Notice how homosexuals, all the way back in that first Book of our Bible, accused Lot of "judging" them. Today, the demonic spirits possessing homosexuals still use the same lines and mob mentality as they did from the very beginning. Freedman said that it was scary to have a mob of students, many of whom were male, following her. She also said that she was explicitly *urged to leave* the university because of her views.

FALLING AWAY FROM THE FAITH

In 2018, "The State of Theology" in America was examined by Ligonier Ministries in a survey conducted by *LifeWay* Research. The survey was based on interviews with 3,000 Americans, and it was the third time that Ligonier and *LifeWay* conducted the study. The others were done in 2014 and 2016. Ligonier said the survey helps uncover what Americans think about God, Jesus Christ, sin, and eternity. As with studies I'd shared in the previous book, the results are alarming and they highlight the *sad state* of Theology in America's churches. While it was a survey of all Americans, I want to zero in on shocking responses by Evangelical Christians.

On the survey statement, "Everyone sins a little, but most are good by nature," 52% of Evangelicals agreed. *More than half* (of what is supposed to be the most Biblically-literate denomination) completely contradict what God's Word teaches. Not one human being on this earth is "good by nature." We live in a fallen world, where we're prone to sin since youth. We are more likely to break God's Moral Law each day than to do good. Like it or not, that is just the way it is. We all sin, and fall short of the Glory of God (Romans 3:23). That's the reason we all need a Saviour. We serve a Holy God, Who cannot dwell in the presence of sin. As long as we're stained in sin, we cannot enter into His Presence. We aren't "good." Every single one of us is a sinner.

The holiest pastor or priest wrestles with sin daily. Agreeing that *most* people are good is 100% against the Bible. Jesus said, when He was called "good," that "there is *none good* but GOD." He was referring to His Father in Heaven, YHWH. Another piece of Scripture, obliterating the view that "most are good," is found in the Book of Romans -

"AS IT IS WRITTEN, THERE IS NONE RIGHTEOUS, NO, NOT ONE: THERE IS NONE THAT UNDERSTANDETH, THERE IS NONE THAT SEEKETH AFTER GOD. THEY ARE ALL GONE OUT OF THE WAY, THEY ARE TOGETHER BECOME UNPROFITABLE; THERE IS NONE THAT DOES GOOD, NO, NOT ONE." - ROMANS 3:10-12

You'd think that would be plain enough to anyone claiming to be a Bible believer, but I guess a lot of Evangelicals today totally glossed over that Chapter of Romans. While it's disappointing for believers to agree with the first statement, their agreeing with the next one is beyond blasphemous. On the statement, "God accepts the worship of all religions," 51% of so-called Christians agreed. Again, more than half! I'm curious as to what version of the Holy Bible that half of Evangelicals are reading (or not reading at all), because their versions are poorly translated. God does *not* accept the worship of other gods or religions in any way, shape, or form. He condemns idolatry all throughout the pages of our Holy Book, in both the Old and New Testaments.

He most assuredly condemns worship of Islam and Allah, as Allah is the "Baal" of our Bible. As I proved in my first book, the Quran is the antithesis of the Holy Bible. The LORD condemns worshipping any false gods, and that would pertain to Buddhism, Hinduism, and all of the other "ism" religions of the world (with the exception of Judaism). YHWH is clear that there is "no other God" but *Him* (Exodus 20:3, Isaiah 44:6-8 and 45:5); and when you put your faith in His Son for your salvation, honoring Jesus equates to honoring Him (Psalms 2:12, John 5:23 and 14:6, Acts 4:12, 1st Corinthians 8:6, and 1st John 2:23). YHWH and Yeshua are "ONE" (John 1:1, 1:18, 10:30 & 14:9, and Isaiah 9:6).

To those 51% of Evangelicals who think that God's okay with us worshipping other gods, or adhering to other religions: you are grossly mistaken. You must have never read the Bible. There is no possible way that you could have. Christians serve one God - the *true God* of Heaven and Earth. There are no others!

FAITHLESS GENERATION

In the same survey, the theological beliefs of everyday Americans were examined. On the statement, "Even the smallest sin deserves eternal damnation," 69% had disagreed - nearly ¾ of Americans! While it may sound harsh to some for me to say that a white lie, gossiping, disrespecting parents, not keeping the Sabbath holy, or coveting property of your neighbor, would result in you having to spend an eternity in Hell... it's 100% *true*. As I said earlier, we all sin. So, it does not matter how little or how big a sin we commit. God is Holy - we are unholy. Therefore, based on our own merits, we can not stand in His Presence unless we accept His prescribed solution to this problem: JESUS.

He Who knew no sin bore the punishment of sin for us, and died for every one that we have committed - or will ever commit. He suffered the just judgment we deserved, so that we unworthy sinners could spend eternity in Heaven. If you don't accept Jesus' sacrifice on your behalf, then, yes, even the smallest of sins will sentence you to eternal damnation. The LORD has made a way so that you would not have to endure the consequences of your sins; but if you don't repent and accept Christ as Saviour, *you condemn yourself* to Hell - not God.

On the statement that "Religious belief is a matter of personal opinion - not about objective truth," 60% agreed. The Bible was penned by the Holy Spirit of God. It is the only real *truth* in this life. If you believe God's Word, you believe the truth. Something that billions of people the world over have believed for thousands of years, which has always held true and never been proven false, can't be considered *opinion*. So, the 60% are dead wrong (Psalms 119:160, John 8:32, 15:26, 16:13 & 17:17, and 2nd Peter 1:21).

Even worse news, coming out of the survey, is that the trend of wider acceptance of same-sex relations continues. For the first time, in nearly a 5-year period of surveys, more Americans (than not) agree that the Bible's teaching on same-sex relationships is "outdated." On the statement, "The Holy Bible's condemnation of homosexual behavior doesn't apply today," 44% agreed. Though every reference to homosexuality in the Bible is clear (in both Old and New Testaments) that it is abominable sin in the eyes of the LORD, many Americans don't believe God cares too much about the issue in our day. They couldn't be more wrong. The rebellion of the homosexual community against Almighty God is bringing judgment after judgment upon this backslidden nation.

On the statement, "The Holy Bible is 100% accurate in all it teaches," only 50% agreed. *Half of Americans* do not believe the Bible to be the Word of God! What a disgusting shame. Anything that can be proven about the Bible has been or is being proved. Anything that has not... *will be*. On the flipside, nothing has ever been disproven that has been recorded in the Holy Bible. *Nothing*. I, for one, will continue to trust the inerrancy of God's Word over the fallible *opinions* of men.

Finally, as to how young adults (Millennials) responded to the survey... just as you'd expect - *not good*. On the statement, "The Bible is not literally true," 53% agreed. That is up 7% from the 2016 survey. On the statement that "Gender identity is a matter of choice," 46% agreed. Even though we were all created with either male or female anatomy, they're saying we can *choose* the gender we *prefer*. This absurd ideology is antithetical to God's Word.

Sadly, it appears the state of Theology in America is getting worse year after year. People are far more concerned with being entertained in church today, rather than learning something about God. They want "feel good" time, and never "reflect and repent" time. Hopefully, those of us who faithfully preach God's truth to a backslidden nation and world will never grow weary. We need to shout His Word from the rooftops, whether people want to hear it or not; because many want to call themselves "Christian," while cooking up their *own* ideas about what the Faith is about. They are transforming Christianity into what they believe that it *should* be, as opposed to what it always *has been* and *is*.

Just like our Lord and God in Heaven, the Word of the LORD is *the same yesterday, today, and forever*. God doesn't allow us to revise it to better suit the mainstream opinions of our generation. As a matter of fact, He forbids it (Deuteronomy 4:2 & Revelation 22:18-19). His Word has stood the test of time for good reason - it endures *forever* (Isaiah 40:8, Matthew 24:35, and 1st Peter 1:25). You are entitled to believe whatever it is you choose to in this life; but if what you're believing isn't in line with what the Bible says, then you are believing a LIE. Like it or not.

JESUS SAID, WHEN YE SHALL SEE ALL THESE THINGS, KNOW THAT IT (RAPTURE) IS NEAR, EVEN AT THE DOORS.

- MATTHEW 24:33

CHAPTER THREE

MASS SHOOTINGS

IN THE LAST DAYS PERILOUS TIMES SHALL COME.

- 2ND TIMOTHY 3:1

POLITICAL POINTS OF VIEW are all that we ever seem to hear in debates and discussions about mass shootings, and very rarely do we hear a Biblical perspective. I intend to change that.

If you're a Democrat, you probably think that mass shootings have increased under President Trump and that the solution is *gun control*. If you're Republican, you likely believe the tragic events began to increase under his predecessor, Barack Obama, and that *more guns* are the answer - not less. You'd both be wrong. Mass shootings in America had become more frequent and more deadly over time, beginning in 1999. I think it is very interesting that the year includes 6-6-6 upside down. That just so happened to be the year of the infamous Columbine High School shooting. The two perpetrators of the attack were atheist students who were inspired by Adolph Hitler. Those depraved souls murdered a dozen fellow students and one teacher.

A Faith-based film was made about the tragedy and centered on one of the victims, devout Christian Rachel Joy Scott. Masey Mclain portrayed Scott in *I'm Not Ashamed*. If you have not yet seen the film, then I highly recommend it as a must-see. The two demonic shooters carried out the attack on April 20th, which just so happened to be Hitler's birthday. Throughout the course of the next two decades, as our nation drifted further and further away from the LORD, many more kids would follow in the footsteps of the Columbine shooters.

In 2005, a 16-year-old had murdered 7 in Minnesota. In 2007, a 23-year-old student murdered 33 at Virginia Tech University. It became the deadliest school shooting in U.S. history. In 2012, a 20-year-old had shot up an Elementary School in Connecticut. He murdered 26. 20 of the victims were children, aged 6-7 years old. In 2014, a student murdered 4 classmates in Washington. In 2015, an Oregon student murdered 8 classmates and a teacher. In 2018, a 15-year-old slaughtered 2 and injured nearly 20 in his Kentucky school. That same year, a 19-year-old went on a shooting spree at his former Florida high school - murdering 17. Just three months later, another black-hearted teen shot up a High School in Texas. His cold-blooded attack left 10 dead.

It's no surprise that all these young shooters had one thing in common: anti-God influences. The Florida shooter tortured small animals, was anti-Semitic, and testified that demons spoke to him. The Texas shooter idolized the Columbine psychopaths. He wore a long black trench coat like they wore during their massacre. His social media accounts revealed that he, too, was fond of Hitler; as his clothing was adorned with Nazi, Communist, and even Occult symbols. He attributed his "evil side" to the demon Baphomet in a social media post.

These demonic kids are all the consequence of children today not being taught the Laws of God regarding right and wrong; and it's certainly no coincidence that the *least Christian generation* in American history is the most violent. In my first book, I shared a study revealing that more teenagers than ever before say that they identify as atheists. Only 4% of Gen-Z hold a Biblical worldview. And, yet, people wonder why schools have turned into war zones!

I guarantee that mass shootings in schools will continue, and even get worse. It really doesn't matter how many gun restriction laws are passed. As long as the hearts of the youth are evil, Satan will lead their hands to a weapon.

There's only one solution to end America's school shootings epidemic, and that's to put Almighty God back in schools - where He rightfully belongs. Many Americans today are ignorant to the fact that our nation's first schoolbook was the Bible. Ever since it was forced out, along with prayer, the public school environment has rapidly become less safe. In a 1940 survey of teachers, the top disciplinary problems reported were: chewing gum, talking out of turn, running in halls, and dress-code violations. Flash-forward to 2019, and you can see just what America's downward spiral away from the LORD has done to our nation's school system. The top problems that teachers of this generation report are: drug/alcohol abuse, pregnancy, suicide, rape, robbery, assault, and shootings.

Things are unquestionably worse in schools than they've ever been in the history of the USA; and, examining history, we find only *one thing* changed over the course of the past two centuries. At America's founding, did our forefathers own guns? How about in 1940? The answer is yes, on both counts. Did young boys have hormones back then, and desire intimate relations with girls? Yes. Did alcohol exist back then? Yup. So, why no mass shootings in schools? How come as many young girls were not being raped or getting pregnant? Why no assault in schools? Why no widespread alcohol use amongst the youth? What was so different throughout the first few centuries of the United States? The universal answer to all of the above hows and whys is FEAR OF GOD.

Not only was the Lord revered above all, but kids were taught Godly morals from a young age; and God's Word was central to our nation's education system. Teens back then could have never imagined doing any of the abominable things that today's kids do. Yet, here we are… no God in our schools, coupled with a young generation that is inundated daily with lust - gratuitous violence - normalization of drug and alcohol use - immorality - blasphemy - even a bitter hostility toward the God of our fathers - and how can anyone be surprised by where we are as a society? Just examine the history of mass shootings in America; and it's plain to see that after the LORD was pushed out, *evil* filled the void.

In the 50-year period from 1948-1998, there were TEN mass shootings with about 150 victims. From 1999-2018, which is less than half the previous period, there were 19 mass shootings with about 375 victims. In under half the time, shootings *doubled* and the lives lost have *more than doubled*! Still, liberals would rather blame Almighty God for America's ills; rather than acknowledge that we need Him more than ever.

In 2015, a deranged gunman shot up a Planned Parenthood in Colorado - murdering 3 people. As soon as the incident began to headline the major news networks, I knew the lamestream media would demonize Christians because of our strong stance against the baby-murdering organization. As expected, before any details of the shooter had been revealed, the media, Planned Parenthood, left-wing pundits, and liberal keyboard warriors, had labeled the gunman a "right-wing pro-life extremist." Even after the identity of the shooter was revealed, proving he was not a Christian, they continued to place blame on the "extreme" and "hateful" ideology of "conservative Christians."

The shooter was *anything but* a staunch Holy Bible-believing Christian. He was a mentally ill veteran with a lengthy criminal record. Yet, the lefties pushed the narrative that us pro-lifers were *extremists*. First of all, you can't be pro-life and a murderer. That would be an oxymoron. Second, you cannot be a *defender* of life, while at the same time, *destroying* life. So, it was nauseating to watch the libs (who advocate for taking the lives of unborn babies on a daily basis) accuse pro-lifers of bearing responsibility for the senseless murder. It is no secret that most of us Christians oppose

Planned Parenthood. But we *never* call for violence against them or their employees. We never have. We never will. If you do, then you just aren't a true Christian.

There is no justification in the Bible for taking innocent lives (Exodus 20:13, Numbers 35:30, Matthew 19:18). While many in the Planned Parenthood organization are Godless, and downright evil, we must leave vengeance to God alone. We are never to take justice into our own hands. Unless someone is attempting to do you or your family life-threatening harm, it cannot be considered justice to take the life of another human being. I do not care how evil that you may think the other person is - the fate of their life is not in your hands, but God's. If He wants to punish them for their sins, you can be absolutely sure that He will. It is not our job to execute His judgment, by any means.

That is precisely why Christians oppose Planned Parenthood as passionately as we do, because their hands shed innocent blood *every day*. They are responsible for cutting short the lives of over 7-million children of God, and they'll have to answer to Him for it someday. Sadly, they see nothing wrong with murdering babies; but they sure seem to find a heck of a lot wrong with God-fearing Christians. Planned Parenthood's Executive Vice President, Dawn Laguens, released a statement in wake of the Colorado shooting, saying, "One of the lessons of this awful tragedy is words matter, and hateful rhetoric fuels violence." Obviously, she was referring to Christians who speak out against the murder of the unborn.

She added, "It's not enough to denounce the tragedy without also denouncing the poisonous rhetoric that fueled it." Notice that she did not once blame the lunatic who actually murdered three people at the clinic, including a *Christian* cop. She, instead, used the tragedy as a means to demonize her organization's outspoken adversaries. Do you think she would have lashed out at Muslims, or criticized the dangerous rhetoric of the Quran, had the shooter been Islamic? I highly doubt it.

Following any Islamic terror attack, of which there have been far too many to count in the past decade, the lamestream media and the libs come to the defense of Muslims. They say that *not all* Muslims are terrorists, and urge others to not condemn an entire religion due to the actions of *a few*. Yet, when a deranged white guy - neither Christian nor pro-life - shoots up an abortion clinic, the same liberals say, "ALL Christians are extremists and Biblical beliefs are dangerous." Talk about a double standard!

In June of 2016, an Islamic terrorist shot up a gay nightclub in Orlando, Florida, known as The Pulse. In the brutal massacre, about 50 were murdered and over 50 more wounded. At that time, it was the deadliest mass shooting in U.S. history. The shooter, Omar Mateen, called 911 during the attack to publicly declare his allegiance to the ISIS (Islamic State) terror group. A spokesman for the group had called for attacks against Americans during the Muslim holiday of Ramadan, which began just a few days earlier. Mainstream media had dubbed 30-year-old Mateen "mentally ill," conveniently ignoring his Islamic ties. Targeting homosexuals for death was not some new idea cooked up by Mateen. Just like the targeting of Jews and Christians, it is called for in Islam's Quran.

In Islamic nations like Afghanistan, Iran, Mauritania, Nigeria, Saudi Arabia, Somalia, Sudan, the UAE, and Yemen, homosexual activity carries a death penalty. What a contrast with the teachings of Christianity, the Faith which the LGBT community attacks the most. Followers of Christ simply speak out against homosexuality and same-sex marriage, while followers of Muhammad set out to abolish homosexuals by deadly force. Lord Jesus commanded us to show poor sinners the error of their ways, to preach repentance, and lead them to Him. Muhammad, on the other hand, commands his followers to torture, terrorize, and murder them.

I once heard it said, concerning the difference between those who murder in Allah's name and those who murder in the Name of Jesus: "Muslims who murder for the cause of Allah are being *good* Muslims, but Christians who murder for the cause of Christ are being *bad* Christians." Amen. 100% true. So, while the LGBT activists sure do seem to hate Bible thumpers like me, they should be extremely thankful that I'm not thumping a Quran!

In 2017, the toll of a mass shooting in Nevada surpassed that of the Florida nightclub massacre - making it America's deadliest. A 64-year-old, Stephen Paddock, shot dead about 60 people, and injured 500+ others at an outdoor concert. The Route 91 Harvest Festival, which took place just outside Mandalay Bay Resort and Casino in Las Vegas, drew nearly 25,000 concertgoers - making it the perfect target for a demonic madman seeking to end multiple lives. Paddock opened fire on the crowd from a 32nd floor room of the Mandalay Bay Hotel. About 20 weapons were found in his room, including 10 rifles. It was obviously a premeditated attack.

He began shooting during a performance by a country music singer, Jason Aldean, who was closing act of the Festival. After Aldean was rushed off stage, chaos ensued. Thousands of people began to panic, running for cover, and trampling one another in a stampede-like atmosphere. The Mandalay Bay Hotel, from where Paddock had fired, was across the street from the concert venue. It's believed that he fired from two different rooms to get different angles on his victims. His brother told reporters that he had "no religious affiliation and no political affiliation."

Just one month after the Vegas slaughter, a church in Texas was targeted. A 26-year-old avowed atheist, Devin Patrick Kelley, opened fire on the congregation of a Baptist Church in Sutherland Springs - murdering over two dozen and injuring 20 others. It was the deadliest mass shooting in the State, and deadliest shooting in an American place of worship in modern history.

Mass shootings are not always defined by law enforcement as acts of terrorism, but they most certainly are. In a mass shooting, just as in an act of terror, a perpetrator is seeking to end as many lives as possible. And just like with terrorism, as I pointed out in my previous book, mass shootings are not about guns or "mental health." They are the unfortunate result of men not knowing God. When there is no God in the heart of man, evil will always thrive. Whether it be an atheist or Islamic terrorist, evil men are prone to commit murder. Mass shooters are under the influence of Satan. In John 8:44, Lord Jesus said, "You are of your father the devil, and the lusts of your father you will do. He was a *murderer* from the beginning."

Liberals and Democrats who use deadly tragedies to push for gun control obviously don't read the Holy Bible. The gun control argument is always made by people who don't seem to believe in the age-old spiritual battle of good vs. evil and God vs. the devil. In this politically correct nation, liberals don't want to believe that Satan works in the hearts of unbelievers. That doesn't change the fact that he most certainly does. Murder is an abomination to the LORD. Since the irreligious people don't believe in the God who created a moral law, they have nothing that prevents them from committing immoral acts.

Thus, I do not believe that guns have anything whatsoever to do with the plague of mass shootings in America. I believe that the absence of God, in the hearts and lives of many of our fellow citizens, has absolutely *everything* to do with it. I get so disgusted when I hear liberals say, "we don't need prayers, we need action" in the wake of mass shootings. It is that Godless attitude that is allowing demonic murderers to flourish in our society. There is absolutely no legislation that politicians can pass to prevent the deadly incidents in the future. But seeking the LORD in fervent prayer can prevent any and all evil acts.

Liberals can ban every gun in America, and the result would be mass stabbings. Confiscate every knife, and evil men will use pressure cookers or vehicles to take countless lives. You can never stop demonic men from harming others just by taking away their weapons of choice. Murderers will find a way to murder. Do y'all remember Cain and Abel? Will we ever ban *stones*? In order to stop the senseless bloodshed of mass shootings once and for all, it is not the minds of men that need to change - nor the size of the guns that they are allowed to own. It is their *hearts*. And there is only *one way* to change them... It isn't psychiatry. It isn't gun control. It's JESUS, and Jesus Christ *alone*.

EVEN AS THEY DID NOT LIKE TO RETAIN GOD IN THEIR KNOWLEDGE, GOD GAVE THEM OVER TO A REPROBATE MIND, TO DO THOSE THINGS WHICH ARE NOT CONVENIENT; BEING FILLED WITH ALL UNRIGHTEOUSNESS... WICKEDNESS... MALICIOUSNESS... MURDER... MALIGNITY.

- ROMANS 1:28-29

CHAPTER FOUR

RACISM

FOR THE LORD SEETH NOT AS MAN SEETH; FOR MAN
LOOKETH ON THE OUTWARD APPEARANCE, BUT THE LORD
LOOKETH ON THE HEART.

- 1ST SAMUEL 16:7

IN ALL MY YEARS of writing, I have only touched on the issue of racism a few times. This is because I do not believe that we can ever eradicate the disgusting ideology by paying its adherents or their hateful rhetoric any attention. Unfortunately, with the rise of social media in this day and age - which has given a platform to the dregs of our society - hate for others based on their skin color has spread like a plague. So, just as I had felt that the Lord called me to address the hot-button issues of our day - such as abortion and LGBT Pride - from a Biblical perspective in my last book, I believe that He has now led me to tackle this issue.

I will not be addressing this issue from the right or left side of the political aisle either, though it is well known that I lean to the "right" politically as a staunch conservative Christian. I think that the term "right-wing" has been hijacked; because there are far too many unabashed racists claiming to belong to the right side of the political aisle. They most certainly don't belong there. That is not to say that the left doesn't have their share of racists on the fringe of the Democrat Party, because they absolutely do. The brands of racism are different on the opposite ends of the political spectrum, but should all be condemned exactly the same.

Unfortunately, one form of racism is far too prevalent on both sides of the aisle - anti-Semitism. There are the Jew-hating White Supremacists of the alt-right, and anti-Israel Muslims on the left. The Republican and Democrat parties would be wise to condemn them loudly and often. I'd addressed the scourge of anti-Semitism in my previous book, so take a moment to read it if you have not already. In this chapter, I am going to focus on the other forms of racism that are rife in our nation. For starters, there are both white and black Christians who peddle racially-divisive belief systems; and thus I question their faith. Because I do not think that a true believer in Christ could ever see another human "in color."

Our God is *colorblind*. Thus, as His children, we are called to be too. The LORD looks on the hearts of men, and never on the shades of their skin. From the beginning, He has only viewed the human race in two ways - as either believers or unbelievers. You either choose to serve the true God of Heaven and Earth, or you choose to follow false gods. You do one or the other. There is no in the middle. When you do the first, it does not matter if you are white, black, brown, or yellow - God knows you, and you are His child. If you do the latter, then being light or dark-skinned doesn't matter in the slightest to the LORD. He *does not* know you, and you're a stranger to Him. The only thing that ever matters to Him is obedience to His Word and to His will.

If you're defiant and don't accept His Son's sacrifice on your behalf, as atonement for your disobedience, then being born white or black cannot save you. You are going to Hell. Plain and simple. In the end, we will all be judged on our faith alone. Nothing else. We will not be judged in regard to how much money we made, nor by how many kids we had raised; not by worldly positions we held, nor by the size of our homes or businesses; not by how kind or generous we were to others, nor by any good deeds which we had done. All the LORD will care about, come Judgment Day, is whether or not you believed in the Lord Jesus Christ to reconcile your unholy soul unto your Holy Creator.

Today, there are believers all around the world - from every nation, culture, tribe, and color. When we are "in Christ," we are *all equal* in God's Sight. I am not any more favored by the Lord than an African believer, Jewish believer, Arab believer, Spanish believer, or Asian believer. We are all "one race" in Christ Jesus. We're all one family. We're all members of the Church, regardless of denomination. We are all members of one body, of which He is "the Head" (Romans 12:4-5, 1st Corinthians 10:16-17 and 12:12, Ephesians 1:22 - 2:19-22 - 4:15-16 - 5:23, and Colossians 1:18).

Though I'm white, I might actually have more black men and women as "brothers and sisters" than other whites. Whosoever is washed and covered in the Blood of God's Son is my true family. Whosoever isn't is *not* my brother or sister. They are strangers. A black believer in Christ, who believes every word of the Bible as strongly as I do, is more so my family than a blood relative who doesn't believe. That's why I never view others in color. My Faith prevents me from doing so. For there is no skin color that makes any of us superior over another human being. Not one.

Our God wills that all men and women, everywhere - and of every color - would come to Him through His Son, the Prince of Peace. Only then can we experience lasting peace and equality in our divided nation and world. These two long-sought-after things can never be obtained through any government, political leaders, laws, or affirmative action; but are only found in God alone. The ever-growing racial tension that's been sweeping the nation is just one of the many consequences of forcing God out of America - at a time when we need Him more than ever.

As believers, we must not grow weary in preaching His Word - whether our fellow citizens want to hear it or not. If we sit back, resigned to the belief that things will never change, and keep the LORD's unifying message of salvation all to ourselves or only to our churches... America may soon find itself in another Civil War.

We must perpetually place our Faith above our race. Because if any Holy Bible believer is placing their race over the Faith, then their faith is meaningless. You and I are *Christians* above all else. That label should be setting us apart from every other group in the world. We should never be engaged in "race wars," and never be members of race-based groups - especially not those who engage in violent protests or unruly riots to make their voices heard. We should never be known for being Caucasian or African American, nor Asian, Hispanic, Native American, or any other ethnicity. We should be known as Christians. Period. The only race that's ever had a special place in God's heart is the Jew. The rest of us are simply known to Him as Gentiles.

If we ever had to fill out paperwork in Heaven, and there was a "race" section, I suspect that there would only be two options - Jew or Gentile. And the LORD wills that *both* would be united in Christ, King of the Jews and Savior of the world. In the Kingdom of God, there will be no "White Power" or "Black Power." There will only be "Power in the Blood of Jesus." These words might pain the White Supremacists or Black Liberation Theologists, but everything I'm teaching is 100% Biblical. It's the Word of God. It is not my own. Godless men like Richard Spencer, Al Sharpton (who is no "Reverend"), and Louis Farrakhan believe God should favor them (and all those who look like them) because they think that their particular race is superior to all others.

These men, and people who follow their abhorrent doctrines, are of the devil. There is no nice way to say it. Richard Spencer is a neo-Nazi White Supremacist, and is the leader of the "alt-right" movement. He is also an atheist. That explains why he so strongly rejects the traditional "right-wing," especially those belonging to the Christian Right (like myself). Spencer says that "White people should have their own nation, separate from the people of colour." Sadly, as America has increasingly become a Biblically-illiterate nation, he's amassed thousands of followers across the country. A majority of them are anti-Semitic members of the KKK (Ku Klux Klan), neo-Nazis, White Supremacists, and White Nationalists.

Stirring up the racial strife on the other end of the political spectrum are men like Al Sharpton and Farrakhan. These men are the dark-skinned equivalents of Spencer, as they have both made highly controversial statements about Jews and whites. Sharpton has made a career out of profiting off of racial injustices done to African Americans hundreds of years ago, while Farrakhan leads the Nation of Islam and is an unrepentant Jew-hater. Sadly, much like Spencer, they've both accumulated very large cult followings. Sharpton masquerades as a man of God, but is nothing more than a money-hungry race hustler and a habitual blasphemer. He often compares Jesus Christ to young criminals who are shot by police for resisting arrest.

Jesus was *no* criminal. He was falsely accused of being one, and was crucified for the crimes He didn't commit alongside real criminals. To compare Him (the Savior of the world) to immoral, drug-dealing, gun-toting thugs is beyond blasphemous. Sharpton has even said that certain books of the Bible should be "thrown out" because he says they "condone" slavery. He obviously didn't study the Biblical languages of Hebrew or Greek in Theological School. If he did, then he'd know that "slaves" and "servants" in the Bible were *not* the same as African slaves of the 18th-19th Centuries - not at all the same.

The only real slaves we read about in the Holy Bible were the Hebrew Jews in Egypt. Any other time that you ever read about slaves in God's Word, they were what we know today as butlers or maids. They were indentured servants. They were paid wages for their work, and were not whipped nor bound in chains. After the years of their service were complete, they had the choice to go free or to remain with their masters. To say in any way that the Bible condones slavery, as we know it today, is just plain wrong and is theologically irresponsible. If Sharpton truly were a man of God, and sincerely cared about the "equal" treatment of all God's children, then He'd preach everything I'm teaching. He does not.

Instead, he cherry-picks verses from the Holy Bible to fit his racially-divisive agenda. He is also a teacher of "Black Liberation Theology," which just so happens to be pro-Islam and anti-Israel. Bible believers could never hate God's Chosen Nation or support their enemies. Never. Al Sharpton is nothing but a sham. It's such a shame that men like him and the anti-Christian Malcolm X are widely respected, and even adored, in the black community. They have both long been portrayed as champions in the fight against racism. Yet, in reality, they are both the biggest inciters of it!

Malcolm X was spokesman for the Nation of Islam, the black Muslim movement now led by Farrakhan. He and his followers violently rejected Judeo-Christian America, preaching *supremacy* of blacks over whites. Sadly, much of today's black generation is enamored with X's riotous "by any means necessary" approach to fighting racism - as opposed to Martin Luther King Jr.'s "weapons of love." King preached messages like "Darkness cannot drive out darkness, only light can do that. Hate cannot drive out hate, only love can do that." Meanwhile, Malcolm said that "You don't have a peaceful revolution. You don't have a turn-the-cheek revolution. There is no such thing as a nonviolent revolution."

Which of these two famous Civil Rights leaders do you think that Lord Jesus would approve of? If you have to think about your answer for more than a second, then you haven't read your Bible. Unfortunately, most of the young blacks today appear to side with X over King. Just look at the slogan of the popular Black Lives Matter movement: "No Justice - No Peace." If King were alive today, I believe that his message to this group would be:

"Know JESUS - Know PEACE."

No one whom I call a friend would ever say black lives don't matter. All lives matter to God. The trouble with groups like BLM is that their riotous and violent methods are not doing anything to unite this country. They actually only push us further apart. BLM is no better than Richard Spencer's racist alt-right Nazis. Instead of taking a cue from Jesus and Dr. King, the Black Lives Matter activists burn down buildings, vandalize property, assault anyone who disagrees, and clash with police. Their desired end does not justify their means in any way, shape, or form.

The Black Lives Matter movement actually isn't about "black lives" at all. They're a radical left-wing group, who use race as an excuse to push divisive demonic agendas. They support the BDS (Boycott, Divestment, and Sanctions) movement, which supports Palestinian terror against Israel and is for the destruction of the Jewish State. Their Mission Statement states their commitment to "disrupting the nuclear family structure." So, they are against the Biblical model for family - Father (Husband), Mother (Wife), and children. Meanwhile, fatherless homes and abortion happen to be two of the biggest reasons why inner-city black communities have seen so much crime. Yet, BLM *supports both*. They also push the radical LGBT agenda, by "fostering a queer-affirming network."

BLM keeps racism alive and well in this country, as they put blacks into their own category - just like the KKK puts whites in their own category. This should not be so. If they truly wanted all people to be equal, in order to make MLK's dream a reality, then they would stop alienating themselves as "others." As I previously stated, the LORD doesn't see any of us in color! So, why then do we focus so much on the shades of our skin? If you're a Bible believer, you're my brother or sister. The complexion of your skin has no bearing on that whatsoever. Sadly, in a Biblically-illiterate nation and world, not everyone thinks like I do; and not everyone knows our God. Thus, there will always be racists until our Lord comes back down. It is an unfortunate reality.

We Christians cannot change every heart in this world, but we should be placing our focus on the ones we can. Our God is Love. There is no hate in Him. Hate is of Satan. Racism is the epitome of hatred. If we ever want to begin eradicating racism, we need to stop giving a platform to the race-baiters. The lamestream media needs to focus much less on dividers like Richard Spencer or Al Sharpton, and turn their attention to the one true *Uniter* - the Lord Jesus Christ. Everyone needs to stop with the White Pride, Black Pride, Spanish Pride, and every other "Pride"! Because, like hate, pride is of the devil.

As believers, we are all only *one color* in God's sight - RED. That's the color of His Son's sinless Blood - that was shed *for all* on Calvary's Cross, regardless of your skin color. The same Holy Blood that washes, cleanses, covers, and saves me, does the exact same for you. So, let us begin to see one another as our Heavenly Father sees us - as *Family*. We're brothers and sisters in Christ, so let's start acting like it. And when it comes to radical mobs trying to force others to "take a knee" or affirm that just one certain race matters today, we Christians must live by my "only" motto:

> Only bow to the LORD.
> Only kneel to Jesus Christ.
> Only affirm that God is good.

FOR YE ARE ALL THE CHILDREN OF GOD BY FAITH IN CHRIST JESUS. FOR AS MANY OF YOU AS HAVE BEEN BAPTIZED INTO CHRIST HAVE PUT ON CHRIST. THERE IS NEITHER JEW NOR GREEK, NEITHER BOND NOR FREE, NEITHER MALE NOR FEMALE: FOR YE ARE ALL ONE IN CHRIST JESUS.

- GALATIANS 3:26-28

CHAPTER FIVE

HISTORIC WILDFIRES

THE FIRE DEVOURED THE PASTURES OF THE WILDERNESS,
AND THE FLAME BURNED ALL THE TREES OF THE FIELD.

- JOEL 1:19

THE SECULAR MAINSTREAM MEDIA news outlets had found it difficult to describe the historic wildfire outbreaks of 2017-2018 without using Biblical phrases depicting the End Times. Some of the headlines catching my eye were: *Apocalyptic - Armageddon is on - Hell on Earth - Is the World Ending or Something?* Not one of these headlines came from Bible-based news sites, but were all found on secular news sites that are normally known for mocking God. The LORD certainly has His way of getting the attention of even the most hardened skeptics.

While most "Last Days" scoffers say that there have *always* been wildfires in California, outbreaks of the past two years were dubbed as unusual, unprecedented, the deadliest, the largest, and most destructive in State history. While wildfires are common in the States of Alaska, Arizona, California, Florida, Georgia, Idaho, Kansas, Mississippi, Missouri, Montana, Nevada, North Carolina, Oklahoma, Oregon, South Dakota, Texas, and Washington, some of the absolute worst in U.S. history have occurred only in *our generation*. 7 out of 9, or 77.7%, of this country's worst wildfires since 1900 have come within the past fifteen years. I am sure that many of you who read my last book just got goosebumps when seeing that percentage.

As I explained in *The Signs of Our Times*, 777 is attributed to our God and Father in Heaven, YHWH, for so many reasons. It is also attributed to His Father/Son relationship with our Lord Jesus Christ. Whenever I see the number 777, I know that God's Hand is at work. The fact that this number popped up so many times, in relation to rare events that have been occurring in our lifetimes - especially within the last two decades - leads me to suspect that YHWH's Son is at the gates and ready to make His return. Come quickly Lord Jesus. Maranatha!

The top seven worst years for wildfires, since 1980, have all come after 2007. They were 2007, 2008, 2011, 2012, 2015, 2017, and 2018. Anyone else notice the correlation between the years that the United States began turning away from God (more than ever before) and the years wildfires got worse? Like other historic disasters that have recently devastated the USA, you can directly connect the time frame of America's falling away from the LORD to the worst wildfires in our nation's history. And it is not climate change, though Godless liberals would like you to believe it is. In reality, it's God's judgment. It is the consequence of rejecting His Word, forgetting His Laws, and widespread blasphemy.

Both 2017 and 2018 greatly eclipsed this decade's average of 6-million acres burned per year. Roughly 10-million acres of land had been burned across the U.S., and over 2-million acres burned in California alone. In the fall of 2017, there were about a dozen wildfires burning out of control in California. Tens of thousands were evacuated, and thousands of structures were destroyed. Two of the State's largest fires, "Tubbs" and "Atlas," burned an area of wine country 3-times larger than Washington, DC. At their peak, the wildfires were advancing at a rate of more than a football field "every three seconds." A State of Emergency had been declared in affected counties, and President Donald Trump had declared a Major Disaster in the State.

Significant damage was done to at least a dozen wineries, and seven pot farms were completely destroyed. Alcohol and drug use are consistently condemned in God's Word, so I don't believe that these locations were burned by chance. In 2018, Cali experienced its most destructive wildfire outbreak on record. Close to 20 fires burned across the State during the summer. The biggest of them, "Mendocino Complex Fire," became the largest wildfire in State history. The blaze consisted of two fires, the "Ranch" and "River" fires, in northern California. The flames had burned over 450,000 acres. At the same time, the "Carr Fire" burned 230,000 acres in Redding, California.

A record-breaking *Flame Tornado*, dubbed the "Fire Whirl," had sprung up near Redding. The tornado was measured as an F-3 - virtually unheard of in California. The State had not recorded a tornado of that strength in 40 years. President Trump declared a Major Disaster in the State once again. A few months later, in the fall of 2018, the next wildfire outbreak was described in headlines as "Hell on Earth." It consisted of three large fires - "Camp, Hill, and Woolsey." The fast-moving blazes caused evacuations of tens of thousands in north and south Cali, including the home city of Godless celebrities - Malibu. Numerous celebrity homes had been damaged or destroyed, including the home of Miley Cyrus.

The "Camp Fire" in northern California had literally burned Paradise to the ground. The town was home to 30,000 people. Cal Fire Captain Scott McLean said, "The community of Paradise is destroyed, it's that kind of devastation." Thousands of homes and businesses were destroyed and a State of Emergency was declared for Butte County where Paradise was located. The fire had grown uncontrollably, at a rate of "80 football fields every minute." The inferno scorched over 150,000 acres, and it became the deadliest and most destructive fire in State history.

The other two fires had been sparked in Ventura County. The "Hill Fire" originated about 10 miles northwest from the scene of a mass shooting that occurred just one night earlier in the city of Thousand Oaks. The raging flames rolled down the hills and over the 101 Freeway, which had prompted mandatory evacuations for Cal State University campus. The "Woolsey Fire" was sparked at Woolsey Canyon, and burned across the counties of Ventura and Los Angeles. The fire caused authorities to order the mandatory evacuation of the entire city of Malibu. 100,000 acres of land had been burned, and over 1500 homes were destroyed in the blaze.

I believe that Paradise being destroyed in Cali was symbolic. As a majority of the State have turned their backs on the God of gods, how can we be shocked that *Paradise* was taken away from them and their State was turned into a literal *Hell*? And one night after a mass shooting in the State, when many liberals said, "We don't need prayer - We need gun control," they found themselves in desperate need of prayers. The Hill Fire raged just ten miles from the site of that shooting. Poetic justice? It is unfortunate that today's lefties want absolutely nothing to do with God, until He literally brings *Hell on Earth* to their doorsteps. Then they are all about "thoughts and prayers." Well, at least some seemed to be.

Others had lashed out at the LORD for bringing the overdue judgments upon California. The heathen dwelling on the earth in the Book of Revelation mirror this Godless generation perfectly. John prophesied that during the seven-year Tribulation, instead of repenting when the LORD's judgments fall, inhabitants of Earth will blaspheme His Name and curse Him! This generation is the first in American history to seemingly *fulfill* these unimaginable prophecies. God help us.

Too many liberals attribute the record-breaking disasters that America has experienced, throughout the past decade, to a ticked off "Mother Nature." By doing so, they only anger Father YHWH all the more. There is no such thing as Mother Nature! The Father alone is the Author of rare, historic, and unnatural weather we've experienced. It's not *global warming,* and not *climate change.* It's the work of a God who makes the impossible possible, who does whatever He wants - whenever He wants - and who never leaves the wicked unpunished. Articles I had penned about California's wildfires on my website, *BiblicalSigns.com*, were widely mocked by faithless leftists; because I attributed them all to His judgment upon the most Godless State in our Union.

Libs believe that the historic fires in Cali were all randomly caused by climate change, and that they had absolutely nothing to do with Californians breaking just about every Law in God's Holy Book. Well, to all who mocked me for calling it the long overdue judgment of God upon the modern-day Sodom and Gomorrah of our nation: I do not think it is a coincidence that the deadliest, the most destructive, and largest wildfires in the history of California had all occurred in the *exact same year* that the State government attempted to BAN THE BIBLE. How can anyone, believer or not, ignore that undeniable connection?

In my previous book, I warned that California was at the top of the list for coming judgments of the LORD; and I do not take pleasure in saying that I told you so. I wish that all of the heathen in Cali would repent and return to their Maker. He doesn't want to judge them anymore than I want to see them hurt or lose their homes. But the sad and simple fact is that they've made their bed, and now they have to lie in it. I also said in my first book that it is our *sins* causing weather disasters on the earth, and not polluting or failing to recycle. I shared verses from Isaiah in order to prove my statement. I want to share them again in this book, because it is a message that California and many Americans still desperately need to hear today -

"THE EARTH IS DEFILED UNDER THE INHABITANTS THEREOF; BECAUSE THEY HAVE TRANSGRESSED THE LAWS, CHANGED

THE ORDINANCE, BROKEN THE EVERLASTING COVENANT. THEREFORE HATH THE CURSE DEVOURED THE EARTH, AND THEY THAT DWELL THEREIN ARE DESOLATE: THEREFORE THE INHABITANTS OF THE EARTH ARE BURNED." - ISAIAH 24:5-6

Until Californians learn to repent of their Godless ways, their State will continue to burn year after year. They have brought a curse upon their land, and have forgotten the God of our fathers - through whom all blessings flow. Thus, the recent headlines were correct in describing California resembling "Hell on Earth." It is God's Word coming to pass before our eyes. As Californians live like hellions, God turns their State into living *Hell* (Psalms 9:17). Unfortunately, Cali is far from alone. There are many other States across this nation awaiting judgment if they refuse to repent and return to Him. America, it's high time to return to God. REPENT and return to the LORD... before it's too late.

2020 UPDATE

In 2020, five wildfires were added to the list of the Top 10 largest fires in the history of California. Four of them broke the top five! The August Complex Fire eclipsed the Mendocino Complex Fire of 2018 as the largest in State history. It burned over one-million acres. The over 4-million acres burned across Cali and 10-million acres burned nationally in 2020, were the most acreage burned in a single year since record-keeping began over a half-century ago.

I WILL KINDLE A FIRE IN THE FOREST THEREOF... IT SHALL DEVOUR ALL THINGS ROUND ABOUT IT, SAITH THE LORD.

- JEREMIAH 21:14

CHAPTER SIX

PESTILENCES

JESUS SAID, THERE SHALL BE... PESTILENCES.

- MATTHEW 24:7 & LUKE 21:11

IN RECENT YEARS, HEALTH experts from numerous countries have issued warnings that the human race is at a greater risk of experiencing a global pandemic than ever before. They also warn that we're currently ill-prepared to combat a worldwide outbreak. Experts are in agreement, across the board, that it is not a matter of *if* a pandemic will strike but a matter of *when*. An outbreak of SARS, cholera, bird flu, swine flu, Ebola, bioterror, or brand new disease altogether, could kill millions. During 2014-2016's Ebola epidemic, nearly 30,000 people were infected and about one-third of them had died from the disease.

We're at greater risk of witnessing a worldwide plague than at any other time in history due to numerous factors - global travel, growing population, immigration, weather, and terrorism (just to name a few). The fact that the population of the U.S. had grown by leaps and bounds during the Obama years, due to an influx of refugees from the Middle East, means the possibility of a national pandemic has greatly increased. The immigrants pouring in from disease-prone Syria, and Mexico, are prime candidates for being carriers that could bring the next pandemic to America.

It is believed that, within 30 years, nearly 70% of the world's population will live in urban areas rather than less populated rural areas. In cities, interacting with thousands who could possibly be infected increases the chance of contracting disease. City-life also greatly increases the chance for disease to spread quickly, through something as simple as a touch, a cough, a kiss, or a bite. While many of the coming deadly diseases will most likely not originate in the USA, the easiest way they can arrive here is through global travel. Countries like Africa, or Middle East war zones like Syria, are breeding grounds for deadly diseases. An outbreak that begins on the other side of the globe will eventually make its way *here*.

That is exactly what happened with the Ebola pandemic. The disease, which spread rapidly in foreign nations, was undetectable for a few days. So, Americans traveling home from infected areas did not know that they had contracted the disease until they were back on U.S. soil. Luckily, the infected were quarantined and the deadly disease didn't spread as much as it could have. Experts say infectious agents can live in humans during the incubation period - which is the time between infection and the onset of symptoms. This means travelers can transmit an infection to another country before any onset of appearance of sickness. Billions of travelers crisscross the globe annually.

The SARS (Severe Acute Respiratory Syndrome) pandemic of 2003 began through Dr. Liu Jianlun, who developed symptoms of the airborne virus on a trip to China and then went to visit his family in Hong Kong. It is believed that he infected people at his hotel, along with family. In less than 4 months, nearly 4,000 cases and 550 deaths from SARS were traced to Liu's Hong Kong visit. More than 8,000 people became infected and nearly 800 had died, in more than 30 countries worldwide, because of just *one man*.

Country to country infections can be spread through insects and animals. Air travelers became infected with malaria through mosquitoes hitching rides on planes. In 2004, bird flu had crossed borders when Thai eagles had been traded as pets. A year earlier, Guinea rats that were carrying monkeypox were shipped as pets into the USA. The 2009 H1N1 outbreak began in Mexico and had originated from pigs. That pandemic infected at least 60-million Americans, and killed around 12,000. Nearly 600,000 ultimately died from the disease globally.

Another big threat is bioterror. A genetically engineered virus is easier to make than a suicide bomb, and it could kill far more people than any bomb, gun, or even a nuclear weapon. ISIS and Al-Qaeda terror groups, both desiring America's downfall, have made clear their intentions to use bioterrorism against the United States. Instead of suicide vests or running into military complexes with guns-a-blazing, a terrorist could easily weaponize a disease for a suicide bioterror attack by exposing themself to a virus. All they would have to do is enter a crowded airport, subway, arena, or heavily populated building, and touch everyone they could.

This form of terrorism kills far more people than any suicide bomb attack because the perpetrator claims more victims after the disease is spread. This is one of the most disturbing scenarios of a global pandemic that I can imagine. Sadly, it's the most probable. A Naval War College professor, Captain Al Shimkus, told *Forbes*, "If ISIS ever wanted to send half a dozen of their operatives into an outbreak region and intentionally expose themselves to a virus, they very well could. The idea is that once they have intentionally infected themselves, they'd try to interact with as many people in their target city." ISIS leaders have said their fighters are willing to sacrifice themselves by spreading a virus like Ebola.

A bipartisan Congressional report accused the administration of former President George W. Bush of doing too little to address the threat of bioterror. And during Barack Obama's presidency, a Congressional panel gave his government an "F" in preparedness. Sources from the U.S. Border Patrol revealed that their agents had detained at least a dozen ISIS fighters at the U.S.-Mexican border during the Obama years.

Another factor that contributes to the risk of an outbreak is weather. Flooding events, in particular, greatly increase chances for waterborne diseases and disease vectors like mosquitoes. With mosquitoes able to live in new unprotected territories, the risk of an outbreak is high. With the recent flooding from hurricanes like Harvey, Florence, and Michael, there could be numerous diseases spreading across the USA as we speak. Mosquitoes brought Zika virus to America. In 2017, they'd carried it into over 125 cities in California. The Public Health Division of Communicable Disease Control laboratory-confirmed 530 cases of Zika infections there.

The experts agree that an uncontrolled pandemic or bioterror attack could result in the deaths of about 30-million people. They say that if another outbreak of a deadly disease were to occur, the nations of the world are "grossly unprepared." Now, I know this may all sound frightening and is very scary to ponder; but even if a global pandemic were to occur, there is one sure way to keep yourself and your family safe - FAITH. Even if this whole nation and world experience a plague unrivaled in history, believers can take heart that the LORD will keep us far from it. Read Psalms 91:3 - "Surely He shall deliver you from the noisome pestilence," and 91:6 - "We shall not fear pestilence that walks in darkness."

I like to think back to Exodus, and God's promise to "pass over" His people when the plagues came upon Egypt. Believers today are living in a modern-day Egypt/Babylon, and I believe the LORD's age-old promises ring just as true for His children today as they did for the Jews. Instead of marking the doorposts of our homes with the blood of a lamb though, we can now symbolically cover our doorposts and homes in the Blood of the *Lamb of God* - Christ Jesus. If God passed over His people when they'd marked their homes in the blood of a mere animal, how much more will

He now pass over us as we mark our homes in the holiest blood ever poured out on Earth - the Blood of His only begotten Son?

I mark my home in the Blood of Jesus during every Passover feast, and He's kept His promise to keep the destroyer, the spoiler, plagues, disaster, and every evil, far away from my home. He will do the same for you when you dedicate your home to Him, mark it in the Blood of His Son, and believe *by faith*. There is no global plague that can ever claim the life of a believer if we put our trust in God's Word, repent of sin, and diligently seek Him in times of national or personal distress. Here are some of the Biblical verses that I take heart in -

"AND THE BLOOD (OF THE LAMB) SHALL BE TO YOU FOR A TOKEN UPON THE HOUSES WHERE YE ARE: AND WHEN I SEE THE BLOOD, I WILL PASS OVER YOU, AND THE PLAGUE SHALL NOT BE UPON YOU TO DESTROY YOU, WHEN I SMITE THE LAND OF EGYPT, SAITH THE LORD." - EXODUS 12:13

"IF THOU WILT DILIGENTLY HEARKEN TO THE VOICE OF THE LORD THY GOD, AND DO THAT WHICH IS RIGHT IN HIS SIGHT, AND WILT GIVE EAR TO HIS COMMANDMENTS, AND KEEP ALL HIS STATUTES, I WILL PUT NONE OF THESE DISEASES UPON THEE, WHICH I HAVE BROUGHT UPON THE EGYPTIANS: FOR I AM THE LORD THAT HEALETH THEE." - EXODUS 15:26

"YE SHALL SERVE THE LORD YOUR GOD, AND HE SHALL BLESS THY BREAD, AND THY WATER; AND I WILL TAKE SICKNESS AWAY FROM THE MIDST OF THEE." - EXODUS 23:25

"THE LORD WILL TAKE AWAY FROM THEE ALL SICKNESS, AND WILL PUT NONE OF THE EVIL DISEASES OF EGYPT, WHICH THOU KNOWEST, UPON THEE." - DEUTERONOMY 7:15

"HE WAS WOUNDED FOR OUR TRANSGRESSIONS, AND HE WAS BRUISED FOR OUR INIQUITIES: THE CHASTISEMENT OF OUR

PEACE WAS UPON HIM; AND WITH HIS STRIPES WE ARE HEALED." – ISAIAH 53:5

"THE PRAYER OF FAITH SHALL SAVE THE SICK; AND THE LORD SHALL RAISE HIM UP." – JAMES 5:15

"WHO HIS OWN SELF (JESUS CHRIST) BARE OUR SINS IN HIS OWN BODY ON THE TREE, THAT WE, BEING DEAD TO SINS, SHOULD LIVE UNTO RIGHTEOUSNESS: BY WHOSE STRIPES YE WERE HEALED." – IST PETER 2:24

Jesus told us that in the season of His imminent return there'd be *pestilences*. We've seen them popping up more and more over the course of the past decade, and I suspect that they'll only grow worse leading up to His Second Coming. I thank God that we true Bible believers will be raptured before the plagues of the Book of Revelation befall the heathen on Earth.

With so many other "Last Days" signs occurring around us in this generation, I am convinced that a national pandemic or global outbreak could begin any day now in the near future. Since a lot of people in this world are falling away from Biblical Faith, fear and panic will grip the hearts of so many across the globe. While most of the secular world will be seeking out every vaccine under the sun to protect themselves from plagues, believers must follow prescriptions given unto us by our Heavenly Physician. He's said that if we want to live healthy and safe, and stay healthy and safe, then we need to -

- Have faith.

- Love the LORD with all of our hearts, souls, and minds.

- Keep His Commandments.

- Repent of our sins.

- Get washed and covered in the Blood of Jesus Christ.

- Pray without ceasing.

- Trust in the LORD.

Whether it be a physical or spiritual illness, there is no better medicine in the world for all that ails the human race than faith in God. If you don't have it, then you would be wise to FIND IT.

I LOOKED, AND BEHOLD A PALE HORSE: AND HIS NAME THAT SAT ON HIM WAS DEATH, AND HELL FOLLOWED WITH HIM. AND POWER WAS GIVEN UNTO THEM OVER THE FOURTH PART OF THE EARTH, TO KILL WITH SWORD, AND WITH HUNGER, AND WITH DEATH, AND WITH THE BEASTS OF THE EARTH.

- REVELATION 6:8

2020 UPDATE

CORONAVIRUS PANDEMIC

LESS THAN A YEAR after I had published this book, the world experienced much of what I wrote about in this chapter. Now, I'm no prophet. I simply believe every prophecy of the Bible, and that is why I feel the Holy Spirit led me to write these books - because the LORD needs someone to alert the world as to what is coming on the horizon. The question you all need to ask is... if I was right about the global pandemic, prophesied in the Gospels about 2,000 years ago, then *what else* could I be right about?

America (and virtually every other country of the world) was on lockdown for months during Coronavirus (COVID-19). It felt like living out an End Times film about the Apocalypse. Actually, many who don't read the Bible believed it *was* the Apocalypse. It was not. It was just one of many pestilences that Lord Jesus said would come in the days leading up to the Rapture and His return. As I predicted in this chapter, the virus began on the other side of the world (China) and had made its way into America and the rest of the world through global travel. As I also predicted, it sparked great fear in unbelievers - hopefully leading to their salvation!

The pandemic left about 2-million dead globally, with 20% of those deaths in the United States, and about 100-million had been infected around the world. Many say that it's a once-in-a-lifetime event, but my Holy Bible says that THEY ARE WRONG.

CHAPTER SEVEN

WARS AND RUMOURS OF WARS

JESUS SAID, YE SHALL HEAR OF WARS AND RUMOURS OF
WARS: SEE THAT YE BE NOT TROUBLED: FOR ALL THESE
THINGS MUST COME TO PASS, BUT THE END IS NOT YET.

- MATTHEW 24:6/MARK 13:17/LUKE 21:9

THERE ARE MANY UNBELIEVERS who mock Bible Prophecy. One of the things you will hear them say most often is that "there have *always* been wars." While there most certainly have, going back all the way to the days of Abraham (if not earlier), the wars which Jesus had prophesied could only take place after 1948. As I explained in great detail in the first book, that all-important year started the clock on the season of the Rapture. '48 was the year of the biggest prophecy fulfillment since Christ left the earth nearly 2,000 years ago - the rebirth of the Nation of Israel. Without the Jewish State present on the world scene, none of the Holy Bible's "Last Days" prophecies could ever be fulfilled. A reborn Israel is absolutely central to Jesus coming back. It is where He returns!

Not to mention, after He defeats Antichrist and Satan - who come against Israel in the end - it is the Jewish State's Capital of Jerusalem where He will rule and reign from! In a nutshell, what all of this means is that every single war prior to '48 could not be a sign of the End Times. That includes World Wars 1 and 2. They meant nothing concerning Christ's return; but World War 3 *will*. It will be the war to end all wars, and is known to Bible believers as the Battle of Armageddon. The war will be staged in Megiddo in Israel's Jezreel Valley. Virtually all nations of this world will come against God's chosen Nation. When all hope seems lost for Israel, and destruction seems imminent, that's when their Messiah will make His long-awaited return to destroy their every enemy.

Of course, their Messiah is our Lord Jesus Christ; and the war will be the culmination of the seven-year Tribulation on the earth. It is the Antichrist who leads the charge against the Jewish State. Being Satan incarnate, he'll actually attempt to fight Jesus; but he will be swiftly defeated and cast into the *lake of fire* (Revelation 19). Bible-believing Christians will not be here for the seven-year Tribulation, and will be raptured long before Armageddon begins. I believe the wars that Jesus referred to in Matthew 24, Mark 13, and Luke 21, are all wars post-1948 - especially the future Psalm 83 and Gog-Magog wars. The Psalm 83 battle is obviously found in Psalm 83, while Gog-Magog is described in Ezekiel 38-39.

Both wars, like the Battle of Armageddon, are the attempts by ungodly nations of the world to obliterate the Nation of Israel. We read in Psalm 83:4-5, "They have said, Come, and let us cut them off from being a nation; that the name of Israel may be no more in remembrance. For they have consulted together with one consent: they are confederate against you." The last phrase is referring to all Islamic nations mentioned in the Psalm forming a confederacy to make war on the Jewish State. This confederacy will resemble the group of nations that came against Israel in the Six-Day War of 1967. Though, in the Psalm 83 War, Muslim nations bordering Israel will be joined by virtually *all* of the Islamic nations in the Middle East and Africa.

Just like in 1967, the Bible tells us that they will fail and that Israel will have another miraculous military victory. I suspect the defeat of the Muslim armies will lead to those nations crying out to Russia, who is allied with Israel's enemies in the Middle East, and this will lead to the Gog-Magog War. I'd written a good deal about the war in my previous book, so I refer you to the "Enemies of Israel" chapter in *The Signs of Our Times* if you haven't read it already. It'll give you a better knowledge of the war going further. Since I don't want to repeat all I'd covered in the first book, I will just touch on a few key points about the war for anyone who has not yet read it.

I explained why "Gog" is the leader of Russia, and "Magog" is derived from "Magogites," who dwelt in what is today Russia. I connected the other names that were found in Ezekiel's prophecy - "Meshech, Tubal, and Rosh" - to Russia as well. This is why it's undeniable that the largest nation in the world will someday lead the second largest war against the Nation of Israel. Who knows, if Antichrist comes from Russia, the Eurasian superpower may lead the Battle of Armageddon too. Believers will be raptured before Antichrist reveals himself, so we can only speculate about who it could be. I do believe he is alive now and waiting in the wings.

In the first book, I pointed out how Russia is currently closely allied with *exact* nations that Ezekiel prophesied it would be. Iran (Persia) and Turkey (Togarmah) are two of Russia's closest allies in the world. Ezekiel said they'd be the two closest confederates of Russia. His 2,600-year-old prophecy is fulfilled before our very eyes. Gog-Magog will be fought on the mountains of Israel. This would most likely be on the border of Syria in the Golan Heights region. It is very interesting that Russia has military boots on the ground in the Heights *right now* to protect their interests in Syria.

It is not far-fetched to think that a flare-up between the IDF (Israel Defense Forces) and the Syrian army could claim lives of Russians stationed in the area. That could provoke Vladimir Putin of Russia to consider military action against Israel. Russia's made numerous public threats against Israel over the course of the past decade, which leads me to believe that the Gog-Magog War is at the doors. In 2012, Russia warned that an Israeli attack on Tehran (Iran's Capital) would be an attack on Moscow (Russia's Capital). The threat implied that any war between the Israelis and Iranians would lead to the Russians fighting alongside Iran, just as Ezekiel prophesied they would. It's no secret that Turkey's President hates Israel, so it is easy to envision the Turks joining forces with them.

Putin has allied Russia with virtually all enemies of Israel. He has sent an abundance of high-powered weaponry to Iran and has held joint military exercises with them. Putin's military protection of Syria's brutal dictator Assad hasn't just caused deadly chaos in the Middle East region as a whole, but it is in direct opposition to Israeli and U.S. forces on the ground and in the air. Russia fights alongside Iran in Syria's Civil War. Israel recently discovered that Russia has placed surface-to-surface ballistic missiles in northern Syria. The two SS-26 Iskander missiles are vehicle-mounted with launchers capable of carrying nuclear warheads, and their range is 300 miles. Israel is only 50 miles away.

Given all the facts on the ground, it is impossible to deny that the wick of the powderkeg has been lit that could explode into the Gog-Magog War. Vladimir Putin seems to always be itching to go to war, and His regime possesses the most nuclear weapons in the world - even more than the USA. In 2017, Russia had about 2,000 nuclear warheads. It's estimated that they currently possess about 4,400 of them! With America allied with Israel, and the Russians with the Jewish State's enemies, it is inevitable that the U.S. will see war with Russia in the not too distant future.

In 2017, Putin was furious when America's President, Donald Trump, gave the order for two U.S. Navy Destroyers to bombard and destroy a Syrian air base with 60 Tomahawk cruise missiles. The strike had been in response to a chemical weapons attack by the Assad regime in NW Syria, which had left dozens of civilians dead. Not long after, a former spokesman for the Russian Defense Ministry revealed that Russia buried nuclear bombs off the coasts of the USA. Colonel Viktor Baranetz said that the "mole nukes" would be used to trigger a tsunami which could drown major U.S. cities. He explained, "While the Americans deploy tanks, planes, and special forces battalions along Russia's border, we are quietly seeding the U.S. shoreline with nuclear mole missiles."

He said, "They dig themselves into the ocean floor, and they will sleep until given a command to detonate. Oh, it seems that I have said too much, I should hold my tongue." Baranetz claimed that there is no computer technology that can pinpoint location or calculate trajectory of the Russian nuclear warheads. If his claims are true, major U.S. cities such as New York, Boston, and Miami could be devastated by a historic tsunami when the nuclear bombs are detonated. He said the bombs are aligned in a chain to cause a "massive tidal wave" when they are detonated together. Some of America's most populated coastal cities are sitting ducks if such an unconventional attack were to ever be carried out.

Foreign Policy experts believe Russia will employ numerous methods of war against the United States before ever engaging in all-out nuclear war. Their current methods include cyber-attacks, EMP attacks, and the nuclear tsunami option. Russian ships have been spotted off American coasts for years. Iran, during Obama's administration, parked warships off our East Coast many times. I wrote a lot about Iran, and their hatred for Israel, in the previous book. So, as with Russia, I don't want to repeat too much of what I already wrote. Please make sure to read *The Signs of Our Times* to get all of the vital information that has led me to believe we are truly the Rapture generation.

In 2017, a senior commander of Iran's Revolutionary Guards said, "Over one hundred thousand missiles located all across the Middle East are ready to strike Israel at a moment's notice." The leaders of Iran have long called for the destruction of the Jewish State - from their Supreme Leader to the President, and right on down the line. They all desire Israel to be "wiped off of the map."

In a 2018 video of the Revolutionary Guard Corps' military drills, the soldiers chanted "Death to Israel" and "Death to America" as a depiction of the White House and the Star of David were being split by a sword.

Besides Russia and Iran, Israelis could much sooner see a war with the Hamas terrorists in Palestine's Gaza Strip and Hezbollah terrorists in Lebanon. In the 2014 war with Hamas, 5,000 rockets were fired into Israel. In the 2006 war with Hezbollah, Israel had 4,000 of them launched into the Jewish State. For more about the threats that Israel has faced, is facing, and will face in the future, go and read the first book.

Finally, I can't write about *rumours of wars* and not mention North Korea. Currently, the dictator of the country, Kim Jong-un, has actually been playing nice. Since his 2018 Summit with U.S. President Trump, many believe that he is genuine in his pledge to destroy his nuclear weapons in exchange for peace and security for his country. Given the history of North Korea, I am not buying it. With how much of a threat that NK has posed throughout the past few decades, you'd think they'd be mentioned in the Bible. By name, they are not. That's because there was no nation known by that name when the Bible was written. Though, North Korea could be alluded to, along with China, in the Book of Revelation.

In Chapter 16, verse 13, we read "kings of the east" - though some translations read as "kings of the rising sun." I suspect this verse refers to China - the most powerful oriental nation. They're closely aligned with Russia and Iran in a Eurasian Union today. It is likely that the verse is also referring to other Asian nations, as it says "kings" (plural). If it does mean more than one Asian nation, then North Korea is certainly a prime candidate. After all, China's long been one of the few allies that North Korea has in this world. It is also hard to imagine a nuclear war without the trigger-happy North Korean regime being involved.

If the current nuclear talks with Kim Jong-un and the United States were to break down, there is no doubt that he would return to his old threatening ways. Before the Summit with Trump, the leader said his country was on the "brink of war." I highly doubt that North Korea will keep their promises to destroy their nuclear arsenal. They possess at least eight nuclear weapons as I pen this.

Americans laughed at Kim Jong un's failed missile launches for years. But in 2017, as his missiles began to fly much higher - much farther - and for much longer - we began to take the threat a lot more seriously. Missile experts said that Kim's missiles were coming dangerously close to putting major U.S. cities within their range. North Korea's ICBMs (Intercontinental Ballistic Missiles) were already capable of reaching Alaska, Hawaii, and California. Some experts went so far as to say that America's most populated cities, like Boston, Chicago, Denver, Los Angeles, and New York, were *already* within range of NK missiles. In 2017 alone, North Korea launched 14 missiles - equivalent to 2 missiles per month.

Besides the threat of nuclear attack, America currently faces an even greater possibility of falling victim to an EMP attack. An EMP (Electromagnetic Pulse) attack can fry the U.S. power grid, leaving one-quarter to one-half of the USA in complete darkness. We'd return to the Stone Age. EMP is a burst of electromagnetic energy, most known for being emitted from the Sun. Today, it can be man-made. And while EMP warfare is not as devastating as a nuclear attack initially, it proves to be just as deadly over time and much harder to defend against. North Korea has two satellites that are orbiting over America, and they are capable of performing a surprise EMP attack at an altitude and trajectory evading National Missile Defenses.

National Security expert, Peter Vincent Pry, warns that North Korean satellites can be commanded to deorbit to hit a target on the ground, or to explode at a high altitude. Both scenarios would create an EMP effect, knocking out our nation's grid and critical infrastructures that depend on it. By exploding a nuclear warhead in space, within 300 miles above a major city, a blackout of much of America's power grid would ensue after the blast mingles with the magnetic field. I'm sure that you will all be very comforted to know (sarcasm intended), though the Obama administration had been put on high alert to the threat, our grid has been defenseless against such an attack. A powerful Solar Flare from the Sun, or a terror attack, could fry our power grid the very day you read this.

Thankfully, Trump's administration has taken the threat more seriously; but there's still much more action that needs to be taken by the U.S. government to ever defend against such a catastrophe. The North Korean satellites orbit at an altitude of 300 miles, with trajectories that put them over America *daily*. At that altitude, an EMP can impact much of the continental United States, according to EMP experts. Last year, the *Washington Examiner* had reported that NK doesn't plan to give up its nuclear arsenal. Sources close to Jong-un's Communist regime revealed there are plans in place to use the weapons to launch EMP attacks in the near future.

We all take electricity for granted in today's day and age. Our cell phones, television, heating, air conditioning, and refrigerators would all be *useless* after an EMP attack. That is why the experts warn it's the "biggest existential threat that our civilization faces." Homeland Security says an attack on our grid is coming, and that it's not a matter of *if,* but *when.* A Commission of Congress that assesses the threat has said such an attack could wipe out 90% of the population within two years, as a result of disease, scarcity of food, and a complete breakdown of society. How inconvenient is losing electricity for a day or two? Now, think of being without it for months to years! This whole chapter may be scary to ponder, but just know that we are raptured before *the worst* of it begins.

THUS SAITH THE LORD GOD, THOU (GOG) SHALT COME FROM
THY PLACE OUT OF THE NORTH PARTS, THOU, AND MANY
PEOPLE WITH THEE, ALL OF THEM RIDING UPON HORSES, A
GREAT COMPANY, AND A MIGHTY ARMY: AND THOU SHALT
COME UP AGAINST MY PEOPLE OF ISRAEL, AS A CLOUD TO
COVER THE LAND; IT SHALL BE IN THE LATTER DAYS.

- EZEKIEL 38:15-16

CHAPTER EIGHT

"2ND TIMOTHY 3" GENERATION

THIS KNOW ALSO, THAT IN THE LAST DAYS PERILOUS TIMES
SHALL COME. FOR MEN SHALL BE LOVERS OF THEIR OWN
SELVES, COVETOUS, BOASTERS, PROUD, BLASPHEMERS,
DISOBEDIENT TO PARENTS, UNTHANKFUL, UNHOLY,
WITHOUT NATURAL AFFECTION, TRUCEBREAKERS, FALSE
ACCUSERS, INCONTINENT, FIERCE, DESPISERS OF THOSE THAT
ARE GOOD, TRAITORS, HEADY, HIGHMINDED, LOVERS OF
PLEASURES MORE THAN LOVERS OF GOD; HAVING A FORM OF
GODLINESS, BUT DENYING THE POWER THEREOF: FROM SUCH
TURN AWAY... YEA, AND ALL THAT WILL LIVE GODLY IN
CHRIST JESUS SHALL SUFFER PERSECUTION.

- 2ND TIMOTHY 3:1-5 & 12

WHEN IT COMES TO signs of the Rapture and imminent return of Lord Jesus, there are certain Books and Chapters of the Bible that always come to mind. Matthew 24, Luke 17 & 21, Mark 13, Revelation, Daniel, Ezekiel, and Joel, top the list of any Prophecy enthusiast. But you'll find one of the most thorough and detailed Chapters about the Last Days in a very unlikely place - within the letters of Saint Paul.

Paul's Epistles are widely regarded as the foundation for our theology and ethics. His teachings reinforce or expand upon Lord Jesus' teachings, and help us blossom into the believers that God wants us to be. If you are part of a church that doesn't preach the Old Testament, chances are a majority of the pastor's sermons or studies are about Paul's life or teachings from Acts and Romans. Most pastors who teach solely from Acts and the writings of Paul, choosing to omit the rest of God's Word, do so because they don't care about Biblical Prophecy. They want to teach how you can be a better Christian *today,* and are not the least bit concerned with Christ coming back *tomorrow.*

Today, far too many of them are flat-out refusing to teach on the subject of End Times Prophecy. They either do not believe it themselves, or don't think their congregants will. As I pointed out in my previous book, they will say and do just about anything - or exclude just about everything - in order to keep the seats in their Megachurches filled. If only these worldly pastors knew that the *same* Paul, whose teachings they preach to steer clear of Biblical Prophecy, had actually started the doctrine of the Rapture!

He wrote extensively about the Last Days, in detail, and they would know that if they'd ever read past Acts and Romans. Paul revealed "the mystery" of the Rapture, which would precede the Tribulation and Second Coming, in 1st Corinthians 15:51-53 and in 1st Thessalonians 4:16-17. In both letters to Timothy, Paul laid out specific signs that would be occurring in the Last Days - in 1st Timothy, Chapter 4, and in 2nd Timothy, Chapter 3. In the latter, he gave (by my count) 22 unique signs. That is even more signs than Jesus gave in Matthew 24. So, do you think Paul wanted us to be preaching the return of the Lord? You betcha!

Those 22 signs of 2nd Timothy 3 are what this chapter will focus on - to prove, beyond a shadow of a doubt, that we are *the generation* which Paul had spoken of. I will tie each of them, one by one, to our society today. First, Paul warned that **"in the Last Days perilous times shall come**." The word "perilous" can mean dangerous. Have we been living in *dangerous* times? As I pointed out in *The Signs of Our Times,* global terrorism recently reached an all-time high. Mass shootings have become commonplace all across the world. Day after day, wicked regimes are building up nuclear arsenals. Each and every new year, it appears that World War 3 becomes a much greater possibility.

Due to reasons I mentioned in the chapter about pestilences, disease outbreaks are now more possible than ever before. Some of the most powerful earthquakes in history have rattled the world in our generation. Hurricanes are bigger, stronger, and last much longer. And because of this society pushing our God out, immoral men and women are caring less and less for fellow human beings. Violence and rioting have become *cool* to kids of today. There is no one who can argue that this generation has not been living in very dangerous times. Paul also prophesied that men would be...

- **Lovers of their own selves** - Look around, turn on your television, watch any modern Hollywood or Music Award Show, follow top athletes in any popular sport, and play any Rap album out there today... In every single instance, you will find nothing but *vanity*. "You're the best" is what most of today's celebrities long to hear. No humility can be found in the mainstream, except with a few Christians. Virtually everyone wants to be hip and trendy today.

  They want others to love them for just how great *they are*. They desire the most followers or the most likes on social media, a lot of praise and glory, and the biggest fan base they can get. They crave your daily affirmation as a constant reminder of why they are *better than you*. They believe they deserve your adulation. It is somehow owed to them. In their conceited minds, they were "born stars" and feel that they should be treated as such.

  Unlike them, a true Christian does not care about any of that. We live humbly, putting the needs of others above our own. We don't need a lot of followers, but instead are leading others to follow Jesus. We don't care much about being liked, and are more than happy with being hated for preaching the Word of God. We reserve praise and glory for the LORD - never for another human, and especially never for ourselves! Sadly, there doesn't seem to be many of us true Christians left out there.

Today's Godless society tells you to "love yourself." They have got it all wrong. First and foremost, we are to love God - then family - and then others. We don't need to love ourselves. We need to be thankful and comforted by the fact that God loves us, and it should not matter one bit what anybody else thinks of us. When you love God, family, and your neighbor above yourself, everything falls into place. Love yourself first, and everything *falls apart*.

- **Covetous -** We are, no doubt, living in a generation that loves to keep up with the Joneses. Everybody wants what their neighbors have. Our society tells us (in order to be cool) you must drive the newest models of cars, wear the trendiest clothes, possess the most expensive gadgets, and you must have what everyone else around you has, or else you won't fit in. Even some Christians have forgotten that one of the Ten Commandments is: "Thou shalt not covet *anything* that belongs to your neighbor." A lot of modern believers are trying to bring the world into the Church, as opposed to bringing the Church out to the sinful world.

It is hard to tell, in this generation, who is a Christian and who is not. Most everyone walks, talks, and acts the exact same. There are now even "Christian" rappers and heavy metal groups, because they seem to covet what the world outside of the Church has to offer. Honestly, apart from Johnny Cash, most Gospel music is boring. I get it. But that is no excuse to bring Satan's worldly music into

God's House. What may be boring to this world will keep you *holy*. When you bring headbanging, twerking, or hip hop into any church, the door's wide open for the devil to enter in. Satan is comfortable in many "churches" today.

Yet, we wonder how the young believers are far from God in this generation. It is because they have made the world *their god*, instead of making God *their world*. The LORD is clear that coveting does not just entail material possessions or wanting to fit in with the sinful world. He also commands not to covet our neighbor's spouse. With the rapid rise of internet dating sites and apps, it's hard to find a marriage today without a cheater in it. And, sadly, that goes for Christian marriages as much as secular ones.

With the current ease of being able to quench lust at our fingertips, and the ability to talk to attractive strangers discreetly or set up meetings with them over the internet, Satan is tempting every soul he possibly can. The devil is having a field day destroying marriages and it's all due to *covetousness* - the sin of desiring and pursuing that which you can't have. Remember one thing, brothers and sisters - Jesus said that if we *even look* upon someone's spouse with lust in our heart, then we commit adultery with them in our heart (Matthew 5:28). Heed the warning of James from his Epistle in Chapter 1 and verses 14-15 -

"EVERY MAN IS TEMPTED, WHEN HE IS DRAWN AWAY OF HIS OWN LUST, AND ENTICED. THEN WHEN LUST HATH CONCEIVED, IT BRINGETH FORTH SIN: AND SIN, WHEN IT IS FINISHED, BRINGETH FORTH DEATH."

What is the solution to this dilemma that is plaguing so many weak believers, in a culture laden with enticing sexual imagery and temptation around every corner? The

Holy Spirit of God. In Romans 8:6, we are told that "The mind governed by *the flesh* is death, but a mind governed by *the Spirit* is life and peace." Paul tells us, in Galatians 5:16, "Walk in the Spirit, and you shall not fulfil the lust of the flesh." When you truly know God and truly walk in His Spirit, you'll covet no more. You'll still struggle and be tempted. No one is immune to that in this carnal flesh. It is the devil's job, and he is not sleeping on it. He even tempted Jesus!

You can be sure that he'll try you when opportunity presents itself. The next time that he does, how will you respond? Will you fold like an accordion, giving in to the lust and temptation, without putting up any fight? Or will you respond like Jesus did, and rebuke him with the Word of God? Submit yourself to the LORD. Resist the devil, and he will flee from you! (James 4:7) Stand strong, and take heart in 1st Corinthians 10:13 -

"NO TEMPTATION HAS TAKEN YOU BUT SUCH AS IS COMMON TO MAN: BUT GOD IS FAITHFUL, WHO WILL NOT ALLOW YOU TO BE TEMPTED ABOVE THAT YOU ARE ABLE; BUT WILL WITH THE TEMPTATION MAKE A WAY TO ESCAPE, THAT YE MAY BE ABLE TO BEAR IT."

Obviously, the moral of this story is to *stop coveting*! God will provide for our every need, and every good gift is from above. So, don't desire the worldly things that are here today and gone tomorrow; but set your heart on the things that last for eternity. Thank God for the blessings that you already have, such as family, pets, roof over your head, transportation, food, drink, and the clothes on your body. If you covet anything, covet His blessings!

- **Boasters** - I'm sure you've all heard the song, "Anything you can do, I can do better - I can do anything better than you." That seems to be the theme song of this generation. It seems no one wants to build others up these days, only tear eachother down so *self* can be exalted. A majority of this generation, and especially celebrities, desire to be the absolute best at what they do. If they were doing that for the right reasons, such as to honour God or to help others, then that would be praiseworthy. Sadly, most of them do not. They only do it to be braggadocious. Our generation is chock-full of *boasters*.

- **Proud** - Another thing that our generation is filled with is *pride*. I penned an entire chapter about the "pride" of the LGBT community in my previous book. Their pride is no different than that of Lucifer. Pride is rebellion against the LORD and His Will. To be proud is to be self-centered, and to take great pleasure in a certain aspect of your life - whether looks, accomplishments, or lifestyle. Your way is the right way, and you could care less what others have to say or for what God thinks. The LGBTQ movement is a perfect example of the pride of the devil, because in their proud attitude they actually *celebrate* their sin.

    They are more than happy to rebel against Almighty God, because they feel that they're right and He's wrong. A lot of them are well aware that His Word says the way they are living is morally wrong, but they just don't care. As long as it makes them feel good, the opinion of their Creator takes a back seat. It's about *them*, and only them. They remind me of Lucifer with his five "I"s. We read in Isaiah 14:12-14, he said, "I will... I will... I will... I will... I will..." He was so puffed up in pride that he even said he would "be like" God. The LORD rebuked him, and said, no... "you will be brought down to Hell." We all know how things turned out for old Lucifer.

God is saying the exact same thing through His Word to all those who follow in the footsteps of Lucifer today - in their pride, they will be brought down to Hell. There is no escaping that fate until they repent, and turn from their wicked ways and open rebellion against the LORD.

- **Blasphemers** - I've written an entire chapter of this book on blasphemy, because it's become so widespread in our generation. You will read all about it soon.

- **Disobedient to parents** - Growing up, if my brother or I were to act up and disobey our parents, my father would dish out discipline. It was through lashes to our backside from his belt, or by being grounded time and time again, that we had learned right from wrong. In this generation, children can be little hellions. It has to be their way, right away, or else they'll throw a temper tantrum. Some kids actually physically strike or fight with their parents. This was unheard of a decade ago. I've heard many kids raise their voices to their parents, or cuss at them in public. It's so unbelievable that they get away with it.

This generation is the first to see children be blatantly disobedient to their parents. This prophecy has only been fulfilled in *our day*. A big reason behind this downright demonic behavior of today's youth is twofold: the parents wanting to be their child's *friend* instead of authority, and not raising them to fear God. If children were raised in a Christian home, then they'd be learning the Word of God. They would know the Fifth Commandment: "Honor your father and mother." The kids are so disrespectful because they are not being reared according to Proverbs 22:6.

Another verse from the Book of Proverbs, in Chapter 13 and verse 24, says if you "spare the rod" (modern belt) from a child who's in need of discipline, you *hate* them. Think about that... In God's eyes, if you're not chastising your children for doing wrong, then you don't love them. Why should the LORD be concerned with blessing your kids if you don't love them yourself?

Many parents today are afraid to discipline their kids because their children threaten to call the cops or Child Protective Services. I guarantee you, 9 times out of 10, if a police officer shows up at your home and you tell him you spanked your kid for disrespecting you, or for doing something bad, the officer would tell the child not to call again because they got what they had coming. Obviously, Biblical discipline does not entail beating or abusing your child. That is not what I'm talking about. I'm saying that God's just fine with you using that belt around your waist to teach your child some respect.

When I was young, I despised my father for it. Your kids will probably say they hate you for it. But the more my father spared not the rod, the more lessons I learned. I learned to fear him and authority. Because of that, I grew up to fear God and His Authority. If your children do not fear their earthly father and mother, then how can they be expected to fear their Father in Heaven? If they dishonour you, then they'll grow up to dishonour Him. I am forever grateful I'd received discipline as a child. If I hadn't, then none of you would be reading this book. I would not have become the man that I am today. So show these rebellious hellions who's boss, and spare not the rod!

- **Unthankful** - There are many today who would say that this generation is not unthankful. They most likely point to everyone giving thanks on Thanksgiving Day and most always to their family or friends, or to someone who does something nice for them. The "unthankful" that Paul was prophesying meant being unthankful to GOD. When was the last time that you've seen #ThanksBeToGod trending on social media? Sadly, I never have. On Thanksgiving, a national holiday created by our founders for us all to give thanks to the LORD for His countless blessings upon our nation, this generation gives thanks to everyone *but Him.*

I have had arguments with atheists over Thanksgiving many a time, as they try to say that it is a secular holiday having nothing to do with our God. My response to them is, "Who are you *thankful to* for blessings?" Their answer is that it is possible to be thankful to other human beings *without* being thankful to the LORD. No. It's not. *GOD* gives rain upon the heads of righteous and wicked alike. He alone blesses every being on Earth. If someone does something nice for you, to enhance your life in some way, it is the LORD who orchestrates that. If somebody does something evil to you, the *other guy* inspires that (Satan).

The fact is *all* that is good comes from God. There's nothing good that does not proceed from Him. Too many people thank other people all day long, never giving God the thanks, praise, and glory, due Him. I see it too often. This generation wants blessings, but wants nothing to do with the One who gives them. Next Thanksgiving, take a look at what everyone posts on social media about what they are thankful for, and who they're thankful to. Count how many of them mention the LORD. My guess is that you'll be able to count them all on one hand. God forgive this unthankful generation.

- **Unholy** - Is this the most unholy generation since Jesus Christ ascended into Heaven around 2,000 years ago? I'd say that it is. There seems to be no reverence for God or His holy things anymore. Churches are being shut down, boarded up, and bulldozed, more than ever before in U.S. history. People don't want to hear about living *holy* these days. It is a drag to them. There is too much fun found in sin. But for those who actually desire to, how do we live holy exactly? Observe our Holy God's Commandments.

   Obviously, we can't keep them all; but we are called to at least strive to. Lord Jesus said that we should try to be holy and perfect, just as our Father in Heaven is Holy and Perfect. How many around you (even Christians) do you see that are striving to be holy? I, for one, see a lot of in-name-only Christians who are living more *worldly* as opposed to more holy. I'll touch on many unholy things being said and done all around us in the coming chapters, "Demonic Indoctrination" and "Widespread Blasphemy." The worst and most unholy thing that I have witnessed in our generation is irreverence toward the Word of God.

   I wrote in my first book about how I leave boxes of Holy Bibles out in public places for anyone to freely take. Unfortunately, I've found that not only do a lot of people want nothing to do with God or His Word, but some are downright hostile and hateful toward it. Believe it or not, as I couldn't believe it myself, some people have actually *desecrated* the Bibles. They've torn pages and soaked the Bibles in damaging liquids, like milk, mustard, and ranch dressing. I couldn't believe my eyes. It's simply demonic to do that to the Holiest Book in the history of mankind. It bothers me that people like that live in the same town.

   If people can do that to the Bible, then *what else* are they capable of doing? Or should I say... *not* capable of doing? It's one thing if you do not believe in God, but it is a whole 'nother thing to be downright hostile toward your Creator and spit on His Word. I wish that I could say that it was just one lost soul who was possessed by the devil; but, unfortunately, the desecration has been done by more than one person in multiple locations.

Ten years ago, if somebody was caught intentionally defiling the Holy Bible in any way, they would rightfully be excommunicated from town. They'd be the one who was spit on, and would be shunned. They'd accurately be called sick, twisted, disgusting, or evil. Today, because of the utter lack of respect for God's Word, most people will just shake their heads and keep right on walking. There is no righteous indignation anymore. Our society's become the epitome of *unholy*.

- **Without natural affection** - Historically, there have been two ways this has been interpreted. **1:** People would lack the God-given natural feeling to love others - even family. According to Scottish Theologian William Barclay, some people considered children a misfortune in Paul's day. He said that when a child was born, it was laid at the father's feet. If he lifted up the child, then he acknowledged it. If he turned away and left it on the ground, the child would be thrown out - *literally*. There was not a night that went by when 50 abandoned children weren't left in the streets of Rome. Babies that were born deformed were drowned.

Can we make modern-day connections to this lack of respect for life? Sadly, we can. The abortion-on-demand plaguing our society is just like the cold murder of babies in the days of Paul. Instead of the father literally having a baby laid at his feet and walking away from it, some dads today refuse to take responsibility for their children after impregnating the mother. They say that they do not want the "burden" of having to father a child.

There are also mothers today, who consider the baby to be a burden, who turn to the organizations like Planned Parenthood to help them murder the child before it's even born. There are horrific stories of unwanted babies being left inside of dumpsters or on street corners today, just as they were left abandoned in the streets of Paul's days. We are no doubt seeing this prophecy of 2nd Timothy 3 being played out before our eyes *every day* in this generation.

2: Some have also interpreted this prophecy to mean not having affection for others in the natural way that the LORD ordained us to from the beginning. This would be referring primarily to homosexuals and pedophiles. God's natural plan for affection is between a man and a woman. The two love each other spiritually and physically, enter into a marriage union, and then produce children. This is the natural order. Paul explained in Romans (Chapter 1), and God laid it out clearly in the Old Testament as well, that those lying with the same sex are living unnaturally. The LORD called this type of affection "abomination" in Leviticus 18:22.

Do we see this version of the prophecy being fulfilled in our day and age? Homosexuality is more common than ever before in our nation's history, and same-sex marriage is now legal and widely accepted across this country. I'd go so far as to say that unnatural sexual lifestyles are even more prevalent in our generation than they have ever been in world history, since the days of Sodom and Gomorrah. Either way you interpret the prophecy, both meanings of "without natural affection" are being fulfilled today.

- **Trucebreakers** - The word "truce" means an agreement between two parties engaged in battle to stop the fighting, but the word had a much deeper meaning in Paul's day. A trucebreaker, more often than not, was someone who had broken a covenant. Reading this prophecy of Paul in that light, just how many covenant-breakers do we see in this world today? As far as those who break covenant with the LORD, the answer would be: too many to count.

How about those breaking the covenant of marriage? According to a CDC report, titled "100 Years of Divorce and Marriage Statistics," divorce stats were not recorded prior to 1867. Between the years 1867-1900, the divorce rate started at .03% and rose to .07% during the period of 30+ years. By 1930, it had risen to .16%. By 1940, .19%. In 1950, it reached .26%. Up until 1967, it remained right about there and even dropped a bit from year to year. But in 1970, things changed dramatically for the worse, as the divorce rate had jumped to .35%. Throughout the 70's, it climbed every year. By 1979, it skyrocketed to .53%.

Thankfully, that was the peak decade for divorces in our generation - but not for good reason. The divorce rate fluctuated between .40 and .53% up until the year 2000. The reasoning given for the rising trend ending was more women using birth control and less young people getting married in the first place. Both of these things go against God's Will for the human race. In 2000, there were about one-million divorces. Since that time and up until today, there have been between 800,000 to over 950,000 a year. While you'd think it's great that divorces had fallen from over two-million just fifty years ago to under one-million today, it's only because less people are getting married.

A recent study, conducted by the Institute for Family Studies, showed less than 50% of U.S. adults between the ages of 18-64 are married. And, according to census data, this marks an *all-time low* in our nation. So, at the end of the day, our generation is filled with "covenant-breakers"; and many want absolutely *nothing* to do with covenants. Either way is extremely displeasing to our Creator.

- **False accusers** - In today's day and age, if you are a Holy Bible-thumping Christian like me, you are all too familiar with false accusers. We're called "haters" or "bigots," our words are twisted, and the most vile lies are spread about us. In Matthew 5:11, Jesus prophesied this would happen to His followers in the Last Days. We are falsely accused of doing depraved things all the time; because God-haters know that if they can dirty the names of Christians, they can dissuade others from believing what we're preaching by making us look like hypocrites.

    This crowd will especially target those in positions of prominence and authority. Whether a President, Supreme Court Justice, Christian celebrity, or a well-known pastor, the wicked will float the wildest accusations about them to further evil agendas. False accusers are all around us.

- **Incontinent** - The Biblical definition of this word is "not being able to restrain lusts or appetites, particularly of the flesh." It also means to be unchaste or lewd. I often refer to Gen-Z as the Tinder generation. The young adults are not looking for husbands or wives. They are only looking for mates with whom they can satisfy their sexual needs. I've mentioned that the marriage rate in America is at an all-time low, and that is because young people don't want to commit. They only want "friends with benefits."

    Sex is wonderful when enjoyed within the boundaries of God - "on a marriage bed undefiled" (Hebrews 13:4).

Sex outside of marriage makes you a "whoremonger" and an "adulterer" in God's sight. Think about it... in the eyes of the LORD, our generation is full of whoremongers and adulterers. Sadly, this society that needs Jesus more than ever has pushed Him further away than ever before. With the rise of the internet, pornography has become easy to access. Kids stumble across sex-laden websites with little to no effort, often by simply misspelling a search term or web address. Incontinence has *engulfed our continent*.

- **Fierce -** In the Holy Bible, "fierce" is defined as violent, threatening, cruel, savage, and even murderous. I've lived on this earth for 38 years, and I cannot remember a time when the hearts of men have been so cold. Are men today *violent*? These days, protests aren't just protests - they are violent riots. Boxing gloves are considered too tame for our society, so men are now obsessed with maiming each other in MMA fights. The more blood and broken bones, the more the crowds go crazy for it.

  Are men *threatening* today? I once again point to this generation's obsession with violent rioting in order to get their way. When radicals want something, they'll threaten you until they get what they desire. It's all too common in our day and age.

  Are men *cruel*? How many times have you heard the phrase, "it's a cruel world"? You have probably heard it a lot because it's true. Too many people are only concerned about themselves and *their* own needs. They will step on and hurt anyone in the process of getting what they want. Besides using and abusing other human beings, there are those who abuse defenseless animals. As a cat dad, I get so angry when I hear about animal cruelty and torture.

Are men more *savage* and *murderous* today than they were in past generations? Go and read the chapter about "Terrorism" from my previous book, and you've read the chapter on "Mass Shootings" in this book, to find that the answer is a resounding YES.

- **Despisers of those that are good** - In Chapter 15 of the Gospel of John, Lord Jesus said that we would be "hated" for following Him and for believing the Word of God. He said that this evil world would hate us for holding to the Law of the LORD in the midst of society laden with sin. Jesus exposed the sins of the world, and He made us all aware that we all need a Saviour. People who live in sin don't wanna hear that, so they hated Him. Now, they hate us. They persecuted Him. Now, they persecute us. Bible believers who live to please God, keep His laws, and do things that He says are good, are despised with a passion.

  The more sinful this world becomes, the more we are looked upon as the dregs of society. We're reviled all day long. For what exactly? Do we physically harm anyone, or treat people wrong? Absolutely not. We're despised for believing and preaching God's Word of truth in this world filled with Satan's lies. Our Godless society fulfills Isaiah 5:20, which says that "evil will be called good and good evil." Just turn on your television... Things that God calls evil, perverted, and abominable, are *celebrated* as "good" things. Meanwhile, things that the LORD says are good are despised as "evil" - along with us who espouse them.

- **Traitors** - A traitor is someone who betrays their family, friends, or country. Judas Iscariot was the poster child for traitors. They care about no one but themselves, and will betray anyone to save their own hides or to obtain reward.

Treason's long been regarded as one of the worst crimes that a man can commit. How much betrayal do we see in the Church alone? Pastors and priests have been turning their backs on Christ and God's Word, so that they can be friends of this world. How many betrayals are we seeing in relationships today? Far too many cheat on spouses or their significant others. Too many to count.

- **Heady -** Being heady means you are "self-willed." Your way is better than everyone else's way, even better than God's Will for your life. Many in this generation seem to think that they know better than the LORD. His ways are no longer acceptable to them. The liberal thinkers of this day and age feel that the God's Word is outdated, and that it needs to be revised to better suit modern society. They think they're so wise, and many follow after their Godless ideologies. They need to read 1st Corinthians 3:18-20 -

  "IF ANY MAN AMONG YOU SEEMS TO BE WISE IN THIS WORLD, LET HIM BECOME A FOOL, THAT HE MAY BE WISE. THE WISDOM OF THIS WORLD IS FOOLISHNESS WITH GOD. IT IS WRITTEN, HE TAKES THE WISE IN THEIR OWN CRAFTINESS. AND, THE LORD KNOWS THE THOUGHTS OF THE WISE, THAT THEY ARE VAIN."

- **Highminded -** This word goes hand in hand with "lovers of their own selves, boasters, proud, and heady."

- **Lovers of pleasures more than lovers of God -** In the Greek, the word that translates to "lovers of pleasures" in our Holy Bible is "philodonos." This word is a compound of two words: phileo and hedonos. "Phileo" conveys love and affection. The word hedonism stems from "hedonos." Hedonism is defined as a pursuit of pleasure and sensual self indulgence. If you're a hedonist, then you're addicted to doing or obtaining anything that brings you a personal pleasure. You don't care if what you do or want is right or wrong. If it makes you feel good, you will do anything to get what it is that you desire.

Paul was prophesying that, in the Last Days, men and women would be obsessed and consumed with whatever brings them pleasure - as opposed to them doing what is pleasing to our LORD. This generation has drifted further away from God than any other before us; because we've been inundated with more things to preoccupy our minds and senses - which keep us from devoting time to God's Word. While television, radio, and the internet can all be good, when they're used for the right reasons - especially to build up your faith or the faith of others - these things can pull you away from God, and can *keep you away*.

The devil uses every tool at his disposal, even if they were not originally designed to hamper our walk with the LORD. He'll use TV, music, the net, smartphones, social media, video games, and more. One of the tools that he's used most successfully to damage our faith and our lives, in the name of pleasure, is pornography. The addiction to pornography is a disease that's infecting hearts and minds of billions around the globe, even Christians. Porn could forever alter spiritual growth of youth, cause men to view women solely as objects, and inspire the crime of rape. In the U.S., there've been between 200,000-400,000 sexual assaults per year throughout the past decade.

There are so many things that people turn to today for pleasure and happiness, while forgetting the absolute best happiness and serenity can only be found in God. When you love pleasures of this world more than you love Him, you'll never truly be happy. Never. Sure, you'll have brief moments of satisfaction, but they will not last very long. Only the joy and peace that Christ Jesus brings us, from the Father, truly lasts - and lasts forever.

Modern research can prove this Biblical message that I'm preaching. Even with far more toys and gadgets than ever before in history to bring us pleasure, the Worldwide Happiness Index is the lowest on record. That is because if you pursue happiness through anything other than God, and His Word, it will elude you. So, put the Holy Bible at the forefront of your life, and you will find happiness and peace in everything that you do. I guarantee it.

- **Having a form of Godliness, but denying the power of it** - Paul was speaking about Christians who *say* that they believe in God, but who *live* like the devil. How many of those do we see among us? Read the last two chapters of *The Signs of Our Times*, and you will find that the answer is: more than are not. Too many in-name-only Christians either complain that God isn't answering their prayers, or they're entertaining other religions, or they are departing from the Faith altogether. The reason they aren't finding fulfillment in the Faith is because they're not utilizing the power thereof.

   They don't pray without ceasing. They don't believe every aspect of the Word of God. They aren't studying it as diligently as they should. They are not following God's Laws. They don't truly believe - by faith - everything that God has said and promised. Being professing Christians, they may appear "Godly" to others in this secular world - but they will never obtain or realize the power that God's Word brings, while living *like* the secular world. Far too many Christian leaders and churches are concerned with bringing *the world* into the Church, when they should be striving to bring *the Church* out into the world! Until the day they do, they'll be Godly *in-name-only* - that is all.

- **Suffering persecution for being Christians -** This is one prophecy of Paul that's been fulfilled more so than at any other time in history, since the days that he penned it. Go back and read the "Christian Persecution" chapter of my previous book, and the first chapter of this book. We are, no doubt, that "hated by all" generation of Christians that Lord Jesus prophesied would come "in the Last Days."

- **Evil men and seducers who will wax worse and worse, deceiving, and being deceived -** "Evil" is defined as any thought, attitude, or action, that is contrary to God's Will. It is best understood as the polar opposite of "good" - and we know that *God is good.* That is because He is caring, faithful, holy, just, loving, merciful, and the embodiment of truth. His Laws are wholly moral. On the flipside, it is no secret that Satan's evil. He's deceiving, selfish, unholy, corrupt, hateful, cruel, and the father of lies. His ways are wholly immoral.

How many today share the aforementioned qualities of the devil? How many exemplify qualities of the LORD among us? Anyone with a working moral compass has to admit that more men are following after Satan, than being imitators of God (Ephesians 5:1). Whether antichrists or atheists, anti-Semites, animal abusers, rapists, murderers, or flat-out Satanists, they all wax worse by the day. Plus, New Age gurus deceive others with unBiblical nonsense; while being deceived *themselves* by the demons posing as *angels of light* (2nd Corinthians 11:14).

As for the seducers… Most always in the Holy Bible, the word "seduce" means "lead astray". And in verse 13, it can also mean "impostors." These men are best known in our day and age as false prophets. I am going to need a lot more paper to address them, and so this next chapter will be all about the final sign of 2nd Timothy 3.

EVIL MEN AND SEDUCERS SHALL WAX WORSE AND WORSE, DECEIVING, AND BEING DECEIVED.

- 2ND TIMOTHY 3:13

CHAPTER NINE

FALSE PROPHETS

JESUS SAID, MANY FALSE PROPHETS SHALL RISE, AND SHALL
DECEIVE MANY... INSOMUCH THAT, IF IT WERE POSSIBLE,
THEY SHALL DECEIVE THE VERY ELECT (BELIEVERS).

- MATTHEW 24:11 & 24

WHEN SAINT PAUL REFERRED to "seducers" in 2nd Timothy
3:13, I believe that he meant fake Christians. There's definitely no
shortage of them in this generation. These are they who stand in
front of the pulpit preaching their *own* ideas about what it is God
wants for us - as opposed to what His Word actually says. Many
pastors today get their theological degrees, but do not personally
know the LORD. Thus, they preach messages which are any and
everything *but* Biblical. The great preacher, Jack Van Impe, best
described the false prophets of our day and age as having "a head
knowledge of God, but no *heart* knowledge."

So-called pastors and priests, even the Pope, preach self-help
sermons, get-rich quick messages, or are pushing liberal agendas
- all under the banner of Christ. Satan is loving every minute of it,
employing counterfeit Christian leaders to drive souls away from
the eternal truth and into comfortable falsehoods. Thus, instead of
the Church being all about God and what He *did* for our souls, the
prevailing message of so many Christian "teachers" is that it's all

about you and what God can *do* for your bank account. Instead of looking to the Cross for salvation, MegaChurch pastors have you looking to a divine money tree for satisfaction. The seducers are deceiving droves of believers across the globe. At the same time, they themselves are being deceived by Satan.

Many of these pastors probably think that they are doing right by God, with their worldly prosperity preaching, and have no idea that Satan's sifting them (and their congregations) like wheat. The devil is not only leading so-called shepherds astray, but the flocks in the process. Far too many false prophets are in our world today, and they come in various forms. Let me start with the prosperity preachers, who are getting rich off believers struggling financially. Followers of these popular preachers are already behind on bills. Yet, they're told the more they bless their pastor, the more they'll be blessed themselves. These preachers teach that God wants you to be rich and prosperous, but apparently you can only attain your riches *after* enriching *them*.

Now, I'm all for tithing - just not to billionaire false prophets! And I take no pleasure in alienating or calling out other believers. I wish we would all be united around the happy hope that Jesus is coming back soon. At the same time, I cannot remain silent when I see a lot of wolves in sheep's clothing robbing my brothers and sisters in Christ blind. So, I intend to name names. First, I want to start with the name even unbelievers across this world are familiar with: **Joel Osteen**. Joel has refused to preach on Bible Prophecy and the return of our Lord. He dodges questions about hot button social issues of our day, like homosexuality or abortion, and that is how he manages to amass about 50,000 attendees per week at his church (Lakewood) in Houston, Texas.

He, like Rick Warren, knows that this backslidden generation doesn't want to hear about sin, and so he only preaches messages that *they* want to hear - not the message *God* wants them to hear. His style of ministry really reminds me of a verse from Isaiah. In

Chapter 30, verse 10, the worldly sinners say to the men of God: "Prophesy *not* unto us right things, speak unto us smooth things, prophesy *deceits*." A similar verse is 2nd Timothy 4:3 -

"FOR THE TIME WILL COME WHEN THEY WILL NOT ENDURE SOUND DOCTRINE; AFTER THEIR OWN LUSTS SHALL THEY HEAP TO THEMSELVES TEACHERS, HAVING ITCHING EARS."

"Sound doctrine" refers to God's Word - *all of it*. The LORD says that people will no longer want to hear what it is that He has to say about right and wrong in the Last Days. They'll only want to hear about His blessings, and never His judgments for refusing to repent of their sins. Paul said they'd be seeking out "teachers" who would tickle their ears with prosperity sermons. Osteen is at the top of that list of teachers. His preaching style is best summed up by the title of his best-selling book, *Your Best Life Now*. Let's break down the words of this title, and see how it does or doesn't line up with the Holy Bible, shall we?

YOUR... If you took your time reading the previous chapter then you would know that doctrines of self-gratification or selfish ambition are frowned upon by God. Jesus had laid out the selfless example we're to follow as believers. As I previously explained, we're to love God *first* and foremost, then family, then others, and ourselves *last*. If we do this, the LORD takes care of us. When we focus only on *our* needs and not on God, we'll always be *needy*.

The next word Joel used to attract readers is **BEST**. He seems to think we should strive to accumulate as much wealth, material things, fame, and glory as we possibly can in this life. He teaches that you should be desiring the absolute *best* for yourself. This is opposed to what the Word teaches about humbling ourselves and seeking *His best* for our lives. We should all be content with what we have, and with what the LORD provides for us. If God wants you to be financially rich, you will be. I, myself, am content with a roof over my head, a car to drive (even if it's over 20-years old), stocked cupboards and fridge, and in knowing my loved ones are in good health and alive and well. Everything else I'll ever receive from the LORD is just an extra blessing.

In this wicked world, I don't expect to sell a million copies of my books like the Osteens of the world. I know preaching God's truth won't gain me a very large fanbase. Preaching what people want to hear, like Joel, most certainly would. I am called as God's prophets of old were - to preach His Word "in season and out of season," whether the people like it or they don't like it; correcting, rebuking and encouraging, with complete patience and *doctrine* (2nd Timothy 4:2). I do not seek fame, only Heavenly rewards for leading lost souls to God. I don't seek glory, but only to bring the LORD the glory that is due Him.

The third word that Joel used is **LIFE**. He preaches that you should be focusing on *this* life - here and **NOW**. These final two words are the antithesis of what the LORD desires for us. We are not to focus on temporal things of this life, but eternal things (2nd Corinthians 4:18). We should only be concerned with our *eternal* lives, and if we will be right with God in the hereafter. We should not be concerned with enriching our *present* lives, which can pull us away from God. This may be hard for a lot of people to hear, I'm sure. But, look at me, I've now published two books, I am not going hungry, have a healthy family, and am not lacking anything I need in life. God provides for every need, and is giving me the *best days of my life now* because I'm focused on *eternity*.

Again, I may never be a world-acclaimed Best-Selling author. But I know God's pleased with me, and that's all that should ever matter to a believer. Joel, on the other hand, needs his $10-million mansion and $50-million net worth to validate his faith. Do y'all remember how big Lord Jesus' home was? Don't forget, He was God in the flesh. It just so happens, as an adult, Jesus didn't have a home! How about Saint Paul? Was he traveling from city to city in a golden chariot? No. The soles of his feet had been covered in calluses from traveling the Middle East and beyond in some beat up pair of sandals. The disciples all left their homes, families, and possessions, to follow Jesus. Were Paul and the disciples all living their "Best Lives Now"? Not by a longshot!

I know it may seem like I am singling out Osteen, but I most certainly am not. There are others preaching the same prosperity gospel that he does, and who are getting rich off the contributions from their congregations. **Jesse Duplantis** said, "If Jesus were to descend from Heaven and set foot on this 21st-century Earth, He would probably take a pass on riding on the back of a donkey. He would be on an airplane preaching the Gospel all over the world." Preaching the Gospel wasn't Jesus' job - it's ours. He finished His job at Calvary. Rest assured, Christ wouldn't be flying in a golden Learjet if He were on Earth today (even though He is the King of kings and Lord of lords).

Remember that Jesus humbled Himself like a servant, though He was the One who deserved to be served. He chose the donkey to ride into Jerusalem, showing the type of King that He was. He wasn't like worldly kings who are concerned with war and riches. No. He was the Prince of Peace, concerned with helping the poor and needy. Today, I guarantee you that Jesus would still be riding a donkey and certainly not driving a Mercedes Benz. The reason for Duplantis making the "donkey" statement was because he was asking his congregation for $54-million to help him buy a luxury jet to "spread the Gospel" around the world. The jet he'd desired was a Falcon 7x, which would be his ministry's 4th jet paid for by his followers' "offerings to God".

Another preacher in love with luxurious jets is **Creflo Dollar**. In 2015, he started "Project G650," which would be financed by his 200,000 followers. The project would fund the purchase of a $65-million Gulfstream G650 private jet for Dollar's "ministry." **Kenneth Copeland** is another who used his ministry's donations to purchase a Gulfstream V jet, which cost tens of millions. After he acquired the plane, Copeland told his followers that it needed upgrades totalling $2.5-million. He said he needed a new hangar, maintenance equipment, and a longer runway to accommodate it.

Pastor **John Gray**, who had risen to fame as star of a reality TV show on Oprah Winfrey's OWN Network, once worked under Joel Osteen. So, his craving for worldly riches must run deep. He is now a pastor of his own church in Greenville, South Carolina. Last year, he made headlines after purchasing a Lamborghini for his wife's anniversary gift. His excuse was that he is 45-years-old, and shouldn't have to wait until he's 70 to live his *best life*. Where have we heard *those* two words before?

The next dangerous teaching, and teacher, I need to address is "New Testament Only" Christianity and **Andy Stanley**. He is the most well-known pastor advocating for Christians to "throw out" the Old Testament from our Holy Bible. Earlier this year, he made headlines across Christian news outlets for saying that Christians need to *forget* the Ten Commandments. Shame! Maybe he *should* forget the Old Testament, because he obviously needs a whole lot more study of the New! Stanley teaches that Jesus only wants us to focus on *one* singular commandment: "love one another." Yet, *thousands* of words are attributed to Christ in the Bible. If all He wanted us to remember was one phrase, then why did He tell the disciples and Paul to record everything else that He said?

If one commandment was all He came to teach us, then why would He have His followers write nearly 185,000 words, making up roughly 8,000 verses, in 260 Chapters? Sure seems to me that Jesus wanted us to learn and remember a whole lot more than just 3 words. It certainly appears that way, doesn't it? While "love one another as I have loved you" is an important teaching, and central to our Faith, we can't live by that one command alone. According to Stanley's logic, Jesus doesn't care if we sin every second of our day - so long as we love one another. So, you can blaspheme the

Spirit, worship false gods, take the LORD's Name in vain, live as a prostitute or porn addict or pedophile, sleep with family, and the list could go on and on - so long as you just "love one another."

Can you see how Stanley's view of the Holy Bible is flawed? Also, in advocating that we throw out the Old Testament, he is in total disagreement with Jesus Himself. As believers in the Triune God - Father, Son, and Holy Spirit - we believe that Jesus and the Father YHWH wrote the *entire* Bible together, through the Holy Spirit. So, Jesus actually wrote the Ten Commandments with the Father. Why then would He want us to throw them out? Answer: He wouldn't. He commanded us to *keep them* in Matthew 19:17. Jesus said that there was an even *greater* commandment than His command to "love one another." If Andy Stanley would actually study the Bible he supposedly preaches, then he would know that.

In Matthew 22, verses 37-38, Jesus said, "You shall love the Lord your God with all your heart, with all your soul, and with all your mind." He said that this is the first and *great commandment*. When we love the LORD and obey His commands, we will love one another. Stanley's heretical teaching is not just theologically irresponsible, but it's spiritually dangerous. He portrays Jesus, not as Holy Son of Almighty God, not as co-Creator of the Universe, not as the Living God who came down to dwell among us, not as Saviour of the world, but as a hippie who preached "groovy peace and love." His Jesus belongs on a Woodstock poster.

Yes, Christ is love. God is love. You can never know true love in this world unless you know our Father in Heaven and the Lord Jesus. But He isn't some teacher like Gandhi or the Dalai Lama. He was, is, and forever will be *GOD*. He's the King of kings and Lord of lords. So, He had a lot more to teach us poor sinners than just "love one another." Men like Stanley don't care though. They only want to keep seats in their megachurches filled. That is why they preach messages that everyone on this earth can get on board with. Stanley has around 30,000 members at his church. Anyone else notice that the pastors who preach the *least* Biblical truth and doctrine always seem to have the *most* followers?

I have got a piece of advice for everyone... If you are seeking a church today that truly preaches the Word of God, look for the smallest building on the block that has the smallest congregation. I guarantee they are preaching the truth, and their church is empty because nobody wants to hear it! One reason for the backslidden churches booming today is another popular pastor, **Rick Warren**. In the "Falling Away From the Faith" chapter of my first book, I addressed his "purpose-driven" plan for churches in great detail. I'd also highlighted other false prophets, like those promoting or endorsing the sins of Gay Marriage, transgenderism, or abortion - not to mention, those teaching the demonic doctrine that our God is "gender-neutral"; as opposed to *the Male* He portrayed Himself as throughout the *entire* Bible.

Someone else who I had mentioned in the previous book was **Pope Francis**. I constantly refer to him as the uber-liberal Pope. He's so far to the left, on so many issues, you would think he was a politician - rather than the leader of over one-billion Christians worldwide. In *The Signs of Our Times*, I pointed out just some of the blasphemous things he has said and done. In this book, I have selected the most heretical statements of Francis that I could find to show why I believe him to be a false prophet. He has said...

"Many think differently, feel differently, seeking God or meeting God in different ways. In this crowd, and range of religions, there is one certainty that we have for all: we are all children of God."

"I belong to this religion, or that one. It doesn't matter!"

Oh, it matters! Our Holy Bible is clear that we're *all children of God by faith in Christ Jesus* (Galatians 3:26). Anyone who is not washed clean of sins by our Lord, and anyone following after false gods like Allah, Krishna, Buddha, etc., is *not* a child of God! They may have been created by Him, as all human beings are, but they are *illegitimate* children.

"It is true that the idea of conquest is inherent in the soul of Islam. However, it is possible to interpret the objective in Matthew's Gospel, where Jesus sends his disciples to all nations, in terms of the same idea of conquest."

"It is wrong to equate violence with the religion of Islam, and characterization of Islam as violent is untrue... If I speak of Islamic violence, I should also speak of Catholic violence. I believe that in pretty much every religion there is always a small group of fundamentalists."

First off, Islamic conquest involves violence, terror, and war, as called for by Muhammad and Allah. Jesus' Great Commission to His disciples and to all future believers was in no way, shape, or form, the *same idea* of conquest. Those peacefully preaching the Gospel of God's grace and salvation to strangers all across the globe is a polar opposite of Islamic invasion of non-Muslim lands and *forcing* the inhabitants of those lands to worship their god or else. Francis says "all religions have violent fundamentalists, and Islam is no more violent than Catholicism." Where on Earth did this man ever get his theological degree? Clown College?!

So many of his statements totally contradict the Holy Bible. How in the world can someone with such little knowledge of the Word of God be elected to lead an entire global denomination of the Faith? It is dangerous to have someone like him shepherding a large portion of the Lord's flock across this world. He should read chapter 3 of my previous book, where I point out the differences between Islam and Judaism/Christianity. There is no possible way that the two Gods could be the same. I had listed verses from the

Quran itself to prove my point. Whether politically correct or not and whether Francis likes to admit it or not, Islam's been the most violent and deadly "religion" on Planet Earth since its inception.

"We all love Mother Earth, because she is the one who has given us life and safeguards us."

There is no "Mother Earth" - only a "Father in Heaven." It is HE Who has given us life and safeguards us. As the Pope, Francis should know this basic fact of the Faith. You would think!

"When we read about Creation in Genesis, we can run the risk of imagining God was a magician, with a magic wand able to do everything, but that is not so."

"Evolution is not inconsistent with a notion of Creation."

The LORD was absolutely able to do everything in Creation! Not because "He's a magician with a magic wand," but because He is GOD! And, as I also explained in the first book, evolution is 100% inconsistent with the notion of Creation. Living things did not evolve. They were *created*. If you don't believe that, then you just don't believe God's Word. I, for one, will forever believe the LORD over mentally ill men like Charles Darwin.

"There is no Hell."

The reason why I refer to Francis as the "uber-liberal" Pope is because he so very often sacrifices Biblical doctrine at the altar of political correctness. Of course, most people do not want to hear about everlasting torment in unquenchable fire - where there will be weeping and gnashing of teeth. It is a scary thought. The fact is Hell is *just as real* as Heaven. If there were no Hell, then Jesus would have laid down His life for nothing. His sacrifice would be meaningless. If we are all going to Heaven at the end of the road, and there is no punishment for sins against a Holy God, then why would He have suffered and died to keep us from some *imaginary* place of eternal torment?

Jesus was with Father YHWH "in the beginning" (John 1:1). He was there when everything was created, both seen and unseen. In fact, Hebrews 1:2 tells us that it was "through Lord Jesus" that God created "the worlds" (Universe). So, Jesus did what He did for us because He knew *for a fact* that Hell was all too real. The good news of Christ is that not one human being on this earth has to go there if we'd all put our faith and hope in Him. His precious shed Blood cleanses us of *all* sin. All that you and I have to do is repent, and do our utmost best to turn from wicked ways. If there were such a thing as a "Get out of Hell free" card, it would bear an image of our Lord on the Cross!

If the Pope were to actually study the Holy Bible, which over one-billion Catholics on Earth expect him to represent, then he'd find that one person had talked about Hell more than anyone else. Was it the Apostle Paul, as so many think? No. How about one of the Old Testament prophets, who spoke a great deal about God's judgment? Nope. Maybe Noah? Abraham? Moses? King David? The answer is no - on all counts. Then who spoke about Hell the most? The answer to the question might shock you. Believe it or not, it was Lord JESUS. He taught about Hell around sixty times in the New Testament. All the "many paths to Heaven" believers, who ignore "Hellfire and brimstone" preaching because they *only listen to Jesus*, obviously need to read a lot more about Him!

I have compiled a few verses where He described the eternal reality of that place called Hell -

"THE SON OF MAN SHALL SEND FORTH HIS ANGELS, AND THEY SHALL GATHER OUT OF HIS KINGDOM ALL THINGS THAT OFFEND, AND THEM WHICH DO INIQUITY; AND SHALL CAST THEM INTO A FURNACE OF FIRE: THERE SHALL BE WAILING AND GNASHING OF TEETH." - MATTHEW 13:41-42

"AND IF THY HAND OFFEND THEE, CUT IT OFF: IT IS BETTER FOR THEE TO ENTER INTO LIFE MAIMED, THAN HAVING TWO HANDS TO GO INTO HELL, INTO THE FIRE THAT NEVER SHALL BE QUENCHED: WHERE THEIR WORM DIETH NOT, AND THE FIRE IS NOT QUENCHED. AND IF THY FOOT OFFEND THEE, CUT IT OFF: IT IS BETTER FOR THEE TO ENTER HALT INTO LIFE, THAN HAVING TWO FEET TO BE CAST INTO HELL, INTO THE FIRE THAT NEVER SHALL BE QUENCHED: WHERE THEIR WORM DIETH NOT, AND THE FIRE IS NOT QUENCHED. AND IF THINE EYE OFFEND THEE, PLUCK IT OUT: IT IS BETTER FOR THEE TO ENTER INTO THE KINGDOM OF GOD WITH ONE EYE, THAN HAVING TWO EYES TO BE CAST INTO HELL FIRE." - MARK 9:43-47

"BE NOT AFRAID OF THEM THAT KILL THE BODY, AND AFTER THAT HAVE NO MORE THAT THEY CAN DO. BUT I FOREWARN YOU WHOM YE SHALL FEAR: FEAR HIM, WHICH AFTER HE HATH KILLED HATH POWER TO CAST INTO HELL; YEA, I SAY UNTO YOU, FEAR HIM." - LUKE 12:4-5

"IF A MAN ABIDE NOT IN ME, HE'S CAST FORTH AS A BRANCH, AND IS WITHERED; AND MEN GATHER THEM, AND CAST THEM INTO THE FIRE, AND THEY ARE BURNED." - JOHN 15:6

"THE FEARFUL, AND UNBELIEVING, AND THE ABOMINABLE, AND MURDERERS, AND WHOREMONGERS, AND SORCERERS, AND IDOLATERS, AND ALL LIARS, SHALL HAVE THEIR PART IN THE LAKE WHICH BURNETH WITH FIRE AND BRIMSTONE: WHICH IS THE SECOND DEATH." - REVELATION 21:8

Francis teaching that there is no Hell is in direct opposition to the words of Christ. It is also a dangerous teaching. When people believe that there's no eternal punishment for doing evil, then evil will increase. Francis has to be the most Biblically-illiterate Pope in history. In my first book, I'd mentioned that he doesn't seem to care very much about God's love for the Nation of Israel. He was the first Pope to ever recognize and embrace a State of Palestine. If he picked up the Bible sometime, then he would know that the LORD loves the Jewish State more than any other nation in all of history. By befriending the enemies of Israel, the Pope is standing with the devil (1st Chronicles 21:1) - not the God that he *claims to be* representing.

This Pope could be the False Prophet of Revelation (Chapter 13). The Christian *impostor* will hold a great authority over most believers on the earth, and will lead them astray from the truth to follow after Antichrist. He will establish and lead the "One World Religion." Given all of the statements of Francis that I've shared, it is obvious that he'd love to lead a religion that incorporates all faiths of the world into one global body. If you are a Catholic that follows after the Pope, or if you're an Evangelical following men like Osteen or Stanley, I am not condemning you for teachers you have chosen. I do, however, have a piece of advice for you - and I hope you will take it...

If what your Pope, preacher, pastor, or priest, is teaching does not match up with what the Holy Bible says, then FORGET IT. It is not of God, and it is not worth remembering!

THERE WERE FALSE PROPHETS AMONG THE PEOPLE, EVEN AS THERE SHALL BE FALSE TEACHERS AMONG YOU, WHO PRIVILY SHALL BRING IN DAMNABLE HERESIES, EVEN DENYING THE LORD THAT BOUGHT THEM.

- 2ND PETER 2:1

CHAPTER TEN

DEMONIC INDOCTRINATION

NOW THE SPIRIT SPEAKETH EXPRESSLY, THAT IN THE LATTER
TIMES SOME SHALL DEPART FROM THE FAITH, GIVING HEED
TO SEDUCING SPIRITS, AND DOCTRINES OF DEVILS (DEMONS).

- 1ST TIMOTHY 4:1

MAINSTREAM MEDIA TODAY IS no doubt under the control of
Satan. Broadcast television has become nothing short of demonic.
In just the past few years, there have been popular TV series that
have been all about the devil himself. A majority of them actually
paint him in a good light. A FOX drama (now on Netflix) is titled
Lucifer, and it portrays Satan as a likable guy in human flesh. The
show's main character, Lucifer Morningstar, is supposed to make
the devil look "cool." He drives a fancy car, owns a nightclub in
L.A., and is irresistible to women. He is described as "a good guy
who is bored and unhappy as the keeper of Hell."

In the script, Satan resigns his throne, abandons his kingdom,
and "retires" to Los Angeles. God sends an angel to convince him
to return to the underworld. Morningstar questions the angel, "Do
you think I'm the devil because I'm inherently evil or 'cause dear
ol' Dad decided I was?" The question is supposed to make people
rethink the Biblical teachings about good and evil, and about God
and Satan. It's spiritually dangerous for viewers, especially young

people who don't know much about the Word of God. A similar series, titled *Damien*, which had been cancelled by A&E after just one season, presented the Antichrist as another likable young guy who didn't seem that inherently evil.

Meanwhile, Christ Jesus and the Bible are being consistently blasphemed and mocked across network and cable television. On an episode of AMC's *Preacher*, the main character tore pages out of the Holy Bible to use them as rolling paper for smoking weed. The NBC comedy, *Superstore*, had deeply offended Christians by suggesting that Jesus "not only supported Gay Marriage," but that "HE was gay." I'll bet NBC would never say those things about Muhammad of Islam. A blasphemous Adult Swim series, called *Black Jesus*, portrays our Lord as a foul-mouthed, weed-smoking, liquor-drinking, gang-related African American man in Compton. Where's the outrage?!

What's worse, if that were possible, so-called Family-friendly networks are regularly promoting sinful trash to the youth. Disney has incorporated gay characters into popular series and cartoons; as well as in popular films, like 2017's remake of *Beauty and the Beast*. ABC Family went so far as to air a first-ever televised kiss between two underage boys. Netflix recently rolled out a remake of the lighthearted sitcom *Sabrina the Teenage Witch*, and retitled the series *The Chilling Adventures of Sabrina*. In a departure from the original, the revamped version is dubbed "extremely Satanic." It targets the same audience as its predecessor - teenage girls, but is filled with plenty of blood and gore, and even features demons.

America's youth are being subjected to far more sex, profane language, and violence, during traditional early-evening "family hours" of broadcast television viewing than ever before. There's a watchdog group, known as the Parents Television Council (PTC), that studied animated shows ranked highest among viewers aged 12-17. They had monitored them for about a month, and viewed around 125 episodes. They found a total of nearly 1,500 incidents of explicit sex, drugs, and/or offensive language, within 57 hours of programming. Another study found sexual content rose nearly 25% from 2001 to 2007. That was over ten years ago. I can only imagine what those numbers are like today.

Parents today must be especially vigilant in monitoring what their kids watch, because gone are the days of leaving them alone for hours in front of the tube. Satan wants all our souls; and if he can't get yours, then he wants your children. He's using the media as his outlet to do that. If not TV or movies, he'll use music. Most of today's popular musicians have a form of demonic messaging in songs, videos, and performances. Whether Ariana Grande and her song *"God is a Woman,"* Jay Z and his obsession with Occult symbolism, Beyonce's demonic rituals in her live performances, Lil Uzi Vert - whose name is a nod to Lucifer, or Marilyn Manson tearing up the Bible, there is no shortage of Satanic indoctrination (even worship) going on in the music world today.

The devil has his hands all over the internet as well. Besides flooding the net with pornography, he's inspired the big three tech giants to be extremely hostile toward Bible believers. Read about the neverending suppression and censorship that I've endured on Facebook over the years on my website, *BiblicalSigns.com*. Also, Twitter was recently exposed for "shadowbanning" conservative Christians. And it has long been thought by Holy Bible believers that Google holds an anti-Christian bias. In early 2018, we found undeniable proof to confirm our suspicions.

Christians who use the smart device, Google Home, which is similar to Alexa from Amazon, recorded videos of what appeared to be a blatant omission of Jesus Christ by Google programmers. The virtual assistant voice in the Google Home device (and some smartphones) gave detailed biographies for every religious figure in the world, except one... JESUS. Google could tell you all about Allah and Muhammad of Islam, Buddha, Krishna, and other false gods; but as for the Saviour of this world, God in the flesh, King of kings, and Lord of lords, absolutely *nothing*. His Name is more well known than any other figure in history and He's so important to mankind that we keep time by Him (BC and AD). Yet, Google had *no clue* who He is! Or they did, and didn't want *you* to know.

It was obvious censorship of "the Name above all names." In videos documenting Google's cluelessness when it came to Jesus, users had asked the device who some other religious figures were. In one viral video, a Google user asked who Allah was. She got a very long thorough response from the Google assistant. She went on to ask who Buddha, Krishna, and some other "gods" were. She received detailed profiles for every single one of them. Others had asked about Satan, Muhammad, or Joseph Smith of Mormonism, and also got long descriptions for them all. Yet, whenever Google Home or Google smartphones were asked about Jesus, the virtual assistant replied, "Sorry, I don't know how to help with that yet," or "My apologies. I don't understand."

Sadly, it was not the first time Google had been called out for appearing anti-Christian. 2018 marked the 18th year in a row that the Google company didn't recognize Easter in their main page's Google Doodle; and Christmas has only ever been represented by secular images like snowmen, toys, and Santa Claus. The Doodle is a graphic that displays the company name above the search tab on Google's website. The images commemorate special occasions and major holidays... *except* the ones that are Biblical apparently. Throughout Google's history, there have been Doodles for Islam's Ramadan, Hindu religious festivals, and even for LGBT Pride.

I recently read a study which found Google Search is biased in favor of left-wing and liberal domains, but against conservative and Christian sites, with a confidence of 95%. Well that explains a whole lot! I've attempted to submit my website as a News outlet to Google many times since its inception, and it's always rejected. Meanwhile, search Google News today and you'll find websites littered with nothing but ads - or even blogs with less than 10,000 visitors. You would think that never having to retract or correct an article, and having over 1-million visitors, makes my site worthy of inclusion into Google News; but obviously none of that matters to them. They don't want you hearing my *Biblical* point of view.

Google and the lamestream media don't want you to be a free thinker. They want you to think how *they* tell you to think. There is a whole lot of brainwashing going on in the media today, which is why we must stay rooted in God's Word. The powers that be at Facebook, Twitter, Google, New York Times, the Huffington Post, Washington Post, CNN, NBC, PBS, and others in the mainstream media, aim *to shape* your worldview. The absolute last worldview they want you to hold is one that is Bible-based. Since they can't stop you from picking up a Holy Bible at home, or from attending church, they force-feed you beliefs and opinions that are contrary to your Faith. They're obviously dead set on reprogramming your minds to think like they do. Are you going to let them?

One man that they want you to hate is the current President. Now, I've never been a superfan of Donald J. Trump, but I do not dislike him either. Unlike most Americans, I've been pretty much neutral when it comes to the 45th President. He's done some fine things for Christians and for Israel, and for that he has earned my respect. I bring him up, because it is no secret that the lamestream media loathes him *with a passion.* Yet, the exact same "unbiased" media had praised Barack Obama. You never once saw a negative story about the former President ever air on CNN. Today, they're anti-Trump 24-7. It's often too nauseating to watch. It is not just Donald Trump who they hate though. It is also anyone who holds firmly to the traditional Biblical worldview.

They have demonized Christian role models like the patriarch of *Duck Dynasty,* Phil Robertson, as well as Tim Tebow, and the Benham Brothers. If I were more well known in the mainstream, I'd make headlines as an intolerant, closed-minded, homophobic,

Islamophobic, Bible-thumping bigot and hater. That is why I call the liberal media out for what they are: CHRISTIANOPHOBIC.

Given all that I've shared in this chapter, it is no wonder that Christianity's been on the decline in America throughout the past decade. What's even worse is that something has to fill the void. That explains why Satanism and Witchcraft are thriving in 2019. There are now more Americans who identify with Witchcraft than the entire Christian denomination of Presbyterians (1.5-million). In 2018, there were stories about witches across the U.S. placing hexes and curses on President Trump and Supreme Court Justice Brett Kavanaugh. One witch who'd led a hex against Kavanaugh, Dakota Bracciale, said that she was "absolutely willing to cause physical harm" through her witchcraft. She should be arrested!

The rise of Satan in America is the reason so many Godless liberals today want you *gone* if you dare disagree with them. I've actually heard some left-wingers say that Christians "need to die." Nothing, and no one, but the devil himself could inspire that kind of hatred toward another human. Satanic temples are popping up all across the USA, and Satanic monuments have been displayed at State Capitols to protest Nativity Scenes or 10 Commandments monuments. America is a fallen nation, and is in desperate need of revival more than ever before in history. If we Christians do not courageously stand up to the demonic spirits that are infiltrating our nation and corrupting the soul of America, then the USA may soon suffer the fate of Babylon the great.

THE ANGEL CRIED MIGHTILY WITH A STRONG VOICE, SAYING, BABYLON THE GREAT IS FALLEN, IS FALLEN, AND IS BECOME THE HABITATION OF DEVILS, AND THE HOLD OF EVERY FOUL SPIRIT, AND A CAGE OF EVERY UNCLEAN AND HATEFUL BIRD.

- REVELATION 18:2

CHAPTER ELEVEN

WIDESPREAD BLASPHEMY

IN THE LAST DAYS... MEN SHALL BE BLASPHEMERS.

- 2ND TIMOTHY 3:2

"THERE IS NO FEAR of God before their eyes." This verse, from Chapter 3 of Romans, has come to my mind too often throughout the course of the past decade. Whenever I think that the utter lack of respect for God cannot possibly get any worse, someone sets a new low. In *The Signs of Our Times*, I highlighted many cases of blasphemy. I found it necessary to pen a whole chapter on the sad subject in this book because of how common and widespread it's become. I don't think there's ever been a generation, since Jesus ascended into Heaven, that has ever been more irreverent toward our Creator. I'm beginning to think that the God-haters are trying to outdo each other, regarding how far some of them go to slander the Holiest Book on Earth.

Just last year, I read one of the most blasphemous things that I have ever heard in my life. Brian G. Murphy, a gay activist who actually calls himself a "Christian," is co-founder of the website "Queer Theology." In a video that he made for the website, he'd claimed that Jesus is "polyamorous," and that believers should be too. "I'm Christian and I'm polyamorous. I'm also kind of a slut. A reclaimed empowering kind of a slut – *like Jesus*," he said. He went on to say, "If you're one of those Christians who believe in having a personal relationship with Jesus Christ, well He's having personal relationships with billions of other people. He's kind of a relationship slut." This ignoramus called the Saviour of the world a "slut"! Are you kidding me?!

What's the world coming to when that kind of garbage being spewed about the Son of Almighty God has become acceptable? How can anyone, even with the wildest imagination, ever accuse the only Being in the history of mankind - who *never* sinned - of being a slut?! This confused soul can call himself a Christian all that he desires, but I guarantee that he is not and never will be - as long as he promotes such demonic lies from the pit of Hell.

He claims that the Book of Ephesians supports his theology. He said, "In Ephesians 5, Paul uses the word marriage to refer to Jesus' relationship with us. Repeatedly, Paul has reminded us that Jesus gave himself for us. Us. The Church - which Paul described as the whole body of believers. In this marriage, He isn't married to just one person. He is married to the entire body. Jesus is in a pansexual, polyamorous relationship with us. So, Christians can be polyamorous. It is a Biblical model of relationships." This guy has obviously never thoroughly studied the Holy Bible. He is just another, in a long line of cherry-pickers, who takes verses out of context in order to support his perverted beliefs.

First off, Murphy says the Church is made up of all believers. On that statement, he is right; *but* what he conveniently failed to mention is that the Holy Bible always refers to Christ's Church in *female* terminology. Read what Paul says in the *same* Chapter that Murphy claims backs up his theology -

"HUSBANDS, LOVE YOUR WIVES, JUST AS CHRIST LOVED THE CHURCH AND GAVE HIMSELF UP FOR HER, THAT HE MIGHT SANCTIFY HER, HAVING CLEANSED HER BY THE WASHING OF WATER WITH THE WORD." - EPHESIANS 5:25-26

Not only did the LORD inspire Paul to distinctly describe the Church with a female pronoun, but He made him repeat the word "her" *three times*! When God speaks, we are to listen attentively. When He repeats Himself, we must pay extra close attention. God made sure to liken the marriage of the Church unto Christ to the marriage between a *husband and wife*. So, NO Murphy, Jesus is not in a "polyamorous" relationship with the Church. He is most certainly not "pansexual" either. For those who don't know what that lingo means, it is defined as having a sexual attraction toward others "regardless of their sex or gender identity."

Factually, Jesus Christ was not, is not, and will never ever be attracted to other men. Never - no matter how much the perverts in the LGBT community try to twist verses of the Holy Bible to make it appear so. He was and is the sinless Son of God. He was and is "God in the flesh." In Revelation 22:15, He had mentioned unrepentant homosexuals in a list of those who won't be entering Heaven at the end of the road. So, how could He ever *engage* in homosexual relations? He couldn't, didn't, and won't! This sick nonsense needs to stop. It really ticks me off when homosexuals, ignorant to the Bible's teachings, claim God says something that He most certainly has not and does not.

Yet, there's something that riles me up even more - when men from *inside* "the Church" teach abominable lies to other believers. Believe it or not, one such man recently blasphemed even *worse* than this "Queer Theology" boy. I am speaking of a professor at the College of the Holy Cross in Massachusetts. Tat-Siong Benny Liew was appointed as the university's Chair of New Testament Studies in 2013. Someone needs to pull the Chair out from under him! Because things that he teaches, in a Catholic school no less, I can't even print in this book. His words are much too vulgar and blasphemous. I'll do my best to convey the filth he's propagating to students, without using the same profane language that he has.

Liew's said that Jesus Christ is not just the King of Israel and King of the Jews, but also a DRAG KING! What Liew's implying is that Lord Jesus was a crossdresser! This kind of heresy makes me sick to my stomach. I hate to entertain such a ridiculous belief but I have to make sure that I teach the truth of what God's Word actually says. Jesus was with the Father in the beginning, and He co-authored *every word* of the Holy Bible through the Holy Spirit (2nd Peter 1:21). Chapter 22, and verse 5, of Deuteronomy says -

"THE WOMAN SHALL NOT WEAR THAT WHICH PERTAINETH UNTO A MAN, NEITHER SHALL A MAN PUT ON A WOMAN'S GARMENT: FOR ALL THAT DO SO ARE ABOMINATION UNTO THE LORD THY GOD."

There is no way that Jesus would have ever crossdressed! He kept the Law of YHWH perfectly while on Earth, living a sinless life to become the acceptable unblemished sacrifice on behalf of our sins. Liew's statement is downright ludicrous. And while you would think that there could not possibly be a more blasphemous claim any worse than that, Liew actually made quite a few more. He has said that, in the Gospel of John, there are many verses that show Jesus exhibited "homosexual tendencies." How in the world could a Christian school give this idiot the time of day? It is bad enough that he got the job as a teacher at the college, but it's even worse that he still holds the position of authority six years later!

In yet another preposterous statement, Liew said that John's constant references to Jesus "wanting, giving, and leaking water," spoke to "gender indeterminacy" - and that led to "cross-dressing and queer desires." Whaaaaaaat?! Liew's head is in a fantasy land far far away. How does anyone, in a right state of mind, concoct such perverted ideas while reading the Holiest Book on the earth? He is a pervert of the highest degree. Speaking such blasphemous drivel about the Lord of our souls should be illegal everywhere on

Earth. I don't want to go on writing about what else this so-called "professor" said about Christ but, sadly, I have to - to prove that this generation is unparalleled when it comes to blasphemy.

Liew has also said (as I try to prevent myself from vomiting) that "the episode of Jesus washing the disciples' feet at the Last Supper was suggestive... a literary striptease... even seductive... because it showed and withheld at the same time." Sick! This guy belongs working behind the counter of an Adult Video Store - not teaching at a Christian college! Finally, in statements that I cannot clean up enough to print in this book (they are words found only in pornographic material), he implies that Christ desired and *had* sexual relations with His disciples and (in the most blasphemous thing you will ever hear) even with our Father in Heaven! Okay, now I really have to puke. This guy has major issues.

Normally, right about now, I'd give all of the Biblical verses in which God condemns homosexual sex and incest; but I should definitely not have to do so in this instance. I'd hope every person on Planet Earth, believer or not, should know that our Holy God would not engage in "incestuous" relations with His Holy Son. If that is even remotely conceivable in your mind, then I don't want to know you. I don't ever want to live in a world so perverted. It pains me physically to have to write this garbage in my book, but I'm hoping it has gotten my point across that blasphemy, heresy, and sacrilege have never been worse in history. I cannot conceive how it could ever be any worse than what I just recorded.

To this day, Liew still possesses a theological degree. How it has not been revoked yet, and how he has not been terminated and excommunicated from the school and church, is unfathomable. At this point, they'd be better off giving an unbeliever his job. They'd probably have more respect for the Holy Bible than he does! God forgive him for all the imbecilic garbage he has spewed to young impressionable souls during his career. While I believe that Liew takes the cake for some of the most blasphemous things that I've ever heard, there is actually a world leader who comes very close. The President of the Philippines has publicly called God "stupid."

In a 2018 Davao speech, President Rodrigo Duterte spoke on the Creation account from our Bible. He talked about Adam and Eve eating the forbidden fruit, and about the concept of original sin. "Adam ate it, and malice was born... Who is this *stupid* God? He's a stupid son of a b*tch if that's the case. Creating something perfect, and then thinking of an event to tempt and to destroy the quality of your work." Sadly, it is not the first time that he spoke so unbelievably disrespectful about our Creator. He has called the doctrine of the Trinity - the Father, Son, and Holy Spirit - "silly." He even used vulgar language to attack our Lord Jesus Christ, and what He did for us on the Cross. He said, "Your God was nailed on the Cross. F**k! How unimpressive."

As I questioned how Liew could still hold his job after such sacrilegious remarks, how in the world can Duterte remain chosen leader of an *entire country* after those inconceivable blasphemous words? His statements are beyond the pale. Yet, he is not the only one in the public eye who regularly mocks and disrespects God. Comedian Sarah Silverman and musician Marilyn Manson have become notorious for it. Last chapter, I mentioned Ariana Grande and her blasphemous song, *"God is a Woman."* Since most of the liberals today hate our God's Laws, especially those prohibiting abortion and same-sex relations, many echo Grande's opinion.

At 2018's *Emmy Awards*, the actress Thandie Newton said, "I don't even believe in God, but I'm gonna thank HER tonight." 20 years ago, that comment would have (and should have) destroyed her career. Unfortunately, she received a rousing standing ovation for her blasphemous remarks. Liberals also mock and disparage a specific holy figure of our God, and that happens to be the holiest Woman that ever lived - the Mother of our Lord Jesus, the Virgin Mary. They don't like how she lived her life so chaste, holy, pure, and submissive to the LORD. Feminists seem to hate pretty much everything about her. Meanwhile, God has said that she is blessed above all other women - past, present, and future - and *she should be*. Don't tell the left-wing women that, as they will go bonkers.

During an International Women's Day protest in Argentina, in 2017, feminists staged a mock abortion on a woman portraying Mary. Photos of the disgusting act showed blood and baby parts gushing out from between Mary's legs, as the woman dressed as Mary pumped her fist in the air. She was wearing a rosary around her neck, no less, and laughed throughout the sickening spectacle. This had taken place in front of a cathedral. Pro-life priest Frank Pavone said to LifeSite, "This act shows what is at the foundation of hardcore pro-abortion people. They hate the Church, and they literally want to abort Jesus off the face of the earth." Pavone was spot on, as a placard at the U.S. Women's March read - "If Mary had an abortion, we wouldn't be in this mess."

Another marcher carried a sign depicting Mary as a bloody vagina. She is also disrespected at Christmastime. The God-haters don't want to hear about the miraculous birth of our Saviour, and so they've been trying to push Him out of the global celebration of His birth for years. Thankfully, they've failed. We God-fearing believers do our best each year to remind people who the Reason for the season truly is, and that Christmas begins with CHRIST. Since antichrists among us haven't succeeded in their attempts to push Him out, many have resorted to blaspheming Him instead.

Not only are the atheists putting up Satanic monuments next to Nativity Scenes, but some have created their own nativities to mock our Lord. For instance, a zombie Nativity Scene contained the baby Jesus resembling a creature out of a horror film. Others have vandalized Nativities or have stolen the figure of Jesus from them. These people must really hate our God with a passion. One of the most blasphemous protests to Christmas that I have seen is the trend of *Gaytivity* scenes. A few years ago, a comedian posted an image on Twitter of a Nativity Scene that featured two Josephs

- with Mary being *removed* altogether. LGBT advocates ate it up, and had erected Gaytivity scenes of their own. The Josephs were painted pink, and knelt beside baby Jesus.

Upon sharing her sacrilegious image, Carmen Esposito wrote, "Our neighbors' two Joseph nativity is up and I'm beaming." She was actually celebrating her neighbors making a mockery out of our Lord's birth. Her post had gone viral, and received more than 3,000 retweets and over 20,000 likes. Twitter erupted with others sharing images of Gaytivities, and tweeting messages of support for the disgraceful decor. Comments that had really disgusted me were: "Here come the three wise men. Now it's a party" ... "The Bible says that Jesus had two dads" ... "Jesus, Marty & Joseph." Someone even shared a lesbian Gaytivity, featuring two Marys.

The "three wise men" comment obviously meant to transform the Bible's most important story into a gay orgy. No words could ever describe the disgust I feel for such repulsive blasphemy. As to the argument that "Jesus had two dads." It may be true, but not in the way that they want it to be. Jesus had His Father in Heaven, Almighty God YHWH. Jesus was also given an earthly father by YHWH, to raise and protect Him when He was a child - Joseph. So, while Jesus did have two Dads, they most certainly were not "romantically involved" like the Twitter user grossly implied. One Father was in Heaven, and one was on the earth. Period. Nothing "homosexual" can ever be construed by that.

As to "Jesus, Marty, and Joseph," people tweeting it must be atheists, because they're slapping God in the Face and spitting on His Word. The depraved souls took the event that began the Love Story between God and man, and perverted it into homosexual filth. They must be convinced that there is no God, because how else could you blaspheme the Saviour of your soul and His Godly parents? As much as the LGBT advocates love to reinterpret the Bible, in order to justify sinful lifestyles, the fact is that they can never change the truth. When God-haters come to this realization, they stop trying to alter God's Word and attack it instead - either verbally or violently.

One example of such an attack on the Holy Bible (which has sadly become all too common in this generation) involves Kelsey L. Munger, a contributor to dirtrag websites like Huffington Post and Salon. Her blogs are mostly attacks on Christianity and God's Word. Her absolute worst was published on the HuffPost website, and it was about "ripping up" her Bible. Now you see why I have such a hatred for the Huffington Post. Of all writers in this world, with important things to say, this news outlet thought a blog about desecrating God's Word is great reading material.

Munger wrote, "This is a violent and sacrilegious assault on a holy book - THE Holy Book. It is a declaration of my freedom… Rip rip rip… I never thought I would want to destroy a book, but now I feel as if I won't find peace until the job is done… Rip rip rip…" After a very long profane description of her destruction of the Holiest Book on Earth, she said, "Finally, when nothing is left but a pile of paper shreds, I stop. The Bible no longer exists. I've forcefully ripped it out of the present tense and damned it to the past tense. It is gone." Just how demonic has our society become to allow such unholy filth?! On top of that, to be published on one of the top 5 news sites on the net? How far our nation has fallen!

Meanwhile, liberals have the gall to ask why the LORD can allow California to be burnt to the ground in historic wildfires, or major U.S. cities to be flooded by the record-breaking hurricanes. Their rebellion is all fun and games until the LORD shows up to rain on their parade. As for examples of violent blasphemous acts against the LORD and His Word, two were carried out just a few months before I published this book. A deranged man broke into a church in Virginia in 2018, vandalized it, and then proceeded to tear pages out of the Bible. One month later, security footage had captured a vandal urinating on two angel statues before smashing them to the ground outside a New York church. I cannot recall a time in history where God's been so disrespected.

This leads me to believe that the Rapture is nearer than ever before, because it appears the seven-year Tribulation of the Book of Revelation is just around the corner. In the 16th Chapter of the Book, inhabitants of Earth blaspheme God *three times* when vials of His wrath are being poured out. This is the ultimate blasphemy because, in this case, they are blaspheming all three members of the Trinity - Father, Son, and Holy Spirit. Just two decades ago, it was impossible to imagine a majority of this world blaspheming the LORD with one accord. Now, it appears much more plausible. Thank God *we* will not be here when they do. Come Lord Jesus!

MEN BLASPHEMED THE NAME OF GOD, WHICH HATH POWER OVER THESE PLAGUES: AND THEY REPENTED NOT TO GIVE HIM GLORY... AND BLASPHEMED THE GOD OF HEAVEN BECAUSE OF THEIR PAINS AND THEIR SORES, AND REPENTED NOT OF THEIR DEEDS... AND MEN BLASPHEMED GOD BECAUSE OF THE PLAGUE OF THE HAIL.

- REVELATION 16:9, 11 & 21

CHAPTER TWELVE

SIN ABOUNDS AND LOVE WAXES COLD

JESUS SAID, BECAUSE INIQUITY SHALL ABOUND, THE LOVE OF
MANY SHALL WAX COLD.

- MATTHEW 24:12

IN MATTHEW, CHAPTER 24, after Lord Jesus had prophesied
to His disciples many of the signs that I have written about in my
books, He said that iniquity (sin) would abound in the season of
His return. The Greek word for "iniquity" means "lawlessness."
So, not only will the world be drenched in sin, but any respect for
God's Law will be thrown out the window. It will be because of a
lack of Godly morality across the globe why Jesus said "the love
of many shall *wax cold.*" These words can mean two things...

One: In the sense of the whole world, He means that people
will become selfish and hate one another; and the love He came to
teach will be hard to find. Two: In the sense of us Christians, He
means (due to widespread departure from God's Laws within the
Church) dissensions will arise and brotherly love will cease to be.

Also, due to all of the other signs that I have written about -
persecution, spiritual deceptions, emerging false religions, God's
Law being at odds with modern-day social norms, lack of Biblical
truth being preached from pulpits, perilous times, false prophets,
and doctrines of demons - many will fall away from the Faith and

lose their love for God. Can we see this prophecy of Jesus coming to pass in either of the ways that I described above? The answer would unfortunately be *absolutely* - on both counts. As far as the world's concerned, whether you call it iniquity, transgression, sin, or lawlessness, evil is unquestionably blanketing the earth.

So, how exactly have historically-Christian nations fallen so far away from the LORD in these Last Days? As technology has increased, the devil seems to find more and more tools that he can use to pull us away from God's Word. Whether television, radio, smartphones, or the internet, Satan has taken things that could do a great deal of good for the Kingdom of God and has used them to destroy faith. I have written about this in the previous chapters, so I should not have to explain how he's utilizing these things to pervert minds, defile hearts, and spoil souls all around the world. He has inspired Godless people to use these tools to propagandize the population of the United States.

Little by little, the servants of Satan have chipped away at our country's Judeo-Christian foundation and have succeeded a great deal in turning a majority of this generation away from God. My friends, the Benham Brothers, have done some great research on this subject; and they have described the devil's agenda to destroy America as happening in three ways:

1. By eliminating traditional (Biblical) values
2. By creating or infiltrating new rules
3. By exterminating Christian influence

The Bros have said, "traditional values have been entrenched for so long in American culture and government that atheist and Communist groups have formed to create systematic strategies to eliminate these values." They refer to a book written in 1958, *The Naked Communist*, as a prime example of anti-Christian strategies that Satan has successfully utilized. The book has long served as a step-by-step guide for all God-hating Americans, teaching them how to erode the moral foundation of our country. Here are some steps laid out in the book -

- Eliminate prayer in schools on the grounds that it violates the principle of separation of Church and State.

- Discredit the nuclear family as an institution. Encourage promiscuity and easy divorce.

- Get control of the schools. Use them as transmission belts for socialism. Soften the curriculum, and seize control of teacher associations.

- Eliminate all laws governing obscenity by calling them censorship and a violation of free speech and free press.

- Break down traditional standards of morality - promoting pornography in books, magazines, films, and television.

- Present homosexual and promiscuous lifestyles as being normal, natural, and healthy.

- Infiltrate the press. Gain control of key positions in radio, TV, and motion pictures.

- Infiltrate churches, replacing revealed religion with social religion. Discredit the Bible.

Sound like modern America? I want to go down the list and see if the Godless radicals have achieved any of these goals.

Eliminate prayer in schools - check. Discredit the institution of the nuclear family - check. Encourage promiscuity and divorce

- check. Get control of schools - check. Eliminate laws governing obscenity - check. Break down the basic standards of morality by promoting pornography - check. Portray homosexual lifestyles as normal, natural, and healthy - check. Infiltrate the press (just how many times have I written about the Godless mainstream media?) - check. Infiltrate the churches - check. Replace revealed religion with social religion - check. And then, there's the final step - the step that would make all of the other goals achievable - discredit the Holy Bible... check.

To discredit something is to harm its good reputation. Now, I (and hopefully everyone reading this) could never view the Word of God in a negative light - as that is impossible for a true believer to do. But there are sadly many Americans who've been deceived and programmed to do so. A Biblically-hostile media mocks the Bible on a daily basis, and promotes lies that it is just a bunch of stories and moral laws written for a different time in history. They paint God's Law as archaic, bigoted, discriminatory, and hateful. So, have they succeeded in discrediting the Holy Bible?

Stand in a crowd of people at your job, a secular venue, or on the street, and say these phrases aloud: "I believe in the One *True* God, the God of the Bible" - "Jesus is the *only way* to Heaven" - "The LORD *created* the Universe" - "Humans are created by God and *did not evolve*" - "Islam, Buddhism, Hinduism, and all other faiths besides Judaism and Christianity are false and *of the devil*" - "Abortion is *murder*" - "There are only *two genders:* Male and Female" - "I *oppose* Gay Marriage." Would you feel comfortable saying these things out loud? Most likely not. Why would you not feel comfortable saying these things publicly if you truly believe them? We should boldly state these things whenever - wherever.

The reason some won't is because they know our society has been brainwashed into believing whatever the media tells them to believe; and the powers that be want you to believe *everything but* the Holy Bible. Thus, they've done their best to discredit it. If you believe, preach, and stand up for it, then you will become *public enemy number one* in today's America. The Benham Bros pointed back to a Guide Magazine from 1987, titled *"The Overhauling of Straight America."* The article had laid out a number of steps for homosexual activists, like the *Naked Communist* did, that would lead to normalization of homosexuality in America. It would also lead to demonization of Bible believers, and anyone who opposed the "Gay Rights" movement. The final step had read:

*"At a later stage in our campaign for rights, it will be time for us to get tough with remaining opponents. To be blunt, they must be **vilified**. We intend to make those opposed to us look **so nasty** that average Americans will **disassociate** themselves from such types."*

Welcome to 2019 America. They've done exactly what they said they would. "By any means necessary" is the battle cry of all Americans who've opposed Christianity and the Holy Bible, and that's how we have gotten to where we are today. Sin abounds all around us. It's been allowed to fester unchecked by much of the Church for decades. Thus, love has grown cold in our country and hate is widespread. Either Christians are hated by this "anything goes" society, or some Americans are hating everyone who is not of the same political persuasion. This is where love for neighbors has waxed coldest in this nation today: in the world of politics.

Obviously, if you've read my previous book, you can derive that I don't vote for Democrats. I don't vote for every Republican either, but I side with them a whole lot more because they stand for my Biblical values far more than the Dems do. I don't believe that either party can *save* the nation, to be clear - only Jesus can do that. I don't think that either will *make America great again*, because only the LORD can do that. Sadly, some Christians today become so entrenched on their political side of the aisle that they don't even view the other side as human beings - hating political adversaries with a passion. I cannot recall a time, throughout my life, in which the political climate of the USA was so polarized.

While the left-wing liberals oppose just about everything that I stand for, I still don't hate them. Like I had said in my previous book, I hate Islam and LGBT Pride, but I don't hate the Muslim people or homosexuals. You can hate an idea, but don't ever hate people behind the idea. You can dislike what it is they stand for, but don't ever wish evil upon them. If they wrong you, then leave vengeance to the LORD. It is possible to love someone that you disagree with. Lord Jesus commanded us to "love your enemies," and to "do good to those who persecute you."

That is what separates believers from the rest of humanity. No other faith teaches such things. Our calling is to lead others to the Lord. How can we do that if we're constantly shouting or cursing at those with whom we disagree? We cannot. We should calmly debate adversaries and preach truth to them. If they want to shout us down, let them. We should behave like Jesus Christ. No matter how much we're persecuted for our beliefs in this world, we must never become so bitter that we allow hate to enter into our hearts. Hate is a product of the devil. God is love. And we must always represent our loving God to this unbelieving world. We can never stoop to their level.

When Jesus was hung on the Cross, He *prayed for* those who put Him there. He asked His Father to forgive them. Our God has the right to hate us all every day, because we are all covered in sin - and He *hates* sin. Still, He loves us even though He hates what we do. That is what we are called to do - love our neighbors, even though we may hate what they do. God loved us poor sinners so much that He sent His Son to die for us so we could be reconciled unto Him. Now, He expects us to love like He does. You can hate what someone stands for all day long; but as for the person, you need to love them. Period.

On my website, and in my books, I have constantly criticized men and women - by name - for abominable things that they have done. Whether those people are Presidents, Popes, popular actors, musicians, false prophets, or atheists, I've always rebuked anyone if they say or do anything against God. Yet, I pray for them - that the LORD would open their eyes to understand Him. I criticize, I rebuke, and then I *pray* for my enemies - but I *never* hate them. I know this may sound difficult to do in our highly charged political climate, as we're more divided than any other time since the Civil War, but we can never allow our contentions to turn into hate. As Christians, there are three steps to follow concerning enemies:

1. **PRAY** for your enemies. Do not prey on them.

2. **BLESS** them, and do not curse them.

3. **DO GOOD** to them, even if they do nothing but evil to you. For we cannot overcome evil *with* evil, we can only overcome evil with GOOD (Romans 12:14-21).

In our generation, the Matthew 24:12 prophecy of Lord Jesus is being fulfilled in the Christian community just as much as it's been in the world. Lawlessness abounds in the Church more than ever before in history since the Dark Ages. Megachurches refuse to preach on sin, priests molest kids, pastors are sexually abusing vulnerable young women, preachers use tithes to enrich their own lavish lifestyles while their flocks starve, and some churches even celebrate sin, such as abortion and LGBT Pride. Because of all of this, as with the world, the love of Christians has waxed cold.

There are some who refuse to even enter a church because of a scarring experience in the past, and others depart from the Faith altogether because of abuse from wolves in sheep's clothing who posed as men of God. There are also those who develop a hatred for God, Himself, because of sinful things that were done to them or that they'd seen done in "the Church." The Lutherans disagree with Evangelicals, or Baptists spar with Catholics, and so on and so forth. There are billions of Christians globally and yet so much dissension. The devil loves to divide us. In the earliest days of our Faith, all believers were one in Christ. In the days of the apostles, due to doctrinal disputes, the Church was divided into two sects; but brotherly love still continued despite the disagreements.

Flash-forward to today, and there are dozens - if not hundreds - and some say thousands - of Christian denominations. What we are seeing isn't a minor doctrinal dispute here and there, but many so-called believers think they know better than everyone else does - and that *their* way is the *only way* to know God. They're arguing about baptism, Sabbath-keeping, healing, tithing, grace, prophecy, pre or post-Trib Rapture, is the Bible literal or allegorical, etc.

Debates are healthy, especially in the Church, because truth is revealed when wise and learned men of God - who are filled with the Spirit - come together and reason with one another. What isn't healthy is when believers get puffed up in pride, and shout down other believers who dare disagree with their opinion on the Word. We see too much of this today. It is a shame. While it is nothing new for believers to disagree, what is new (and extremely sad) is how Christians can flat-out hate each other. Brothers and sisters, this should not be so! We must realize what the first two Christian denominations realized: we have one important thing that unites us all... our Lord and Saviour, JESUS CHRIST.

I personally don't care if you are Adventist, Baptist, Catholic, Evangelical, Lutheran, or belong to any other denomination under the sun; as long as you believe Christ was born of a Virgin, died on the Cross for our sins, rose from the dead, and is coming back down to Earth again, then you're my brother and sister. It is that simple. While the love of the world may be waxing cold, it should not be so amongst us believers; because our King is coming!

It is about time that we live - *and LOVE* - like He is.

HE WHICH TESTIFIETH THESE THINGS SAITH, SURELY I COME
QUICKLY. AMEN. EVEN SO, COME, LORD JESUS.

- REVELATION 22:20

ACKNOWLEDGMENTS

TO GOD - THANK YOU for mercifully pulling me out of a life of sin and into service to You. If someone would have told me 20 years ago that I would be studying Your holy Word every day, and preaching a message of repentance to sinners, I'd have said they were crazy. Yet, You knew from my Mother's womb what You'd willed for me to be and were beyond patient in waiting for me to finally come around.

I'm so grateful to know You LORD, through Your Son, and I pray that You will continue to draw closer to me each and every new day. Words cannot express just how humbled I am that You allow me to serve You. Thank You for being such a Good Father. Thank You for every gift and blessing that You've ever bestowed upon me. Thank You especially for Jesus and Your Spirit. I love You forever YHWH.

To Christ Jesus - I wrote in the dedication how thankful I am to You, and for You, and there will never be enough human words to ever fully describe how much I love You Lord. Glory to You.

To the Holy Spirit - You are the Author of my books. I'm just the vessel that You have used to put Your thoughts onto paper. I in no way claim that every word I have written in my books comes directly from You, as I'm an imperfect human being who is prone to mistakes; but I do attribute any words that lead to the salvation of souls all to You. I've done my best to convey all that You have placed on my heart, and I pray that You will continue to guide me and perfect my craft to glorify You, Lord Jesus, and the Father in Heaven, always.

To Mom, Dad, Bro, Jacob, and Family - I love you all more than you will ever know. I thank God for every one of you daily, and pray the LORD blesses and keeps you all healthy and well all the days that we share on Earth. May God be with you all forever.

To Jason and David Benham - I can't thank you guys enough for all you've done for me and my website over the years. You've taken time out every year for the annual Christmas Special, and I am honoured to share your articles. As busy as the two of you are, you still take time to respond quickly whenever I reach out to you about anything. I don't believe that there could ever be two men of God in this world that I could ever admire more. God bless you and your families always. Love ya' Bros!

To all those who've supported my website and books - I hope that your faith has been strengthened by my words. Thank you for the interest that you have shown, as it encourages me to do more study, research, and writing each new day. These books would not have been possible without the support of you all. As long as you continue to enjoy them, I will continue to write them as the Spirit guides me to do so.

NOTES

CHAPTER ONE: THE SIGNS OF OUR TIMES CONTINUE

1. "END ANTI-SEMITISM: I'm A Christian - Therefore, I Love the Jews," BiblicalSigns.com, October 30, 2018, https://biblicalsignsintheheadlines.com/2018/10/30/end-anti-semitism-im-a-christian-therefore-i-love-the-jews/

2. "MODERATE ISLAM?: Linda Sarsour Calls For Jihad in America, Tells Fellow Muslims Not to Assimilate," BiblicalSigns.com, July 6, 2017, https://biblicalsignsintheheadlines.com/2017/07/06/moderate-islam-linda-sarsour-calls-for-jihad-in-america-tells-fellow-muslims-to-not-assimilate/

3. "WAR ON CHRISTIANITY: Liberals Are Relentless in Their Attacks on Bible Believers," BiblicalSigns.com, August 17, 2018, https://biblicalsignsintheheadlines.com/2018/08/17/war-on-christianity-liberals-are-relentless-in-their-attacks-on-holy-bible-believers/

4. "ISRAEL VS. HAMAS: Everything That You Need to Know About Their Clashes in 2018," BiblicalSigns.com, July 25, 2018, https://biblicalsignsintheheadlines.com/2018/07/25/israel-vs-hamas-everything-that-you-need-to-know-about-their-clashes-in-2018/

5. "ANOTHER RARE SIGN IN THE HEAVENS: Longest Blood Moon of the Century Rises," BiblicalSigns.com, July 27, 2018, https://biblicalsignsintheheadlines.com/2018/07/27/another-rare-sign-in-the-heavens-longest-blood-moon-of-the-century-rises-tonight/

6. "THE FORERUNNER?: Alaska's 7.0 Magnitude Earthquake Could Be First of Many Powerful Quakes to Rattle USA,"

BiblicalSigns.com, November 30, 2018,
https://biblicalsignsintheheadlines.com/2018/11/30/the-forerunne
r-alaskas-7-0-magnitude-earthquake-could-be-first-of-many-pow
erful-quakes-to-rattle-usa/

7. "HURRICANE MICHAEL: The Storm I Have Long Warned
    About Has Arrived, And It Is Making History,"
    BiblicalSigns.com, October 10, 2018,
    https://biblicalsignsintheheadlines.com/2018/10/10/hurricane-mic
    hael-the-storm-that-i-warned-of-has-arrived-and-it-is-making-hi
    story/

CHAPTER TWO: MORE SIGNS CONTINUE

1. "CONFORM OR ELSE: Transgender Activists Threatening
    Those Who Refuse To Embrace Their Radical Ideology,"
    BiblicalSigns.com, December 7, 2018,
    https://biblicalsignsintheheadlines.com/2018/12/07/conform-or-el
    se-transgender-activists-threatening-those-who-refuse-to-embrac
    e-their-radical-ideology/
2. "THE SAD 'STATE OF THEOLOGY': New Survey Reveals
    Americans (Even Some Christians) Are Biblically-Illiterate,"
    BiblicalSigns.com, October 19, 2018,
    https://biblicalsignsintheheadlines.com/2018/10/19/the-sad-state-
    of-theology-new-survey-reveals-americans-even-some-christians-
    are-biblically-illiterate/

CHAPTER THREE: MASS SHOOTINGS

1. "AMERICA DOESN'T NEED GUN CONTROL - AMERICA
    DOESN'T NEED MORE GUNS - AMERICA NEEDS JESUS,"
    BiblicalSigns.com, May 18, 2018,
    https://biblicalsignsintheheadlines.com/2018/05/18/america-does
    nt-need-gun-control-america-doesnt-need-more-guns-america-ne
    eds-jesus/
2. "YOU CANNOT BE "PRO-LIFE" AND A MURDERER, IT IS
    AN OXYMORON," BiblicalSigns.com, December 1, 2015,

https://biblicalsignsintheheadlines.com/2015/12/01/you-cannot-be
-pro-life-and-a-murderer-it-is-an-oxymoron/

3. "DEADLIEST SHOOTING IN U.S. HISTORY: Islamic Terrorist Massacres Gays," BiblicalSigns.com, June 12, 2016, https://biblicalsignsintheheadlines.com/2016/06/12/deadliest-mas s-shooting-in-u-s-history-muslim-terrorist-massacres-gays/

4. "OF THE DEVIL: 'Irreligious' Terrorist Commits Deadliest Mass Shooting in U.S. History," BiblicalSigns.com, October 2, 2017, https://biblicalsignsintheheadlines.com/2017/10/02/of-the-devil-ir religious-terrorist-carries-out-deadliest-mass-shooting-in-u-s-hist ory/

CHAPTER FOUR: RACISM

1. "RACISM: What Does God Have to Say About It?," BiblicalSigns.com, October 19, 2017, https://biblicalsignsintheheadlines.com/2017/10/19/racism-what-d oes-god-have-to-say-about-it/

2. "A NATION DIVIDED: 'No Justice, No Peace' Must Become 'Know Jesus, Know Peace'," BiblicalSigns.com, July 9, 2016, https://biblicalsignsintheheadlines.com/2016/07/09/a-nation-divi ded-no-justice-no-peace-must-become-know-jesus-know-peace/

CHAPTER FIVE: HISTORIC WILDFIRES

1. "JUDGMENT BY FIRE: 'Apocalyptic Scenes' in California As Wildfires Rage," BiblicalSigns.com, October 11, 2017, https://biblicalsignsintheheadlines.com/2017/10/11/judgment-by-f ire-apocalyptic-scenes-in-california-as-wildfires-rage/

2. "HOLY FIRE: 'Largest Wildfire in California History' May Be Long-Overdue Judgment Upon Godless State," BiblicalSigns.com, August 6, 2018, https://biblicalsignsintheheadlines.com/2018/08/06/holy-fire-apo calyptic-wildfires-may-be-long-overdue-judgment-of-god-upon-g odless-california/

3. "HELL ON EARTH: 'Paradise Destroyed' in California As Wildfires Once Again Rage Across Godless State,"

BiblicalSigns.com, November 9, 2018,
https://biblicalsignsintheheadlines.com/2018/11/09/hell-on-earth-paradise-destroyed-in-california-as-wildfires-once-again-rage-across-godless-state/

CHAPTER SIX: PESTILENCES

1. "THERE WILL BE PESTILENCES: Greater Risk of Global Pandemic Than Ever Before," BiblicalSigns.com, April 4, 2017, https://biblicalsignsintheheadlines.com/2017/04/04/there-will-be-pestilences-greater-risk-of-global-pandemic-than-ever-before/

CHAPTER SEVEN: WARS AND RUMOURS OF WARS

1. "RUMOURS OF WARS: Biblical Battles on the Horizon," BiblicalSigns.com, April 7, 2017, https://biblicalsignsintheheadlines.com/2017/04/07/rumours-of-wars-biblical-battles-on-the-horizon/
2. "ALLIED AGAINST ISRAEL: Is the Gog-Magog War At the Door?," BiblicalSigns.com, February 14, 2018, https://biblicalsignsintheheadlines.com/2018/02/14/allied-against-israel-is-the-gog-magog-war-at-the-door/
3. "NUCLEAR TSUNAMI: Russian Bombs Detonated on Sea Floor Could Drown Major U.S. Cities," BiblicalSigns.com, May 2, 2017, https://biblicalsignsintheheadlines.com/2017/05/02/nuclear-tsunami-russian-bombs-on-sea-floor-could-drown-major-u-s-cities/
4. "NUCLEAR NORTH KOREA: The Threat Is Real," BiblicalSigns.com, July 30, 2017, https://biblicalsignsintheheadlines.com/2017/07/30/nuclear-north-korea-the-threat-is-real/
5. "EXISTENTIAL THREAT: Enemies of America Plot EMP Attacks," BiblicalSigns.com, April 25, 2016, https://biblicalsignsintheheadlines.com/2016/04/25/existential-threat-enemies-of-america-plot-emp-attacks/

CHAPTER EIGHT: "2ND TIMOTHY 3" GENERATION

1. "I STAND AGAINST PRIDE: Christians Cannot Stand With God AND the LGBT Movement (So Pick A Side)," BiblicalSigns.com, June 10, 2017, https://biblicalsignsintheheadlines.com/2017/06/10/i-stand-agains t-pride-christians-cannot-stand-with-god-and-the-lgbt-movemen t-so-pick-a-side/

2. "KAVANAUGH CONTROVERSY: Dems Aren't About Protecting Women - Only About Preserving A Liberal SCOTUS," BiblicalSigns.com, September 24, 2018, https://biblicalsignsintheheadlines.com/2018/09/24/kavanaugh-co ntroversy-dems-arent-about-protecting-women-only-about-prese rving-a-liberal-scotus/

3. "CONFIRM KAVANAUGH NOW: The Christian Case For Why He Should Be Sitting On the Supreme Court," BiblicalSigns.com, October 5, 2018, https://biblicalsignsintheheadlines.com/2018/10/05/confirm-kava naugh-now-the-christian-case-for-why-he-should-be-sitting-on-t he-supreme-court/

4. "WAR ON CHRISTIANITY: Liberals Are Relentless In Their Attacks On Bible Believers," BiblicalSigns.com, August 17, 2018, https://biblicalsignsintheheadlines.com/2018/08/17/war-on-christ ianity-liberals-are-relentless-in-their-attacks-on-holy-bible-believ ers/

CHAPTER NINE: FALSE PROPHETS

1. "SIN: The Word Nobody Wants To Hear, But Should," BiblicalSigns.com, November 10, 2015, https://biblicalsignsintheheadlines.com/2015/11/10/society-of-sin- why-stopping-it-starts-with-us/

2. "THE POPE'S LOVE AFFAIR WITH ISLAM: Is Francis Revelation's 'False Prophet'?," BiblicalSigns.com, August 1, 2016, https://biblicalsignsintheheadlines.com/2016/08/01/the-popes-lov e-affair-with-islam-is-francis-revelations-false-prophet/

3. "FALSE PROPHET: Megachurch Pastor Tells Christians 'Forget' the Ten Commandments," BiblicalSigns.com, January 10, 2019, https://biblicalsignsintheheadlines.com/2019/01/10/false-prophet-megachurch-pastor-tells-christians-to-forget-the-ten-commandments/

CHAPTER TEN: DEMONIC INDOCTRINATION

1. "DEMONIC INDOCTRINATION: The Devil In Your TV," BiblicalSigns.com, February 9, 2016, https://biblicalsignsintheheadlines.com/2016/02/09/demonic-indoctrination-the-devil-in-your-tv/

2. "TARGETING YOUR KIDS: Disney Joins Forces With Gay Lobby To Push LGBT Agenda On Children," BiblicalSigns.com, March 3, 2017, https://biblicalsignsintheheadlines.com/2017/03/03/targeting-your-kids-disney-joins-forces-with-gay-lobby-to-push-lgbt-agenda-on-children/

3. "SUPPRESSING SPEECH: Exposing Facebook's War On Conservative Christians," BiblicalSigns.com, March 31, 2017, https://biblicalsignsintheheadlines.com/2017/03/31/suppressing-speech-exposing-facebooks-war-on-conservative-christians/

4. "BLATANT OMISSION: Google Home Knows Allah, Muhammad, Buddha, and Satan, But Not Jesus," BiblicalSigns.com, January 26, 2018, https://biblicalsignsintheheadlines.com/2018/01/26/blatant-omission-google-home-knows-allah-muhammad-buddha-and-satan-but-not-jesus/

5. "SATANIC WORSHIP ON THE RISE IN AMERICA," BiblicalSigns.com, November 3, 2015, https://biblicalsignsintheheadlines.com/2015/11/03/satanic-worship-on-the-rise-in-america/

CHAPTER ELEVEN: WIDESPREAD BLASPHEMY

1. "BEYOND BLASPHEMY: Gay Co-Founder of 'Queer Theology' Claims Jesus Was a Polyamorous 'Slut'," BiblicalSigns.com, November 19, 2018, https://biblicalsignsintheheadlines.com/2018/11/19/beyond-blasphemy-gay-co-founder-of-queer-theology-claims-jesus-was-a-polyamorous-slut/

2. "VITRIOL AGAINST THE VIRGIN: The Blasphemy of the Left Knows No Bounds," BiblicalSigns.com, March 14, 2017, https://biblicalsignsintheheadlines.com/2017/03/14/vitriol-against-the-virgin-the-blasphemy-of-the-radical-left-knows-no-bounds/

3. "WAR ON THE CHRIST OF CHRISTMAS CONTINUES: God-Haters Blaspheme, Mock, And Pervert the Birth of Jesus," BiblicalSigns.com, December 1, 2017, https://biblicalsignsintheheadlines.com/2017/12/01/war-on-the-christ-of-christmas-continues-god-haters-blaspheme-mock-and-pervert-the-birth-of-jesus/

CHAPTER TWELVE: SIN ABOUNDS AND LOVE WAXES COLD

1. "CHRISTIANS IN THE CROSSHAIRS OF A DARK AGENDA," BenhamBrothers.com, February 16, 2016, https://benhambrothers.com/christians-cross-hairs-dark-agenda/

2. "LOVE YOUR ENEMIES: Threatening Lives of Political Adversaries Is Not the Way of 'the Right'," BiblicalSigns.com, October 26, 2018, https://biblicalsignsintheheadlines.com/2018/10/26/love-your-enemies-threatening-the-lives-of-political-adversaries-is-not-the-way-of-the-right/

ABOUT THE AUTHOR

MICHAEL SAWDY is the Founder of the website *Biblical Signs In The Headlines*, and the Author of *The Signs of Our Times* book series. In 2006, He had a life-changing experience with the Lord Jesus Christ, which led him to turn from a sinful life and to fully dedicate his life to God. Since then, he's spent thousands of hours studying the Bible - along with teachings by some of his greatest influences: the Benham Brothers, Jack Van Impe, Billy Graham, John Hagee, and Chuck Missler.

Due to the message which he received from the Lord, during his salvation experience, MichaEL believes strongly that Jesus is truly coming back soon. This belief is what inspired him to create *BiblicalSigns.com* in 2015, and to write books about "Last Days" Bible Prophecy - specifically concerning the Rapture. His website had surpassed over 1,000,000 visitors in 2017, and his books have been #1 Best Sellers in multiple Christian categories on Amazon.

VISIT THE WEBSITE:
BiblicalSigns.com
FOLLOW ON SOCIAL MEDIA:
Facebook - /BiblicalSignsInTheHeadlines
/TheSignsOfOurTimesBook
Twitter - @MichaelofYHWH (Personal)
@BiblicalSigns (Website)
@SignsOfTimes777 (Books)